TH

THE GLOBAL DEVELOPMENT CRISIS

BENJAMIN SELWYN

polity

First published in 2014 by Polity Press

Polity Press
65 Bridge Street
Cambridge CB2 1UR, UK

Polity Press
350 Main Street
Malden, MA 02148, USA

ISBN-13: 978-0-7456-6014-1 (hardback)
ISBN-13: 978-0-7456-6015-8 (paperback)

A catalogue record for this book is available from the British Library.

Typeset in 10.5 on 12 pt Sabon by
Servis Filmsetting Ltd, Stockport, Cheshire
Printed and bound in Great Britain by Clays Ltd, St Ives plc

The publisher has used its best endeavours to ensure that the URLs for external websites referred to in this book are correct and active at the time of going to press. However, the publisher has no responsibility for the websites and can make no guarantee that a site will remain live or that the content is or will remain appropriate.

Every effort has been made to trace all copyright holders, but if any have been inadvertently overlooked the publisher will be pleased to include any necessary credits in any subsequent reprint or edition.

For further information on Polity, visit our website: www.politybooks.com

CONTENTS

v

FIGURES AND TABLES

Figures

Tables

ACKNOWLEDGEMENTS

This book is a collection of essays and something greater. It is a collection of essays because sections of the core chapters have been written or published previously as individual articles. It is more than a collection because I have modified every chapter from the original article, and I have added substantial additional chapters. My hope is that while each chapter can stand alone, together they provide a more integrated argument about processes of development under, against and potentially beyond capitalism.

Each chapter engages with fundamental themes in development studies. The difference between this work and other books that discuss theories of development is that I engage critically and hopefully creatively with rival theories, from the perspective of labour, derived from Marxian political economy.

The chapters in this book draw upon and develop arguments previously published. Part of chapter 2 was published in *New Political Economy* (volume 14, 2009), part of chapter 3 was published in *Global Labour Journal* (volume 4, 2013), a large part of chapter 4 was published in *Economy and Society* (volume 40, 2011), and part of chapter 7 was published in *Economic and Political Weekly*, volume 46, 2011).

In the writing of this book I have incurred many intellectual debts. First and foremost, I wish to thank my colleagues in the Historical Materialism World Development Research Seminar (HMWDRS) who have provided a brilliant forum for thinking through and applying Marxist political economy to questions of development: Elena Baglioni, Liam Campling, Gavin Capps, Owen Miller, Jonathan Pattenden, Jeff Webber and, in particular, Satoshi Miyamura, with whom I wrote an earlier draft of chapter 6. Many people have read and commented on parts of this book. They include Tom Selwyn, Kamran Matin, Kees van der Pijl, Justin Rosenberg, Earl Gammon, John Glenn, Andy Mason, Chris Armstrong, Tony Evans, Ben Fine, Dimitris Milonakis, Cris Kay, Demet Dinler, David Blaney, Knud Erik Jorgensen, Colin Barker, Marcus Taylor, Lucia Pradella and Sandra Halperin. In developing my ideas I have benefited enormously from being a member of the Centre for Global Political Economy and the department of International Relations at the University of Sussex. I owe a long-standing political debt to Mike Pany, George Roe and Martin Chapman. I thank David Held, Susan Beer, Jennifer Jahn and Elliot Karstadt at Polity for supporting this project. A huge debt of thanks, as always, to my wife Mjriam, who read much of this book and suggested ways of clarifying my arguments. Finally, I dedicate this book to Henry Bernstein – teacher, friend and colleague who has taught me so much about political economy.

— 1 —

THE GLOBAL DEVELOPMENT CRISIS

The central paradox of the contemporary world is the simultaneous presence of wealth on an unprecedented scale, and mass poverty. Liberal ideology and practice, as propounded by international financial institutions (IFIs) and heads of trans-national corporations, state leaders and their intellectual supporters explains the relationship between capitalism and poverty as one based around the dichotomy of inclusion (into capitalism) vs exclusion (from capitalism). The global capitalist system, or 'the world market' or 'the free market', is portrayed as a sphere of economic dynamism, an arena where freedom to exchange prevails, and as a source of developmental opportunities for less developed countries.

Within such explanatory frameworks poor countries and their populations are held to be poor not because of the nature of the capitalist world system, but because of their effective exclusion from it. Policies such as trade liberalization and the deregulation of markets (in particular financial, commodity and labour markets) are designed to remove state 'distortions', and thus enable poor countries to harness the dynamism of the market. An example of this way of thinking is provided by Anthony Giddens, who argues that the main problems experienced by poor countries 'don't come from the global economy itself, or from the self-seeking behaviour on the part of the richer nations. They lie mainly in the societies themselves – in authoritarian government, corruption, conflict, over-regulation and the low level of emancipation of women' (Giddens 2000, 129). In this way of thinking the world market is often portrayed as a ladder (of opportunity and wealth), where, once on the bottom rung, poor countries have the possibility of climbing further up and, by doing so, accelerating the human development of their population.

1

The inclusion/exclusion discourse reflects what Henry Bernstein (1992) labels a 'residualist' understanding of the relationship between capitalism and poverty, where 'exclusion' from 'the market' is the main cause of poverty. At the heart of this understanding is the assumption that 'inclusion' (into capitalism, or globalization, or the world market) brings economic growth and development, and improves the incomes and livelihoods of all participants. An example of a residualist perspective is UN Millennium project director Jeffrey Sachs' defence of the proliferation of sweatshop labour across the global south. He argues that 'rich-world protestors ... should support increased numbers of such jobs' and that '[t]he sweatshops are the first rung on the ladder out of extreme poverty' (Sachs 2005, 11) (see chapter 5 for a direct critique of this argument).[1]

The ideological appeal of the residualist discourse to defenders of neoliberal globalization should be clear. It shifts our focus away from investigating how a particular type of economic system (capitalism) simultaneously generates poverty and wealth. It reframes the debate around the axiom that capitalism must, by definition, provide the solutions to the world's poor, and that therefore, the problem of development is not the capitalist system itself, but exclusion from it. Through this discursive act capitalism remains a pristine non-object of analysis (Wood 1991, 1–11).

Neoliberalism represents the contemporary ideological defence and justification of capitalism, where markets are said to operate optimally when they are 'freed' from state and other forms of non-market interference. The ideological power of this definition of capitalism is that markets are portrayed as neutral arenas of exchange that do not favour any particular social group or class. However, behind the ideology, neoliberal policy relies heavily upon states to reshape class relations in favour of capital, in particular finance capital (Harvey 2005, Harman 2008, Panitch and Konings 2009). As shall be argued throughout this book however, capitalist markets are not neutral arenas of exchange, or benign spheres of developmental opportunity. Rather, they are sets of social relations that reproduce the subordination of the greater part of society (labourers) to the minority (owners of capital). Because markets are contested social relations, they are based upon rival interests and visions of how the ownership, control

---

[1] For a highly influential exposition of the residualist framework see the World Bank's (2002a), *Globalization, Growth and Poverty: Building An Inclusive World Economy*. Robert Wade (2005a) and Ray Kiely (2007, 131–60) provide excellent critiques of the World Bank's position.

and consumption of of wealth should be organized. Neoliberal policy and ideology seeks to strengthen the social institutions that 'advance the disciplinary power of markets' over labouring classes (Taylor 2006, 7). Economic thought that understands markets as non-political arenas of exchange logically precludes political economy analysis, as 'politics' are externalized from market activities.

The portrayal of capitalism as a benign sphere of human activity goes hand-in-hand with another firmly held axiom within develop-ment thinking – that development 'policy' consists of enlightened actors (states, entrepreneurs, international institutions and Non-Governmental Organizations) carrying out actions *for* the poor (or at best, constituting the leading 'partner' with the poor). The way 'the poor' are portrayed in much development discourse are as the 'disempowered' who need to be 'empowered' by benign assistance from above. At the sharp end of this mode of thought, the poor need to be forcefully liberated from oppressive state rulers through Western foreign military intervention and effective re-colonization (Collier 2007). Contrary to such paternalist conceptions of develop-ment policy this book argues for a conception of development that is undertaken by 'the poor' themselves – that is, a labour-centred conception of development. Such a conception is premised upon a fundamental critique of capitalism.

It is the argument of this book that if we are to understand the apparent paradox of immense wealth and mass poverty, then rather than following a residualist mode of analysis, we require a deep and sustained theoretical and empirical scrutiny of capitalist processes of development.

In opposition to residualist conceptions of development, Henry Bernstein proposes a relational conception, which

> Investigate[s] the causes of . . . poverty in terms of social relations of production and reproduction, of property and power that characterize certain types of development, and especially those associated with the spread and growth of capitalism. A relational approach thus asks rather different questions [to the residualist approach]: are some poor *because* others are rich (and vice versa)? What are the mechanisms that generate both wealth and poverty as two sides of the same coin of (capitalist) development? (Bernstein 1992, 24, original emphasis)

What are the social relations to be conceptualized and investigated in a relational political economy of development? Again, Bernstein (2010, 22–4) provides us with a useful guide. Four key questions, or registers, that constitute such a political economy are: Who owns what? (the question of property rights); Who does what? (the question of the social division of labour); Who gets what? (the question of the social division of fruits of labour); and, What do they do with it? (the question of the social relations of consumption). These four registers exist and mutually constitute each other nationally and internationally.

Early in their political careers Marx and Engels recognized the paradox of the simultaneous expansion of global wealth and poverty. In the Communist Manifesto, written in 1848, they observed how:

> The bourgeoisie, during its rule of scarce one hundred years, has created more massive and more colossal productive forces than have all preceding generations together. Subjection of Nature's forces to man, machinery, application of chemistry to industry and agriculture, steam-navigation, railways, electric telegraphs, clearing of whole continents for cultivation, canalization of rivers, whole populations conjured out of the ground – what earlier century had even a presentiment that such productive forces slumbered in the lap of social labour?

They also noted how, in the periodic economic crises that beset capitalism since its birth:

> ... there breaks out an epidemic that, in all earlier epochs, would have seemed an absurdity – the *epidemic of over-production*. Society suddenly finds itself put back into a state of momentary barbarism; it appears as if a famine, a universal war of devastation, had cut off the supply of every means of subsistence; industry and commerce seem to be destroyed; and why? Because there is *too much civilization, too much means of subsistence, too much industry, too much commerce.* (Marx and Engels 1848, emphasis added)

While in this text Marx and Engels portray the phenomenon of excess surpluses as a product of periodic economic crisis, it will be argued in the following chapters that it represents a deeper, structural problem of capitalism itself.

It needs to be emphasized at the outset that the argument here is *not* that capitalist states and markets cannot achieve and deliver economic growth. As the above quotes make clear, Marx and Engels understood the immense dynamism of capitalism as dwarfing anything achieved in previous modes of production. Capitalist states and markets generate rapid rates of economic growth, technological innovation and wealth generation. The argument, which will be developed throughout this book, is that while capitalism's productive dynamism represents a potential source of real human development, capitalism's social relations, in particular the non-democratic ownership of wealth

4

and means of creating wealth by a tiny percentage of the world's population, preclude such possibilities.

The discrepancy between capitalism's dynamism and widespread global poverty demands a fundamental questioning and re-thinking of what we understand by development. Does it mean economic growth? Does it mean the ending of global poverty? Does it mean economic 'catch-up', where previously poor states re-organize their resources (natural and human) and achieve rapid rates of economic growth, to become rich and stand alongside leading capitalist states in the world system? Amartya Sen rejects the reduction of development to economic measurements, arguing instead that development consists simultaneously of the 'removal of various types of unfreedoms that leave people with little choice and little opportunity of exercising their reasoned agency' and conjointly, 'a process of expanding the real freedoms that people enjoy' (Sen 1999, xii, 3). While I concur with Sen, I disagree with his understanding of how such a process of development can come about.

It is the argument of this book that capitalism precludes Sen's vision, as it is founded upon the systemic exploitation and repression of the majority (the world's labouring classes) by the minority (the world's capitalist classes and states). Exploitation under capitalism is understood by institutions such as the International Labour Organization (e.g. ILO 1999) and by liberal economists, as, for example, the payment of below-market wages, of excessively long working hours or demeaning working conditions.[2] This book argues that exploitation under capitalism is, rather, the pre-condition and basis of the capital–labour relation, and cannot, therefore, be 'solved' by benign state intervention (as advocated by the ILO) or of better functioning markets (as argued for by liberal economists). Rather, exploitation consists of capital's ability to pay workers a 'fair' wage in the labour market, but then use workers' labour power in the sphere of production to generate greater value (surplus value) than the price of the original wage. Capital can achieve this act based upon its ownership of social wealth and the means of producing that wealth (the 'means of production' in standard Marxist terminology) and worker's need to sell their labour power in order to earn a wage. To be sure, the forms of exploitation that the ILO and liberal economists identify exist across the world (north and south), but even if these forms were eliminated labour would still be exploited by capital.

---

[2] For a critique of the ILO's understanding of exploitation, and its alternative conception of Decent Work see Selwyn (2013), Lerche (2012) and Miyamura (2012).

Capitalism's dynamism, evidenced by its ability to propagate rapid economic growth, technical change and wealth generation is pursued and achieved in the interests of capital (firms) and states, and not in the interests of the majority of the world's population. Capital's ability to systematically and continually exploit labour requires a political-economic infrastructure to reproduce this unequal relationship. Democracy and freedom of choice are therefore limited, often to the sphere of electoral politics and to consumerism (itself determined by workers' relatively limited purchasing power). However, while the relationship between capital and labour is based on an unequal, antagonistic and exploitative relationship, this does not preclude labouring classes from mobilizing to demand improvements in their pay and working conditions and over the extent of their democratic participation within society.

These mobilizations can force capitalist states to engage in progressive actions, such as the establishment of universal suffrage, welfare states and regulation of labour markets and workplaces in order to limit the kinds of exploitation identified by liberals and the ILO. These gains are a product of labouring-class struggles, real and potential, and their ability to threaten the stability of capitalist social relations.

Struggles between capital and labouring classes have short, and medium/long-term institutional and developmental outcomes. Short-term outcomes may reflect more or less concession to labour from capital (for example higher or lower wages). Medium and long-term outcomes become institutionalized in the form and extent of labouring-class representation (e.g. what kinds of actions trade unions can engage in), and in state formation, where labouring classes are more or less incorporated into the state structure (compare, for example, the Brazilian state's structures in relation to labour before and after the 1964 military coup). These processes, in turn, reflect the balance of class power, which describes a situation where representatives of one class are able to formulate their own objectives and force other classes to concede to them (Cliff 1979, 1995; Harman 1984a). Shifts in the balance of power towards labouring classes can have positive institutional and developmental outcomes for labouring classes.

The above arguments about capitalism's incompatibility with human development, and the balance of class power as a core variable in the developmental processes and outcomes of the world's labouring classes, may strike many within the development studies community as counter-intuitive. In the following section I suggest that this is because the evolution of development studies and

6

thinking about development more broadly has been characterized by an intellectual hollowing out, often resulting in explicit or implicit celebrations of capitalism, rather than in a systemic critique of the system itself.

The Rise, Fall and Re-Birth of Thinking about Development/ Development Thinking

Reflection on the nature of development can be traced back at least as far as Aristotle's concept of Eudaimonia (which is often understood to mean the process of human flourishing) or to Adam Smith's conception of different phases of human development (the ages of hunters, of shepherds, of agriculture and finally of commerce).

The systematic and institutionalized study of development and its translation into national and international policy emerged, however, during the moment of de-colonization following the Second World War. The post-colonial moment represented a particular world historical conjuncture, entailing anti-colonial struggles and revolutions, the threat of the global expansion of soviet-style 'communism', the emergence of the United States as the hegemonic power of the economically more advanced Western hemisphere, and the successful Marshall Plan in Western Europe. It occurred in the midst of the Keynesian revolution (Keynes 1936), which, for a generation at least, overthrew established neoclassical ways of thinking.

Northern states and the international institutions that they created at the 1944 Bretton Woods conference sought to incorporate certain Keynesian precepts into their national and international policies, in particular the recognition of the possibility and necessity of states stimulating economic growth. These actions established what, by comparison to the prior colonial period and today's neoliberal-dominated policy consensus, Philip McMichael (2000) labels the 'development project'. States in the emerging 'Third World' were encouraged and assisted by northern states and international institutions in pursuing active development policies. Within this unique conjuncture, institutional space was created in universities, funded by the post-war boom and relatively progressive fiscal policies, in particular in economics and sociology departments, for the study of the problems faced by the world's poorer countries (Leys 1996).

The post-colonial moment, then, generated a rich proliferation of thinking and debate about development. From Rostow's (1960) modernization theory to Frank (1966) and Wallerstein's (1974) dual

7

riposte in the forms of dependency and World Systems theory respectively, themselves drawing on the Latin American structuralist school of development thinking (Kay 1989), to the burgeoning attempts to construct a specific sub-field of development economics by figures such as Hirschman, Gerschenkron, Rosenstein-Rodan, Lewis and Myrdal (discussed in chapter 4), development thinking enjoyed something of a 'golden age'.

Prior to the Keynesian revolution and the emergence of development economics, thinking about development, informed primarily by neoclassical economics, had operated according to a double set of assumptions based on monoeconomics and mutual gains (Hirschman 1981). The monoeconomic assumption was that economic 'laws' were applicable across time and space.[3] The assumption of mutual gains from trade was derived from Ricardo's model of comparative advantage. Albert Hirschman (1981) notes how development economics rejected monoeconomics, but retained the expectation of mutual gains. The rejection of monoeconomics opened the door, intellectually and politically, to diverse forms of industrial, trade and technology policy, and to questions of the state's role in coordinating the economy. The expectation of mutual gains (that advanced economies would gain from poor countries' development) created an institutional environment in the advanced economies favourable to heterodox development thinking.

Within the expanding sub-field of development economics there was considerable scope for investigating and theorizing how capitalism generated simultaneous economic dynamism and stagnation. Development economics represented, to a significant degree, a commitment to a relational political economy. While most of its proponents were committed to establishing viable national capitalist economies, they did not shy away from subjecting capitalism itself to a relatively critical scrutiny. While few of these development economists considered how labouring classes and their struggles to ameliorate their conditions could be constitutive of human development, the rise of development economics nevertheless represented an important moment in intellectual and policy history.

The 'golden age' was not to last however, and gave way, under conditions of world economic crisis, slowing growth and indebtedness across much of the Third World, to what John Toye (1987)

---

[3] Former US Treasury Secretary Lawrence Summers summed up the essence of monoeconomics when he quipped that 'The laws of economics are like the laws of engineering . . . One set of laws works everywhere' (quoted in Klein 2009).

described as the neoliberal counter-revolution. The counter-revolution re-enshrined the principles of monoeconomics within much development thinking. The re-founded dominance of (neo)liberal monoeconomics generated the so-called Washington Consensus, centred around removing state 'distortions' from the economy, which, it was endlessly proclaimed, would lead to renewed growth, poverty alleviation and accelerated human development (Williamson: 1989). Under these intellectual and political conditions, development thinking, with its commitment to heterodox political economy, witnessed a rapid impoverishment, so much so that by late 1980s it was common to describe development studies as having reached an 'impasse' (Booth 1985; Sklair 1988; Kiely 1995).

To be sure, the neoliberal counter-revolution did not eliminate all non-liberal thinking. There were stimulating intellectual developments in gender and development analysis (see Kabeer 1994; Visvathan et al. 1997), in 'Post-development' (Sachs 1992; Escobar 1995) and within Marxism (Warren 1980; Shaikh 1980; Byres 1991). And, as we shall discuss in chapters 2 and 4, Statist Political Economy represented a very powerful counter-position to neoliberal thought. However, these currents were sideshows to an increasingly hegemonic neoliberal monoeconomics.

Despite the intellectual simplicity and hence policy attractiveness, and institutional power of neoliberal monoeconomics, and contrary to many expectations, development studies did not disappear. Rather, and perhaps paradoxically, it was re-born, manifested by the rapid expansion of development studies departments in much of the northern-English speaking world and beyond. Part of the reason for this re-birth was the recognition from the early 1990s onwards, that the Washington Consensus's 'minimum programme' of 'freeing' markets from distorting state activities had not, and could not, lead to the kinds of growth rates that its exponents were promising and hoping for. With this recognition, the Post-Washington Consensus emerged, with a central role for the state (Stiglitz 1998; and for a critique see Fine 1999).

However, rather than a return to the heterodox, relational political economy of the 'golden age', under the hegemony of the Post-Washington consensus, the state was (re)conceptualized as a 'supporting' actor in expanding and delivering market 'opportunities' to the populations of the global south (and north). Consequently, as Bernstein (2005) suggests, while in the 1980s development thinking experienced a process where 'less became more' (based on the assumptions that limiting state activity in the economy would 'free up' market dynamism), in the 1990s and beyond 'more became less' as the myriad policy mechanisms required to 'support' the market contributed to the expansion of development studies' remit, but at the continued expense of its earlier, more critical and relational incarnation. Within its expanded remit development studies (in universities) and development discourse (as propounded by governments, aid agencies and many campaigning organizations) revolves increasingly around a residualist perspective, where solutions, based on ever-greater market integration, are posed to problems ranging from poverty reduction and environmental destruction to anti-corruption and state-reform. As Bernstein (2005, 119) argues

> [N]otions such as 'pro-poor growth' . . . expresses . . . the commitment of contemporary development discourse and doctrine to 'win-win' solutions and its faith that an inclusive . . . market economy . . . contains no intrinsic obstacles to a better life for all.

Bernstein argues that what has been lost to development thinking/ studies as a consequence of the hegemony of neoliberal monoeconomics is 'the wider intellectual, and political, understanding of development as a process of struggle and conflict, and use of the diverse intellectual resources available to advance such an understanding' (Bernstein 2005, 119). It is such an understanding, and the generation of the intellectual tools necessary to support it, that represents this book's rationale. This rationale is reinforced when we consider the nature of the paradox of global wealth and poverty.

Some Considerations on Global Wealth and Poverty

Soon after the onset of the current global economic crisis the World Bank estimated that its effects would generate 'from 55 million to 90 million more extreme poor in 2009 than expected before the crisis' (World Bank 2009, 2). Since then the crisis has deepened and shows little sign of abating. The plight of the global poor contrasts with the fortunes of the world's 100 richest people who, in 2012 alone, became $241 billion richer (Miller and Newcomb 2013). Oxfam calculates that this $241 billion would be enough to end extreme poverty (those living under US$1.25 a day) four times over (Oxfam 2013). These figures only describe documented *income*, and are thus an underestimate of global wealth. The extent of unaccounted-for wealth is significantly greater. By 2010, for example, there was somewhere between $21 and $32 trillion of hidden financial assets

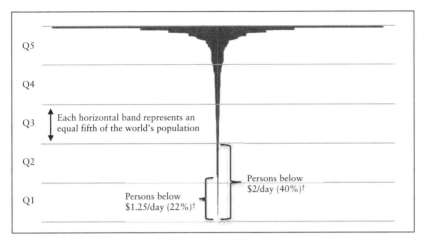

Figure 1.1 Global Income Distribution by Quintiles of the Population in 2007 (or latest available) in PPP constant 2005 International dollars

(Permission to reproduce this figure obtained from the UN.)

Source: Adapted from UNDP (2005) using World Bank (2011), UNL-WIDER (2008) and Eurostat (2011)
*According to the global accounting model
†Based on Chen and Ravallioin (2008)

held offshore, and thus untaxed, by 'high net worth individuals' (Tax Justice Network 2012a, 33).

Figure 1.1 provides a static image of the *global division of wealth by income* by dividing the distribution of world GDP into quintiles (world population divided into fifths). Ironically it is shaped like a champagne glass and shows that in 2007 61 million individuals (around one per cent of the global population) had incomes equal to the bottom 3.5 billion individuals (56 per cent of the global population) (Ortiz and Cummins 2011). A dynamic image of this division of wealth would consider how the *income gap* between the richest and poorest fifth of the world's population has been widening over the last half-century: From 30:1 in 1960, to 60:1 in 1990 and 74:1 in 1997 (UNDP, cited in Glenn 2007,156). One manifestation of this growing income gap is reflected by how 'the relative income share of the poorest 30 per cent of humanity was *reduced* by about one-fifth during the 1988–2002 period: from 1.52 to 1.22 per cent of global household income' (Pogge 2010, 11, 105–6, emphasis added).

While the data shown in figure 1.1 detail patterns of the global distribution of wealth, they tell us relatively little about how wealth is distributed within the countries of the global south. The Tax Justice Network (2012a), however, provides data for 139 'mostly low-middle income countries' and notes that:

> [T]raditional data show aggregate external debts of US$4.1 trillion at the end of 2010. But take their foreign reserves and unrecorded offshore private wealth into account, and the picture reverses: they had aggregate net debts of *minus US$10.1–13.1 trillion* . . . [T]hese countries are big net creditors, not debtors. [However], their assets are held by a few wealthy individuals, while their debts are shouldered by their ordinary people through their governments.

A recent study by Boyce and Ndikumana (2011) shows how:

> [S]ub-Saharan Africa experienced an exodus of more than $700 billion in capital flight since 1970 . . . Africa is a net creditor to the rest of the world in the sense that its foreign assets exceed its foreign liabilities. But there is a key difference between the two: the assets are in the hands of private Africans, while the liabilities are public, owed by the African people at large through their governments.

This is compared to Africa's $177 billion in external debts (Ndikumana and Boyce 2011).[4] If this wealth was subject to some form of democratic control in its distribution, it would be possible to envision an Africa with significantly lower levels of absolute and relative poverty. Democratic control over wealth generation and ownership is not, however, a subject of discussion within mainstream development discourse.

The discrepancies between extreme wealth and poverty reflect deep structural processes within the contemporary world system. According to the Food and Agriculture Organization the numbers of undernourished people in the world increased from 825 million in 1995–1997, to 923 million in 2007 and to 1023 million in 2009. The rapid increase between 2007 and 2009 was in part due to financial speculation on commodities in response to falling profits elsewhere in the world economy. While the numbers of undernourished people fell to 925 million in 2010 this was a consequence of falling (and continually fluctuating) prices, rather than an increase in food security for the world's poor (FAO 2011). The prevalence of global malnutrition does

---

4 See also Tax Justice Network 2012b.

not, however, reflect a lack of food. As the World Food Programme notes 'Food has never before existed in such abundance . . . In purely quantitative terms, there is enough food available to feed the entire global population of seven billion people'.[5] The total quantity of food produced globally is 'more than one and a half times what is needed to provide every person on earth with a nutritious diet' (Weis 2007, 11). As Farshad Araghi notes, we now live in a world where 'hunger amidst scarcity' has given way to 'hunger amidst abundance' (Araghi 2000, 155).

The magnitude of the development crisis that confronts the populations of the global south is caputured well by Thomas Pogge:

> At 18 million per year, the global poverty death toll over the 15 years since the end of the Cold War was around 270 million, roughly the population of the US. If the magnitude of the world poverty problem remains constant, the poverty death toll for the period from the Millenium Declaration [2000] to 2015 will likewise be about 270 million. (Pogge 2003, 17).

Capitalism, Exploitation and Economic Growth

These discrepancies – between immense economic wealth concentrated in the hands of the global elite, and widespread poverty – are the source of resentment and rebellion across much of the global south (and north). Such rebellions were on the agenda even before the onset of the global economic crisis. US geostrategist Zbigniew Brezinski described a situation where '[I]n the twenty-first century the population of much of the developing world is . . . politically stirring. It is a population conscious of social injustice to an unprecedented degree and resentful of its deprivations and lack of personal dignity' (Brezinski 2007, 203). Since the onset of the crisis these rebellions have deepened in their intensity and widened geographically. As Immanuel Wallerstein (2012) puts it 'the geography of protest constantly shifts. Tahrir Square in Cairo yesterday, unauthorized massive marches with pots and pans in Montreal today, somewhere else (probably somewhere surprising) tomorrow.'

Neither (neo)liberals nor their statist critics like to dwell on capitalism's mis-match between ever-increasing global wealth and continued mass poverty. Nor do they incorporate the above-mentioned mass

[5] http://www.wfp.org/hunger/causes.

movements into their consideration of development processes. They are particularly loath to associate the simultaneous reproduction of immense wealth and widespread poverty with exploitation. While they disagree on the precise balance of state-led and market-led economic activity, both camps agree that economic growth is the most effective (almost magical) solution to the problem of poverty (Wade and Wolf 2002). But is it? Not only does such a faith in growth obviate the need to look elsewhere for sources of human development, it also represents a profoundly a-political conception of the capitalist economic system. Gareth Dale provides a sharp explanation for the predominance of the growth paradigm:

> [G]rowth serves as an *idealized refiguration* of capitalist social rela-
> tions; it serves to naturalize and justify the prevailing social order. . . .
> Discussion of the economic by way of biological analogy implies con-
> tinuity (gradual change), and unity (it is the 'social whole' that grows).
> When represented through the discourse of growth, the interests of
> capital come to be identified with the common good, because the
> profitability of capital . . . appears as a necessary condition for the satis-
> faction of all other interests. Without profitable enterprises there will be
> no investment, no employment, no taxation, and no money for workers
> to pursue their goals. (Dale 2012, 106)

Economic growth under capitalism is generated by capital's impera-tive to continually expand. While this expansion is widely interpreted and proclaimed, within liberal and non-liberal ideology, as benefiting all members of society, the following chapters investigate how it is based upon the production and reproduction of exploitative capital–labour relations. Because of this unpalatable fact most political economy, whether liberal or statist, rests upon the continued obfusca-tion of human social relations under capitalism. Indeed 'as a system of competition capitalism depends on the growth of capital; as a class system it depends on obscuring the source of that growth' (Kidron and Gluckstein 1974, 35).

Capitalist exploitation takes place across five distinct but intercon-nected and mutually constituting moments. These are:

(1) Within the sphere of production (the workplace) where surplus value is generated by workers and extracted by capital;
(2) Within the sphere of exchange (the labour market) where workers' labour power is institutionally organized so that it can be sold to capital for its subsequent exploitation in the workplace, and

where workers' wages constitute 'effective demand' for capital's products;

(3) Within the private sphere (the family) where (mostly) women's unpaid labour contributes to the generational reproduction of the labour force (Weeks 2011);

(4) Through 'race' and racism, which facilitates the generation of categories of worker for particular occupations, reproduces cultural 'distinctions' and divisions among labouring classes and 'justifies' unequal economic rewards (Wolf 1982; Callinicos 1995).

(5) In capitalist societies' interface with its substratum (nature) where the latter is commodified and used by capital as an input into production and as a dumping ground for waste production (Foster 2010; Moore 2011).

The following chapters emphasize mainly the first and second moments of capitalist exploitation and reproduction. While questions of gender and race are taken up briefly in this book, I recognize that their coverage is limited compared to my focus on the process of exploitation of labour within the workplace and the labour market. In the future I hope to address the latter moments (points 3–5) more systematically. If it is accepted that capitalism is a system of exploitation, which by necessity reduces the majority of humanity and nature to the status of commodity inputs into profit-oriented production and exchange, then there is a strong case for thinking about non-capitalist alternatives. But where are the actors who can and do resist capitalist exploitation, and who could potentially generate a non-capitalist developmental future? I suggest that the women and men (and sometimes children) who make up this potentially developmental actor exist within the global labouring class.

Labouring Classes Under Global Capitalism

Throughout this book, the term 'labouring classes' is used to refer to 'the growing numbers . . . who now depend – directly and indirectly – on the sale of their labour power for their own daily reproduction' (Panitch and Leys 2001). Over the last four decades or so there has been an enormous expansion of the global labouring class – from 1.1 billion people in 1980 to 3.05 billion in 2005. Women have been increasingly integrated into the global labour force – rising from 38.6 per cent to 40.1 per cent (Kapsos 2007, 13). Fifty-five percent (around 1.7 billion people) of the global labour force is located

15

within East, South East Asia and South Asia. During the above period regional labour forces more than doubled in Central America, the Caribbean and South America, expanded by around 149 per cent in the Middle East and North Africa (making it the fastest-growing labour force in the world), and by approximately 2.7 per cent per annum in Sub-Saharan Africa (Kapsos 2007, 16) (see also Freeman 2006 and Haynes 2011).

In 2010 there were approximately 942 million working poor (almost 1 in 3 workers globally living on under US$2 a day). The ILO notes that '[t]he poor are . . . unlikely to be unemployed' and that the 'majority of persons living in extreme poverty cannot afford to be unemployed' (ILO/KILM 2011). However, it calculates poverty levels using the World Bank's (self-acknowledged) extremely conservative nominal poverty lines of US$1 and US$2 a day (Ravillon 2004). Woodward (2013) suggests a more realistic (and humane) global poverty line, of US$5 a day. If adopted, the ILO would have to concede that the majority of the world's labouring class lives in poverty (see also NEF 2010).

Social classes can be defined as 'common positions within the social relations of production, where production is analysed above all as a system of exploitation' (Wright 1979, 17). The term 'labouring classes' includes urban/industrial workers ('the working class' in traditional Marxian terminology), the 'new middle class' of white-collar workers (Callinicos and Harman 1989) and informal workers that populate the ever-expanding 'planet of slums' (Davis 2006; Standing 2011). The definition extends to some workers in the rural sphere who are sometimes classified as 'peasants' (in particular the poorer peasants) (Bernstein 2009). As Panitch and Leys (2001) note, 'capital is more geographically diversified than it used to be because it now has more working classes to exploit.' The geographical spread and diverse forms that capital take are mirrored by a huge diversity of forms and conditions of labour.

This diversity is manifested in a number of ways that can be illustrated schematically. First, workers employed within globalized production networks, with workshops located in Export Processing Zones (EPZs) north and south, are experiencing an intensification of work driven by capital's attempts at increasing the rate of exploitation. Many of these workers receive poverty wages that are insufficient to meet their social reproductive needs. Naomi Klein described how:

[T]he workday is long – 14 hours in Sri Lanka, 12 hours in Indonesia, 16 in Southern China, 12 in the Philippines. The vast majority of the

workers [in EPZs] are women, always young, always working for contractors or subcontractors . . . filling orders for companies based in the
US, Britain, Japan, Germany or Canada. The management is military-
style, the supervisors often abusive, the wages below subsistence and the
work low-skill and tedious. (Klein 2000, 205–6).

Secondly, and analytically separate from the previous group of
workers, there is a process of 'fragmentation' of labour occurring,
with large swathes of the global labouring class unable to secure
permanent, full-time work. These workers often straddle the rural/
urban, agrarian/industrial divide, live in the urban slums that are
expanding across the global south and have to rely on various and
numerous types of work and sources of employment to secure their
and their families' social reproduction (Bernstein 2009). The expansion of this 'planet of slums' and the informalization of work has been
driven by expulsions from the land. Araghi (2000, 151) estimates,
that about 65 per cent of the growth of the world's urban population
is 'attributable to rural-urban migration'.

Thirdly, while the second group can, at one level of abstraction, be
analytically distinguished from the first group, there are nevertheless
real connections between the two. For example, in her research on
the evolving conditions of South Africa's working class Claire Ceruti
(2007, 22–3) illustrated the interconnections between 'secure' (formal
sector) and insecure (informal sector) workers' conditions. One case,
from Soweto, is instructive:

Mr Khumalo . . . was a teacher and now works as a driver. He lives
with his wife, who is a nurse, and his three children. One child is at
university. He supports his brother and his sister. His brother has been
unemployed for two years after the factory closed.

The conditions of the global labouring class are well captured by
Arrighi and Moore, who argue that:

The underlying contradiction of a world capitalist system that pro-
motes the formation of a world proletariat but cannot accommodate a
generalized living wage (that is, the most basic of reproduction costs),
far from being solved, has become more acute than ever. (Arrighi and
Moore 2001, 75)

This contradiction is as much a product of current economic stagnation, itself rooted in a longer and deeper crisis of profitability and
neoliberal restructuring, as it is to do with the concentration of wealth
within the hands of a tiny global minority. Each of these determinants
of the poverty and near-poverty of the world's labouring classes

(stagnation, neoliberalism, concentration of wealth) is an outcome of processes of class formation on national and global scales and the particular balance of power between classes. It is quite plausible that through a major shift in the balance of class power a significantly greater percentage of the global workforce than at present could earn a living wage. Such a shift would also, no doubt, raise further possibilities for greater democratic control over resource generation and allocation (discussed further in chapter 8).

The simultaneous numerical and geographical expansion, increasing exploitation, immiseration and fragmentation of the global labouring class means that there will not be any spontaneous, homogenous expression of world working-class solidarity and political unity against capital. Political expression will take myriad forms, ranging from reactionary to revolutionary. Throughout this book, however, I argue that exploitation is an inbuilt, constant feature of capitalism. Immiseration is often a pre-requisite and/or continuing requirement of exploitation (and it is increasingly so under contemporary globalization), and that it is not, therefore, unreasonable to expect that resistance by various labouring classes will continue to characterize the relations between globalized capital and labour. Under such circumstances it behoves progressive social scientists, thinkers and activists to consider the extent to which such resistance can be considered 'developmental', that is, whether it can generate human developmental gains in the present and future. It is also necessary to think through how such struggles can contribute to an alternative future vision and reality of human development.

At this point, however, supporters of capitalism, or doubters of alternatives to it, might say that it is utopian to think beyond economic growth, capital accumulation and even capitalism itself. They may also add that surely 'the market' generates and allocates resources far more efficiently than any 'planned' economy.

Human Development Within and Beyond Capitalism

Supporters of capitalism often resort to Hayekian arguments about how market outcomes are optimal compared to any known alternative and the innate inefficiency of attempting to coordinate centrally these decisions:

> Knowledge of the circumstances of which we must make use never exists in concentrated or integrated form but solely as the dispersed bits

18

of incomplete and frequently contradictory knowledge which all the separate individuals possess. (Hayek 1949, 77)

Wan (2011, 9) neatly summarizes the Hayekian position thus: 'centralized planning is bound to fail because of the very nature of knowledge: there simply cannot be a central actor overseeing and controlling all knowledge.' But the Hayekian position conflates the surface appearance of atomized capitalist markets with their underlying social relations. Indeed, to deduce from the appearance of billions of people's seemingly individual choices that the capitalist system is one based upon autonomous decision making is to reify, or attribute real power to the market, which is in fact a deeply complex and coordinated human construction.

It is of course true that the scale of commodity production, exchange and consumption under contemporary capitalism is of a magnitude greater than any prior period of history. But does this mean that these interactions are based upon autonomous decision making? On the contrary, as Colin Barker puts it 'Commodity production has been the social form under which the most completely developed system of *social interdependence* in human history has been achieved' (1998, 3). To put it a different way, global capitalism is the most socially integrated and interconnected system ever known. For example, Peter Nolan (2003) shows how giant Trans-national Corporations (TNCs) play the role of system integrators, simultaneously coordinating the labour of workers in multiple locations. Through their control over proliferating global commodity chains, they engage in internal (within-firm) and external (between-firm) coordination as they attempt to structure the global economy in ways more rather than less favourable to their profit-maximizing objectives.

The concentration of power in TNC hands is highlighted when we consider their ownership structure. As Harman (2008, 28) calculated, the sales of the world's 2,000 biggest companies equalled about half of world output in 2008. He then assumed that around ten directors sit on the board of each of these TNCs. Consequently, 'out of a world population of over six billion, a mere 20,000 [mostly rich white men] exercise decisive control over the creation of wealth.' These figures and the underlying dynamics that support them also suggest, contra the Hayekian position, that planning is not only intrinsic to capitalism, but that it is an increasingly global phenomenon. The implications are, to quote Wan again, that '[T]he real choice before us is not between planning and laissez-faire, but between different modes of planning' (2011, 11). As I will argue in chapter 8, labouring classes potentially can manage the economic affairs of humanity better than capitalist firms and states.

Even if the above arguments are accepted, at this point readers may object to any talk of alternatives to capitalism asking, 'what about the failures of really existing socialism' in Russia and elsewhere? And if these countries did in some way represent an alternative to capitalist development then the reader would be correct, as they have proven to be developmental dead ends. There is, however, an important body of literature that demonstrates with empirical precision and theoretical clarity that the cases of 'really existing socialism' were forms of 'state capitalism'. This literature identifies the Russian revolution of October 1917 as the highpoint (so far) of workers' power, but also how, following international isolation and intervention, famine, de-industrialization and the physical disappearance of the pre-1917 industrial working class, the revolution was defeated from within, by Stalin's effective counter-revolution. In place of any semblance of workers' democracy Stalin established 'socialism in one country' and the first five-year plan in 1928. This literature includes Cliff (1974) and Haynes (2002) on Russia; Harman (1974) and Dale (2004) on Eastern Europe; Harris (1978) and Hore (1991) on China; Binns and Gonzalez (1980) on Cuba; and Zeilig (2010) on myriad Sub-Saharan African cases. These writers show how, following the model of Stalinist Russia, new post-colonial ruling classes used the state to accumulate capital rapidly, based upon the exploitation of their countries' working classes and peasantries, in order to compete in and attempt catch-up with more economically advanced capitalist countries. While these strategies achieved high rates of economic growth initially, they lost competitive ground from the 1980s onwards in an increasingly globalizing world (Harman 2008). To classify these countries as socialist is to accept uncritically their (and their opponents') ideological self-definition. But, as the above authors show, these countries were subject to the same competitive pressures as other states and firms in the world system. They responded to these pressures by implanting strategies designed to accumulate capital as rapidly as possible: consumption subordinated to accumulation, and capital accumulation driven by permanent external competition, based upon the repression and exploitation of labour.

If the 'soviet' states were 'state capitalist' then Marxism has more to offer than 'only' an *analysis* of the contemporary world. Indeed, as Marx himself argued, while philosophers [or political economists] have attempted to understand the world, the point, rather, is to *change* it. But how? This is perhaps the central problematic of critical political economy. On the one hand a vision of socialist equality may appeal to many disheartened or disgusted with capitalism. On the other hand the global dominance of capital makes realizing this vision extremely difficult, and often seemingly impossible. How, then, do we move from here to there? How do we conceptualize a form of development based on the expansion of people's freedoms – as opposed to the accumulation of capital or augmentation of state power? Moreover, how can such a development process be driven by the majority, for the majority, in contrast to the prevailing elitist conceptions of development associated with most of the thinkers we will discuss in this book?

Stuart Corbridge (2007) and Teddy Brett (2009) recognize that development studies must always be simultaneously critical (of theories, actors and institutions), and constructive (suggesting realistic alternatives as part of the critique). It is (relatively) easy, they point out, to deconstruct arguments and theories by counterposing them to abstract and utopian ideals. This strategy was (and is), for example, the modus operandi of neoliberal monoeconomics – where functioning market systems across the 'Global South' are deemed 'imperfect' by comparison to text-book 'perfect market' processes of resource allocation, distribution and utilization.

I agree with Corbridge and Brett's prescription, and accordingly, this book constitutes both a critique of existing ways of thinking about development, and an alternative conception of development – grounded in historical and contemporary processes, struggles and movements. In the chapters that follows I argue for a labour-centred (re)conception of human development. In this conception, labouring-class struggles are re-interpreted as potentially 'developmental' in that they contribute directly to improvements, both materially and in terms of generating more freedoms, of their lives and of their dependants and communities.

Unlike state-centred and capital-centred conceptions of development, that variously ignore or subordinate labouring classes to the requirements and actions of states and capital, a labour-centred development studies does not ignore the actions of states and market actors in attempting to foster their own, respective, visions of development. Rather it views these actions from the perspective of labour, and attempts to interpret them as processes and outcomes of complex relations between social classes. Put differently, state actions do not reflect a simple state 'logic' (as conceived within Realist International Relations theory), or represent actions on behalf of an abstract capitalist class. Rather state actions can be interpreted as an outcome of,

21

and on-going processes of, contested class relations. Within this field of contestation, there is significant room for manoeuvre by labour, if it is able to tilt the balance of power in its favour. It is worth considering in some more detail, then, the nature of the capitalist state and its relation to labouring classes.

States and the Regulation of Labour

States play a central role in constructing and managing the political and legal structures within which capital accumulation occurs. These structures constrain workers' ability to organize, by determining which actions are legally recognized. Jessop's (2001; 2008) conception of the state as a strategic relational actor is useful because he shows how states do not simply command a monopoly over the means of violence in the Lenin–Weber sense. Rather, he suggests that states engage in building institutions designed to structure the behaviour of their citizens, to simultaneously reproduce state power and to guarantee the process of capital accumulation. 'Institutionalization involves not only the conduct of agents and their conditions of action, but also the *very constitution* of agents, identities, interests and strategies (Jessop 2008, 1230, emphasis added).

In a complementary vein, Edwards et al. (1994, 3) propose that the social organization of labour should be understood in terms of the regulation of 'the rules and expectations governing employment which develop from the interaction between states, employers, unions and workers'. Edwards and Elger's (1999) framework suggests that such regulation consists of the following:

(1) Employment relations under capitalism are based on an antagonistic relationship and are therefore inherently conflictual.
(2) Capitalist development is based to a large degree on the management of this conflict through a combination of domination and accommodation.
(3) This regulation involves the state in institutionally structuring the work process, the labour market, collective representation within and beyond the enterprise and the political representation of labour.
(4) Forms taken by such regulation vary both spatially and temporally.
(5) States are neither neutral actors in capital–labour relations nor do they simply represent the needs of an abstract 'capital' or specific

capitals. Rather they can best be considered as attempting to manage the process of capitalist development.

(6) Such regulation is continually undergoing transformation as the entities involved change in their relations to each other and in relation to other entities (e.g. in relation to changing global markets).

The production and reproduction of state institutions, 'is incomplete, provisional, and unstable, and . . . coevolve[s] with a range of other complex emergent phenomenon' (Jessop 2001, 1228, 1230). And state institutions, ranging from those established to manage the capital–labour relationship (ministries of labour) to their welfare functions, to their democratic forms, can themselves be understood as outcomes of prior and on-going struggles between capital and labour.[6] The implications of this conception of the state, and of the concept of the balance of class power is that through their struggles labouring classes can extract human developmental gains from states and capital (for example, in the form of better wages and conditions, greater state provision of welfare, and greater democratic participation). In fact, such struggles are a constant feature of capitalist societies, and it is in part, the dominance of monoeconomic and residualist conceptions of capitalist development that has kept them beyond the pale of development theory and practice. More profoundly, of course, most development thinkers' commitment to establishing viable capitalist states and economies precludes consideration of how labouring-class movements can challenge, in developmentally positive ways, capitalist social relations.

Organization of and Rationale for this Book

This book is about human development under and beyond capitalism. It addresses the question of how such development occurs and can occur, through a critical and constructive engagement with some of the most influential political economists of the last two centuries – Friedrich List, Karl Marx, Leon Trotsky, Joseph Schumpeter, Alexander Gerschenkron, Karl Polanyi and Amartya Sen. The rationale for discussing these thinkers is that they are the principal non-(neo) liberal theorists that students of development (within and outside universities) encounter. They also represent, in various ways, a rejection of residualist and moneconomic conceptions of development.

---

[6] See Bergquist (1986) for an outstanding illustration of this interrelationship.

It should be noted immediately that there are many more writers, originating from the global south, who deserve to be discussed at length as representatives of alternative visions of development. These include at least Mahatma Gandhi, Raúl Prebisch, Celso Furtado, Samir Amin, Ruy Mauro Marini, Frantz Fanon and Paulo Frierie. Nevertheless, the authors I have chosen to focus on are the principal representatives of non-liberal political economy within development thinking. That they are mostly from the global north (with the exception of Amartya Sen) reflects, in part, the hegemonic influence of northern thinkers upon issues of the transformation of southern societies.

Each of these political economists address issues of perennial importance in our attempts to understand strategies and processes of human development: strategies of catch-up development (List and Gerschenkron), the nature and socio-economic impacts of industrial innovation and economic growth (Schumpeter), the inner structures, expansive dynamics and social relations of capitalism (Marx and Trotsky), the possibilities of regulating, or in his words, 'embedding' the market in order to ensure human dignity (Polanyi) and the possibilities of human development taking the form of the expansion of individual freedom (Sen). Each of these political economists informs ways of thinking about post- (or non-) neoliberal development.

What distinguishes this book from other recent treatments of theories of development (for example, Willis 2005; Jomo 2005; Jomo and Reinert 2005; Jomo and Fine 2006; Rist 2008; Brett 2009; Payne and Phillips 2010) is that it approaches these political economists from the perspective of labour and how, specifically, they conceptualize the relationship between development and labouring classes (see table 1.1).

Each chapter presents these political economists' core ideas and then engages with them critically, by employing analytical concepts and categories derived from Marx. Marxism, I argue, potentially provides us with the deepest comprehension of capitalist development and alternatives to it, for three reasons. First, of the thinkers considered in this book only Marx and Trotsky were concerned principally with the nature of the capital–labour relationship as a determinant of capitalist development. For progressive thinkers, scholars and activists, an ignorance of the capital–labour relation is myopic, irresponsible and dangerous. This is because, as Michael Denning (2004, 224) reminds us 'the workplace remains the fundamental *unfree* association of civil society' (cited in Weeks 2011, 23, original emphasis). For those of us concerned with pursuing real human development,

Table 1.1 Key Thinkers in the Political Economy of Development

Key Thinker	Formative Influences	Intellectual Relationship to Labouring Classes	Key Problem of Investigation	Core Conception of Development
Friedrich List (1789–1846)	German weakness in face of Britain's Industrial Revolution; Positive impression of United States' industrial policy and subsequent economic growth.	Developed concept of 'productive power' to obscure nature of capital–labour relation.	How (some) agricultural countries could achieve industrial status and economic parity with advanced industrial countries.	Shift from peripheral agricultural economy to internationally competitive industrial economy.
Karl Marx (1818–1883)	First-hand experience of English industrial revolution under new capitalist class; Witness of emergence and self-organization of world's first industrial proletariat, and their struggles against the capitalist class.	Explained workers' exploitation by capital through labour theory of value, and why such a form of exploitation generated resistance from workers.	How industrial workers in particular and labouring classes generally could attempt and succeed at creating a future classless society.	Human development determined by struggles between classes; Human development as a process of individual and collective flourishing.

Table 1.1 (continued)

Key Thinker	Formative Influences	Intellectual Relationship to Labouring Classes	Key Problem of Investigation	Core Conception of Development
Leon Trotsky (1879–1940)	Writings of Marx and later Marxists; Analysis of rapid economic growth, structural change and class struggles in Russia at turn of nineteenth/ twentieth centuries; Experience of the first Russian Workers' Councils ('Soviet') of 1905.	Identification of Russian working class as having the ability to lead Russian revolution, thus triggering world revolution.	How states could pursue and achieve rapid industrialization through 'skipping stages' of economic development; How 'catch-up' development generated new social classes, tensions, and revolutionary possibilities; How new social classes could lead socialist revolution.	As with Marx, human development determined by struggles between classes; Human development as a process of individual and collective flourishing.
Joseph Schumpeter (1883–1950)	Influenced by Marxism and Marginalism; Witnessed emergence of giant firms, and 'socialization' of the economy under firm and state control.	Fear that labouring classes in particular and non-dominant classes generally would be able to achieve political and economic power through democratic means.	Capitalist innovation and dynamism and how it simultaneously generated rapid economic growth and expansion and economic recession and stagnation.	Entrepreneurial innovations leading to rapid capitalist expansion and economic structural transformation.
Alexander Gerschenkron (1904–1978)	Rejection of emergent 'modernization theory' in 1950s US; Trotsky's writings on Russian development;	Conceived of labouring classes as resource (to be exploited) for catch-up industrialization, but also as a threat to catch-up attempts.	Institutional innovations necessary to generate successful catch-up development.	Like Friedrich List, a conception of development entailing catch-up industrialization.

Karl Polanyi (1886–1964)	Conscious of dangers of failed attempts at late development – as exemplified by the Russian revolution. Influenced by but critical of Marxism. Critical of reigning marginalist economics Witness to 'Red' Vienna Advocate of Christian Socialism.	Ambiguous: on the one hand viewed labouring classes as foremost participants in generating societal 'counter-movements' against ravages of the free market. On the other hand viewed labouring classes as simply another social group in a potentially united society, alongside capitalists and other social classes.	How the capitalist market became all-encompassing, leading to the 'fictitious' commodification of labour, land and money and thus to potential societal breakdown; How 'society' confronted this potential breakdown with a 'counter-movement' leading to an 'embedded' market economy.	Development as human dignity and the struggle to prevent the free market from undermining it.
Amartya Sen (1933–)	Bengal famine (1942) in British-ruled India; Critique of economic growth-based conceptions of development.	Conceives of progressive social change as being generated by states and social elites (e.g. journalists, academics); Role of labouring classes restricted to their participation in democratic process.	How to transform a growth-centred conception of human development into a freedom centred conception.	Development as a dual process: of removing unfreedoms/ restrictions and of increasing individual freedoms.

27

such an ignorance is all the more perilous because the lack of freedoms associated with the workplace in developed countries are often magnified in late-developing countries.

The second reason for employing Marxism is that, as noted above, there has been an enormous expansion of the global labouring class over the last four decades. This (continuing) expansion, I argue, *increases* the relevance of Marx's analysis of capitalism. Some readers may object, however, that a focus on workplace relations represents only one facet of the conundrum of human development under (and potentially beyond) capitalism. The intention of the discussions that follow, however, are to explore how, through a creative and critical engagement with the above-mentioned political economists, we can understand the capital–labour relation as constituting far more than the relations between managers and workers at the point of production. To be sure, the purposive management of capital–labour relations lie at the heart of attempts at boosting economic growth and achieving catch-up development, through enhanced exploitation of labour in the workplace (see the chapters on List and Gerschenkron). However, an examination of these relations can also inform our comprehension of the form and content of global capitalist expansion and stratification (see the chapter on Schumpeter), the commodification of labour and its dehumanizing effects on the world's poor (Polanyi's key concern) and the limits to human freedom within and beyond the workplace, not least in the ability to secure a basic livelihood (Sen). This book does not, of course, claim to address every facet of capitalism's developmental crisis – issues such as environmental degradation, land grabbing and the dispossession of indigenous people's livelihoods and heritage, racial oppression, bio-piracy and the myriad forms of women's oppression are not discussed in any depth here. One book can only do so much.

There is a third reason for employing Marx. Not only does he provide the most fundamental critique of capitalist development, but he constructed historical materialism as a tool for labouring classes to combat and overcome their exploiters in order to create a world free of exploitation. At its best, Marxism represents a double pedagogy – of the oppressed and of hope (Frierie 1996; Van der Pijl 2007).

— 2 —

FRIEDRICH LIST AND THE FOUNDATIONS OF STATIST POLITICAL ECONOMY

A country like England, which is far in advance of all its competitors, cannot better maintain and extend its manufacturing and commercial industry than by a trade as free as possible from all restraints. For such a country, the cosmopolitan and the national principle are one and the same thing. (Friedrich List 1856 [1841], 79)

History is not without examples of entire nations having perished, because they know not and seized not the critical moment for the solution of the great problem of securing their moral, economical, and political independence, *by the establishment of manufacturing industry, and the formation of a powerful class of manufacturers and tradesmen.* (Friedrich List 1856 [1841], 82, emphasis added)

We begin our investigation of the major non-liberal political economists of development with a discussion of Friedrich List, author of the *National System of Political Economy*, first published in 1841. List's ideas have either directly influenced, or have neatly captured, a central strategy of late developing countries as they have attempted to achieve economic catch-up with already advanced countries. List was writing at a time when Britain's industrial revolution was enabling its capitalist class to dominate world markets. As the epigraph suggests, List was acutely aware that countries, or regions (such as his own German confederation of states) that did not employ protective counter-measures would experience industrial decimation at the hands of more competitive British industrial exports. He formulated the infant industry argument, based on historical investigations (reflecting his inductive methodology, see below) to guide economically backward countries as they sought to catch up with economically advanced ones. His central insight – that economic development under capitalism requires an extensive role for the state in generating and directing resources – is incontestable. '[N]o country has developed its industrial base without resorting to infant industry protection' (Shafaeddin 2005, 42).

List's *National System of Political Economy* can be considered as the founding text for what I will label statist political economy (SPE) (Reinert 1998; Chang 2002). Contemporary exponents of SPE represent some of the best-known opponents to neoliberal development theory and policy within and beyond the academy. They include Ha-Joon Chang, Robert Wade, Linda Weiss, Alice Amsden, Eric Reinart, Mehdi Shafaeddin, Peter Evans and Atul Kohli.

List's infant industry argument is represented within much contemporary development studies and political economy as constituting an anti-imperialist, pro-poor strategy that enables nations of the global south to pursue meaningful socio-economic development. For example, Ha-Joon Chang argues that 'most countries will be better off in the long run with a more activist development strategy than with the bankrupt Washington orthodoxy' (Chang 2012).

List's conception of state-led development emerged through a three-sided engagement – against the prevalent ideas of free trade associated with Adam Smith and David Ricardo, through his first-hand experience of attempts at economic statecraft of the recently independent United States and through an examination of the historical record of industrialization in Europe. Interestingly, in his intellectual and political formation List intersected with Marx in various ways.

Marx and List had much in common, in particular in their opposition to German autocracy. Consequently, they were both exiled (List to the United States, Marx to France, Belgium and finally the UK). It is less well known that they were both associated at some point with the critical and often censored liberal German newspaper *Rheinische Zeitung*, which they either edited (Marx) or of which they were offered the editorship (List). They both criticized British foreign rule and trade policy, justified by Smithian and Ricardian political economy, as based upon double standards and hypocrisy. However, despite these similarities Marx and List were protagonists of the two rivals to economic and political liberalism: communism from below and nationalism from above (Szporluk 1988).

Friedrich List and the Infant Industry Argument

List's Influences

List was influenced profoundly by his experience of exile (from 1825 to 1832) in the US, where, working as a journalist he became aware of and then took special interest in the 'American System' of political economy. Prior to this exposure he had been a free-trade advocate (Reinert 1998). When he arrived in the US he responded to an invitation by one of George Washington's trusted generals, Lafayette, and '[a]s a member of [his] entourage he visited New England, Pennsylvania, and Virginia and was able to observe many aspects of the development of the United States. He met a number of prominent Americans such as President John Quincy Adams [and] Henry Clay' (Henderson 1983, 68).

Many of the ingredients of *The National System* that List presented as a programme for the future development of Germany, and which were employed there after unification in 1871, were already present, in thought and practice, in the US half a century earlier. The key originators and exponents of this American system were Alexander Hamilton (first US Treasury Secretary 1789–1795), John Quincy Adams (sixth president of US 1825–29), Henry Clay (secretary of state 1825–29) and later Henry Carey (chief adviser to Abraham Lincoln 1861–65). For example, Henderson (1983) notes how Hamilton's (1791) *Report of the Secretary of the Treasury on the Subject of Manufactures* was the first attempt to formulate the 'infant industry' argument, by advocating combinations of import duties and import prohibition.

On the US senate website Henry Clay is referred to as 'the most influential member of the senate' during the 1830s and 1840s:

Henry' Clay's 'American System,' devised in the burst of nationalism that followed the War of 1812, remains one of the most historically significant examples of a government-sponsored program to harmonize and balance the nation's agriculture, commerce, and industry. This 'System' consisted of three mutually re-enforcing parts: a tariff to protect and promote American industry; a national bank to foster commerce; and federal subsidies for roads, canals, and other 'internal improvements' to develop profitable markets for agriculture. Funds for these subsidies would be obtained from tariffs and sales of public lands.[1]

---

[1] http://www.senate.gov/artandhistory/history/common/generic/Speeches_ClayAmericanSystem.htm.

Similar sentiments were expressed in Henry Carey's *The Harmony of Interests: Agricultural, Manufacturing and Commercial*. The intellectual justification of the American system prefigured two central aspects of List's political economy – first, the comprehension that political economy had geo-political foundations based in a nation state's sovereignty and its ability to regulate domestic economic relations, and second, a critique of British free trade policy as representing not general cosmopolitan, but particular national, imperialist, interests. In Clay's words, as he defended the system in the US senate against proponents of free trade:

> When gentlemen have succeeded in their design of an immediate or gradual destruction of the American System, what is their substitute? Free trade! Free trade! ... It is not free trade that they are recommending to our acceptance. It is, in effect, the British colonial system that we are invited to adopt; and, if their policy prevail[s], it will lead substantially to the recolonization of these states, under the commercial dominion of Great Britain.[2]

Contrary to the US senate website's claim that this system 'emerged in a burst of nationalism' it was was no quick fix following independence from Britain, but one that grew in strength over time. 'Coinciding with the start of European Liberalization, and accelerating after the North's victory in the Civil War, the United States economy began its period of import substitution industrialization behind rising tariff barriers' (Bairoch and Kozul-Wright 1996, 7). In fact, Bairoch (1993, 30) classifies the US as 'the mother country and bastion of modern protectionism'.

This system of political economy did not stop at the newly established national boundaries of the United States. The US developed, simultaneously, a specifically novel foreign policy – the 'Monroe doctrine'. It ostensibly aimed at assisting its (South) American neighbours achieve political freedom from decadent European (Spanish and Portuguese) power, while integrating them into an expanding US-dominated economic sphere. However, as Wood (2003) and Steadman Jones (1970) observe, this policy represented an adaption and extension of English 'free trade imperialism' by a rising capitalist power – resting on a combination of dollar and gunboat diplomacy in Latin America and internal territorial consolidation (against the native populations) and further expansion of the frontier. This double

---

[2] http://www.senate.gov/artandhistory/history/common/generic/Speeches_ClayAmericanSystem.htm.

aspect of the emerging US political economy – internal economic cohesion and external expansion – would figure centrally in List's political economy.

List against Smith

One of List's main objectives was to critique what he viewed as the cosmopolitan political economy associated with Adam Smith. He argued that Smith's 'fundamental error' was to confound 'cosmopolitical (sic) and individual economy with political economy' (cited in Bolsinger 2004, 5). Between individuals and the world market, stood the state: 'All human association ought to be considered under two points of view . . . the cosmopolitan, embracing all the human race, and the political or . . . national' (List 1856, 73). Bolsinger (2004, 12), argues that 'whereas Smith represents the culmination of the age of liberalism in the field of political economy, List stands for the rising age of nationalism and the ascendancy of the nation state.'

List (and Marx) opposed liberal political economy's abstract and deductive methodology that sought to generate future predictions based upon theories assuming the gains from trade (Smith's absolute and Ricardo's comparative advantage) (Milonakis and Fine, 2009). List's political economy was premised upon an inductive methodology, where future predictions are based on the observation of past historical patterns, and was later associated with the German historical school (Chang 2002). In List's Germany the social sciences were compressed into the field of *Staatswissenschaften*, sciences of the state, typical of anti-liberal contender states (Van der Pijl 2006). Wallerstein (2001, 192) notes that *Staatswissenschaften* was the first 'current of resistance' to the liberal universalism as developed by Smith and later Bentham and Mill. From Friedrich List to Gustav Schmoller, German political economists had contested that Germany could develop by following the British free-trade model but should rely on its own history, and on state power as a key defensive mechanism.[3]

List's critique of Smith was only partially correct however. Smith certainly recognized the importance of state actions and expenditures

---

[3] However, the 'Historical School' of Schmoller came under attack from Carl Joseph Menger, a top civil servant in Austria-Hungary, who adopted the marginalist position derived from the utilitarian premises developed by Bentham and Mill. 'In this debate . . . the Austrians symbolically cast in their lot with the British against the Prussians' (Wallerstein: 2001, 193).

in areas ranging from educational provision and the delivery of justice, to infrastructure construction the regulation of money and trade and military support for overseas commerce (see Smith 1976, 723–816). As the late Giovanni Arrighi noted, far from propounding an early form of laissez-faire, Smith's political economy

> [P]re-supposed the existence of a strong state that would create and reproduce the conditions for the existence of the market; that would use the market as an effective instrument of government; that would regulate its operation; and that would actively intervene to correct or counter its socially or politically undesireable outcomes. (Arrighi 2007, 43)

While List erred in the extent to which he portrayed Smith as an anti-statist cosmopolitan, he correctly identified the latter's free-trade ideology, to be imposed upon colonies and former colonies such as the United States, as a form of imperialism. And it is this latter element of List's political economy that partially explains its progressive colouration within contemporary development studies. Hence, in one of his most famous formulations, List accused Britain of attempting to 'kick away the ladder' from those attempting to emulate it in order to preserve its role as sole producer of high-value manufactures:

> It is a vulgar rule of prudence for him who has reached the pinnacle of power to cast down the ladder by which he mounted, that others may not follow ... A nation which by protective duties and maritime restrictions has built up a manufacturing industry and a merchant marine to such a point of strength and power as not to fear the competition of any other, can pursue no safer policy than to *thrust aside the means of elevation*, to preach to other nations the advantages of free trade ... (List 1856, 440, emphasis added)

List's conception of the division of the world into nation states reflects a hard political realism at the core of his political thought. He warns emerging states of his time (Germany in particular) of the need for industrial policy and national unification in the face of more advanced states:

> A nation that greatly values its independence and its safety, must make a vigorous effort to elevate itself as fast as possible, from an inferior to a higher state of civilization, uniting and perfecting as quickly as possible, its own agriculture, manufactures, navigation, and commerce. (List 1856, 72)

National unity and state coordination of the economy overcome many of the collective action problems associated with late development

– ranging from the high costs of social overhead capital (investments in infrastructure and research and investment) to inter-sectoral articulation, for example, between industry and agriculture, that require collective rather than individual investment. Without such actions grave dangers lie ahead:

> History is not without examples of entire nations having perished, because they know not and seized not the critical moment for the solution of the great problem of securing the moral, economical, and political independence, by the establishment of manufacturing industry, and the formation of a powerful class of manufacturers and tradesmen. (List 1856, 82)

For List states play a central role in the economic coordination necessary for industrialization through developing 'productive power' (see below). This is an early recognition of the need for purposive articulation between economic sectors.[4] While individual endeavour, motivated by wealth acquisition, was a necessary ingredient of industrial development, it required more than the 'hidden hand' of the market, but also the guiding, visible, and coordinating hand of the state:

> Individuals would be in vain labourious, economical, ingenious, enterprising, intelligent, and moral, without a national unity, without a division of labour and a co-operation of productive power. A nation cannot otherwise attain to a high degree of prosperity and power, nor maintain itself in the permanent possession of its intellectual, social and material riches. (List 1856, 74)

In his presentation of the infant industry argument List has often been accused of being anti-trade. Was he, indeed, an outright opponent of Smithian/Ricardian free trade? On the contrary. Despite his critique of 'cosmopolitan' free trade theory, he accepted many of its precepts. For example:

> International trade, by rousing activity and energy, by the new wants it creates, by the propagation among nations of new ideas and discoveries, and by the diffusion of power, is one of the mightiest instruments of civilization, and one of the most powerful agencies in promoting national prosperity. (List 1856, 70–1)

As Shafaeddin (2005, 53) notes, the distinguishing feature of List's argument was 'his stress on the idea that trade is only an instrument

---

[4] For a rich discussion on inter-sectoral articulation see Karshenas (1996).

– and not an end – of development'. As we shall see below, List actually accepted many of the arguments made by Ricardo.

The *National System* taught how 'every separate nation can be raised to that stage of industrial development in which *union* with other nations equally well developed, *and consequently freedom of trade,* can become possible and useful to it' (List 1856, 201, emphasis added). But for freedom of trade to benefit all countries 'the less advanced nations must first be raised by artificial measures to that stage of civilization to which the English nation has been artificially elevated' (List 1856, 207). List was attracted by the beauty of the cosmopolitan vision of Smith and his school, where, following Kant, free trade would be complemented by peaceful political relations. But he argued that such a 'universal republic ... can only be realized if a large number of nationalities attain to as nearly the same degree as possible of industry and civilization, political cultivation, and power' (List 1856, 201).

However, despite his claim that 'every separate nation can be raised to that stage of industrial development', List was adamant that only certain countries had the material and cultural attributes to aspire to the status of advanced industrial state: 'The countries of the temperate zone are especially fit for the development of manufacturing industry; for [it] is the region of intellectual and physical effort' (List 1856, 75). By contrast:

> A country of the torrid zone would make a very fateful mistake, should it try to become a manufacturing country. . . . It will progress more rapidly in riches and civilization if it continues to exchange its agricultural productions for the manufactured products of the temperate zone. (List 1856, 75)

List was clear that following this course of action would mean that

> [T]ropical countries sink thus into dependence upon those of the temperate zone, but that dependence will not be without compensation, if competition arises among the nations of temperate climes [presumably rising Germany against dominant Britain] . . . This competition will not only ensure a full supply of manufactures at low prices, but will prevent any one nation from taking advantage by its superiority over the weaker nations of the torrid zone. (List 1856, 75–6)

This statement represents a tacit acceptance by List of the Ricardian concept of comparative advantage. List's division between nations possessing and lacking pre-requisites for industrialization enabled him to argue that the possession of colonies was *necessary* for industrializing countries and *beneficial* for the countries of the torrid zone: 'The crowning success of manufacturing industry . . . lies in the possession of colonies' (List 1856, 351). And:

> The mother country supplies her colonies with manufactured goods, and receives in exchange the surplus of the latter in agricultural products and raw materials. This trade animates her manufactures, increases her population . . . Its surplus population and capital, its spirit of enterprise, finds in colonization an advantageous outlet. (List 1856)

Further, '[t]hese exchanges explain specially the progress of industry in the manufacturing countries of the temperate zone, and those of civilization and labour in countries of the torrid zone (List 1856, 346). Once incorporated into dependent relationships with the industrialized economies List argued that colonized nations would reside there in perpetuity:

> [B]etween countries of the temperate and those of the torrid zone, this exchange will be perpetual, for it accords with nature. This is the reason why the East Indies have been deprived by England of their manufacturing industry, and their independence; and all the warm regions of Asia and Africa must fall by degrees beneath the dominion of the manufacturing and commercial nations of the temperate zone. (List 1856, 352)

As we shall see below, SPE has jettisoned these element of List's argument, while expanding upon his infant industry argument. At the centre of his argument, List advanced the concept of productive power.

The Concept of Productive Power

Economists who adopt the theory of comparative advantage generally argue that a global division of labour based upon individual country specialization is the fastest and most assured way to increase the productivity of all participating nations, to raise total global output, and through trading surplus allocate increased gains from trade to all. Here, specialization is the most rapid route to capital accumulation, investment, increased output and rising prosperity for individual nations and for the world as a whole.

List's concept of productive power starts from a diametrically opposite position: capital accumulation and specialization are products, not causes, of economic development (Shafaeddin 2005, 48). Economic development must come first, and must be based on the generation and expansion of productive power. List notes that an aspiring developing nations' objectives should 'not [be] to increase directly by means of commercial restrictions the sum of exchangeable values in a country, but its productive power' (List 1856, 253), and that:

> The causes of wealth are quite a different thing from wealth itself. An individual may possess wealth, that is, exchangeable values; but if he [sic] is not able to produce more values than he consumes, he will be impoverished. An individual may be poor, but if he can produce more than he consumes, he may grow rich. (List 1856, 208)

For List, the ability of states to engender productive power enables them to participate in world trade on a value-adding basis, through producing goods that embody relatively high levels of skills and command relatively high prices on international markets. The lack of productive power in an economy dooms a country to importing goods of higher value than those it exports – leading to debt and underdevelopment.

Productive power comprises three types of capital: natural, material and mental (Levi-Faur 1997). The first comprises land, sea, rivers and mineral resources. The second comprises all objects that are used directly or indirectly in the production process, such as raw materials and machines. The third comprises skills, training, enterprises, industry and government. The creation of wealth is the outcome of the interaction between these three types of capital within a nation, leading to enhanced productive power. In particular, List prioritized mental (in today's terms 'human') capital formation as a key component of states' attempts at catching up with their more advanced competitors. The creation of a skilled workforce and managerial cadre was central to the production of higher-value goods. As Levi-Faur (1997, 160) notes, 'List was able to offer an analysis that connected government education policies and the notion of human capital with the desired outcome of economic development.' His focus on mental/human capital was complemented by an analysis of the state's role in coordinating different economic sectors (for example industry and agriculture) in order to enhance the country's productive power. The economic benefits of specialization and a division of labour required an adequate system of infrastructure, communication and transport. This technical coordination was to be complemented by an ideological 'coordination' designed to pull a country's population behind the development project.

Shaun Breslin (2011, 1334) describes how List's ideas – of state coordination, direction of, and investment in the economy – were not only derived in part from his experience of the 'American System', but crucially, informed the theory, policy and practice of the most successful (developmental) states, from the second half of the nineteenth century onwards – Germany and Japan in the last quarter of the nineteenth century, Japan again in its post-World War 2 reconstruction, South Korea and Taiwan from the 1960s onwards, and as we enter the twenty-first century, contemporary China. It is fitting then, to investigate more closely how List's ideas were put into practice and have been interpreted by his contemporary followers. The next section does so in two steps. First, it discusses how List's ideas have been used to interpret hegemonic (to a large degree US and European-dominated) policies and institutions designed to shape less-developed country development policy, and second it highlights some of the processes of state-led development in late twentieth-century East Asia, as this is the region that has stimulated most 'neo-Listian', or SPE, analysis.

Contemporary Statist Political Economy vs Neoliberalism

Ha-Joon Chang's (2002) *Kicking Away the Ladder: Development Strategy in Historical Perspective* arguably does more than any other contemporary text to popularize List's concept of infant industry protection, while also showing how contemporary development discourse and practice has dispensed with the concept in favour of neoclassical precepts associated with the theory of comparative advantage. He shows how developed countries used the same infant industry strategies to accelerate catch-up development that they now deny to today's developing countries. And elsewhere Chang (2007) classifies the US and other advanced countries as 'Bad Samaritans' who tell the rest of the world 'do as we say, not as we did' in order to take advantage of less developed countries' relatively disadvantageous position *vis-à-vis* more advanced countries.

In a similar vein to Chang, Alice Amsden (2007, 10) is scathing about how Britain presided over an Empire where the 'sun never set . . . and wages never [rose]'. She also castigates the US since the 1980s for enforcing a homogenous set of free trade rules on the developing world. Robert Wade (2005b) also directly evokes List's analogy of 'kicking away the ladder' by focusing on treaties affecting North–South relations within the World Trade Organization (WTO). For example, he argues that through strict enforcement of copyrights and patents the Trade Related Aspects of Intellectual Property Rights

(TRIPS) agreement significantly increases the cost of developing countries' access to scientific knowledge.

In stark contrast, Linda Weiss (2005) characterizes the WTO as an upgrading club for advanced capitalist countries – where the organization attempts to deny developing countries the 'right' to utilize infant industry protection strategies associated with successful late development, while facilitating developed countries' governments' support for their own fledgling industries.[5]

Statist Political Economy advances a compelling alternative narrative to mainstream neo-classical economics. It provides clear illustrations and analysis of policies implemented past and present by successful developing and developed countries, in particular in their accounts of South Korea and Taiwan's rapid post-war economic growth. And it suggests an alternative non-neoliberal policy agenda for contemporary developing countries. At the heart of Statist Political Economy approach lies the state.

Statist Political Economy and Development Strategy

Wade (2004), Chang (2005) and Amsden (1989, 1990) provide empirical accounts of how the East Asian states of Japan, South Korea and Taiwan purposively managed and facilitated industrialization and economic catch-up. They demonstrate how they managed tightly foreign trade and foreign direct investment, and how they regulated domestic firms, subjecting them to performance requirements as well as providing supportive subsidies. These states implemented sectoral upgrading programmes based on technology transfer, facilitated by well-educated managerial cadres, based on the shop floor and in R&D agencies, and hence closely coordinating firm requirements with state investments. They used price controls to prevent domestic monopolies benefiting at the expense of national catch-up objectives. In their accounts, these authors dismantle, piece by piece,

---

[5] For example, under the Subsidies and Countervailing Measures (SCM) agreement, state subsidies are divided into different categories – 'trade-distorting' subsidies, which are outlawed (as Wade notes), and 'permissible' subsidies, which are permitted. The trade-distorting category refers to where subsidies will damage competition, such as export subsidies designed to assist local producers break into global markets. However, the permissible category refers to 'pre-competitive funding' – investments and subsidies that are not held by the WTO to damage competition, and include investments in research and development (R&D), venture capital and fledgling industries that are neither export-oriented nor subject to significant import competition.

neoliberal explanations of 'market-friendly' East Asian growth (cf. World Bank 1993).

Derived from their analysis of successful late-developing countries, Chang and Grabel (2004, 66–188) propose a set of policies that contemporary developing countries could use to facilitate economic catch-up. These include: protection of strategic industries to ensure long-term national growth; prioritizing organizational reforms over privatization; prioritizing the education of the population and specifically the workforce as a means of stimulating intellectual advance (as opposed to supporting rigorous intellectual property rights); tying FDI to national development strategy rather than allowing it free rein; subordinating the financial sector to national development needs via, for example, currency and capital controls and state-directed lending; and using monetary policy to pursue growth rather than (as under the contemporary orthodoxy) to reduce inflation. Similarly, Wade (2004) proposes a number of measures to improve state effectiveness, including establishing a pilot agency or 'economic general staff' to guide the catch-up strategy and developing effective institutions of political authority prior to democratization. All of these policies require a 'strong' and effective state.

Statist Political Economy and State Efficiency

SPE's comprehension of the effectiveness of state economic policy, where policy objectives materialize into productive outcomes, derives not only from List, but also from Max Weber (see especially Weber 1978). The latter complements List because both share a concern about effective resource allocation. Weber's concept of bureaucratic and economic rationality provides a framework to investigate states' ability to allocate resources based on 'rationalized' decision making, and capital's ability to best organize the production process.

Weber discusses how, in all societies, resources are allocated based on institutionally defined rules. When these rules allocate resources based on 'tradition' and ascriptive characteristics, rather than based on calculation, then economic interactions occur under non-rationalized conditions. When institutions and rules function to enable actors to calculate how to use and allocate resources in more rather than less efficient ways, they can be characterized as 'rationalized' (Allen 2004). From SPE's perspective, then, what is central is how the processes and outcomes of institution building impact on state capacity to pursue economic resource allocation, based on more

41

rather than less rational calculations (see also Migdal 1988 and Evans 1995).

Weber's conception of economic rationality also entails the firm subordination of labour to capitalist managers. He argues that 'free' labour (in Marx's sense – free from personal ties and free to sell itself on the labour market), and the complete ownership and control of the means of production by capitalists create 'the most favourable conditions for discipline' (Weber 1978, 138). Labour's complete dispossession from the means of production 'is crucial because it allows for the full realization of economic rationality in production' (Wright 2002, 8). As Weber states:

> It is generally possible to achieve a higher level of economic rationality if management has extensive control over the selection and the modes of use of workers, as compared with the situation created by the appropriation of jobs or the existence of rights to participation in management. The latter conditions produce technically irrational obstacles as well as economic irrationalities. In particular, considerations appropriate to . . . the interests of workers in the maintenance of jobs ('livings') are often in conflict with the rationality of the organization. (Weber 1978, 137–8)

Before continuing further, it is worth noting how Weber's advocacy of labour's total subordination to managerial control as an essential component of economic rationality is shared by neoclassical economic and statist political economy alike. Both perspectives regard any worker-generated restriction on managerial control within the workplace as generating efficiency losses (Wright 2002, 32).[6]

A prime example of the appropriation by SPE of List and Weber is Atul Kohli's (2004) *State-directed Development: Political Power and*

---

[6] However, unlike Statist Political Economy and neoclassical economics, Weber was acutely cognisant of the limitations to the rationality of the capitalist system. He wrote that 'the fact that the maximum of formal rationality in capital accounting is possible only where the workers are subjected to domination by entrepreneurs is a further specific element of *substantive irrationality* in the modern economic order (Weber 1978, 138, emphasis added). Erik Olin Wright notes how 'running throughout Weber's work is the view that rationalization has perverse effects which systemically threaten human dignity and welfare, particularly because of the ways in which it intensifies bureaucratic domination'. Wolfgang Mommsen (1985, 235, cited in Wright 2002, 51) argues that '[a]lthough [Weber] vigorously defended the capitalist system against its critics from the left . . . he did not hesitate to criticize the system's inhuman consequences. . . . [in particular] the severe discipline of work and exclusion of all principles of personal ethical responsibility from industrial labour . . .'.

Industrialization in the Global Periphery. Kohli proposes a typology of state types: at one end 'cohesive capitalist states' (CCS) represented by South Korea; at the other 'neo-patrimonial states' represented by Nigeria; and in between 'fragmented multi-class states' represented to different degrees by India and Brazil. He argues that the presence of 'effective states' generally precedes industrialization because state support for investor profits is a precondition for the emergence of industry. Effective states not only protect infant industries, but also direct resources into and coordinate industrial sectors to cultivate globally competitive firms.

Crucially for Kohli, disciplining the labour force is central to succesful late development as it both increases capital's profits, hence enabling further and greater re-investment and accumulation, and prevents organized working-class influence on state expenditures (diverting resources away from capital accumulation), for example on a relatively generous welfare state. Kohli compares directly cohesive capitalist states to inter-war European fascist states, writing that 'in an earlier draft, I had used the term 'neo-fascist states'' (Kohli 2004, 10, fn. 14), and quoting the formulation that:

> Fascist states had certain characteristics and aspirations in common. In their political systems, they created police states [and] one party systems led by a charismatic dictator.... Fascist regimes mobilized and disciplined societies to transform themselves far more rapidly than would have been the case under laisssez-faire system. (Segre 2001, 274–6)

Kohli (2004, 13) observes how cohesive capitalist states successfully combine 'repression and profits' where the former 'was a key component in enabling private investors ... to have a ready supply of cheap, "flexible" and disciplined labour'. In a similar vein, Alice Amsden (1990, 13–4, 18) recognizes how '[h]igh profits in Korea's mass-production industries have been derived not merely from investments in machinery and modern work methods ... but also from the world's longest working week.' Alongside effective investments, 'cheap labour' and 'labour repression is the basis of late industrialization everywhere' (Amsden 1990, 18). Amsden also observes the impacts of the gender division of labour on women workers:

> The average wages of women workers ... have lagged far behind those of men, enabling employers in the labour intensive industries to remain internationally competitive alongside the growth of a mass-production sector. Wage discrimination against women in Korea and Japan is the worst in the world. (Amsden 1990, 30)

These examples of heightened labour exploitation illustrate the uncomforatable disjuncture between the political regimes that SPE aspires to (democratic and liberal) and those they assert are required for high-speed catch-up development (authoritarian). Hence, discussing the Brazilian growth 'miracle' of 1964–80 under conditions of military dictatorship, Kohli (2004, 195) notes that 'the repressed, purged and even tortured were initially leftists . . . but the category rapidly broadened' and 'Labour strife was brutally put down'. Here Kohli documents the measures undertaken by the military to enable the state to operate in a more (Weberian) rationalist direction. Put differently, Kohli interprets the 'populism' of the pre-1964 period as generating less rational resource allocation, while the post-1964 period of harsh authoritarianism freed state bureaucrats from constraints on more rationalist policy decisions. Kohli concludes his study by stating that authoritarian regimes are a necessary but insufficient component of late industrialization and summarizes the core characteristics of Cohesive Capitalist States:

> Generally right-wing authoritarian states, they prioritize rapid industrialization as a national goal, are staffed competently, work closely with industrialists, systematically discipline and repress labour, penetrate and control the rural society, and use economic nationalism as a tool of political mobilization. (Kohli 2004, 381)

Wade (2004) comes to similar conclusions about the exclusion of labour, albeit with significant reservations. He advocates developing 'corporatist institutions as or before the system is democratized' (Wade 2004, 375). The necessity of such institutions are rationalized as follows:

> Inclusion of labour is obviously desirable in principle. But note that if labour exclusion is part of a set of arrangements which generate high-speed growth, workers are protected to some extent by high labour demand. Labour exclusion also gives a government more room to manoeuvre when austerity comes, and that latitude can be used to restore fast growth more quickly. (Wade 2004, 376, fn. 18)

Note the irony here, of a statist political economist turning to the market as a source of labour protection.

However, elsewhere Wade (2005b, 94) moves from hard corporatism to what could be termed a soft paternalism. He argues that while under neoliberalism workers' wages are predominantly conceived as mere costs by capitalists and state bureaucrats, under a more 'articulated' economy 'robust political coalitions between capitalists and employees become possible ... because capitalists, employees and the government recognize a common interest in wages as a source of sales and economic growth, not just as a cost of production'. In a similar vein Chang and Grabel (2004, 203–4) note that they are 'encouraged by the number and strength of new cross-border social movements opposed to neoliberal, corporate-led globalization and anti-democratic multilateral institutions and agreements'. It appears then that these statist political economists' favoured political outcome is one of soft paternalism, or even state actions guided by social movements, but that their analysis of late development in East Asia pushes them to concede the need for hard corporatism in facilitating rapid economic catch-up.

The reasons for such diverse and sometimes contradictory statements regarding the state's role *vis-à-vis* the working class lie in SPE's use of Weber's (limited) view of the state. SPE's (often implicit) incorporation of Weber's concept of bureaucratic rationality and (again implicitly) his understanding of the state as monopolizing the means of legitimate physical violence over a defined territory, enable them to make two apparently contradictory observations. While they note how late-developing states have 'excluded' labour, they also generally shy away from the normative argument that in the future states *should* exclude labour. This is for the obvious reason that if they were to do so too loudly, their claim that SPE represents an alternative, superior, form of development to neoliberalism, would be undermined. Hence, second, Wade, Kohli, Chang and Grabel all hope that labour can be 'included' or that a more 'social democratic' based form of development, perhaps with some pressures from subaltern social movement can contribute to non-neoliberal development strategies. These hopes, however, do not fit these authors' empirical findings. The following section investigates further the root causes of SPE's necessary advocacy of labour repression, by revisiting a critique of List, written by the young Karl Marx.

Against Statist Political Economy

Marx's Critique of List

Four years after the publication of the *National System*, Marx wrote a rarely commented-upon draft critique of List's book. (It was first published in Russian in 1971.) Marx and Engels had discussed List's work and agreed that a critique should be published for the benefit of the emerging German workers' movements. Marx's review of *The*

National System is characterized by extreme language (at least by present-day standards). He describes List and his ideology as 'dirty', and based upon *'hypocrisy, deception and phrase-mongering'*. The reasons for his use of such strong language in his critique of List are two-fold. First, Marx regarded List as a representative of the rising German bourgeoisie, who, as its organic intellectual, was inherently antithetical to the German working class. Second, that unlike Adam Smith's comprehension and explication of capitalism in eighteenth-century Britain, Marx regarded List as mystifying the nature of later capitalist development in Germany (and by extension of other late developers).

For Marx, List's political economy articulates the ideology of the aspirant German bourgeois who:

> ... puffs himself up into being the 'nation' in relation to foreign countries and says: I do not submit to the laws of competition ... the German philistine wants the laws of competition ... to lose their power at the ... barriers of his country! He is willing to recognize the power of bourgeois society only insofar as it is in accord with his interests, the interests of his class! He does not want to fall victim to a power to which he wants to sacrifice others. (Marx 1846)

To be realized, these aspirations required protection from more competitive foreign trade and exploitation of labour at home:

> We German bourgeois do not want to be exploited by the English bourgeois in the way that you German proletarians are exploited by us and that we exploit one another. We do not want to subject ourselves to the same laws of exchange value as those to which we subject you. We do not want any longer to recognize outside the country the economic laws which we recognize inside the country. (Marx 1846)

The German bourgeoisie needed the state to do their work for them because they were too weak to generate the capital to invest in industry in the face of superior competition from British manufactures. And domestically they existed as subordinate political actors to the landlord class and nobility. They required therefore, not just state assistance in raising and investing capital, but also in regulating domestic political relations in their favour, as opposed to the interests of landlords and labourers. The former stood to benefit from integration into the world economy based on principles of comparative advantage, as under such arrangements they would preside over the most productive and valuable sectors of the economy. The latter needed to be 'convinced' that industrial capital represented the 'national interest', rather than a sectional, exploitative, class inter-est. As Dale (2012) notes 'List's prospectus was the domination of town over country, of Europe over the world, and of industry over agriculture.'

Acceptance of the economic role of the state in presiding over and (re)producing capitalist social relations required elevating it into an institution representing the 'general interest' of the nation, as opposed to the narrow, sectional interests of manufacturers or capital more generally:

> However much the individual bourgeois fights against the others, as a *class* the bourgeois have a common interest, and this community of interest, which is directed against the proletariat inside the country, is directed against the bourgeois of other nations outside the country. This the bourgeois calls his nationality. (Marx 1975, original emphasis)

The development of manufacturing requires 'making the majority of people in the nations into a "commodity"' (Marx 1975). In his concep-tion of productive power List argued for the need for the development of 'mental capital', entailing industrial training to establish a cadre of skilled workers. But he was deliberately vague as to how this would impact on new industrial working classes. To this Marx responded:

> Under the present system, if a crooked spine, twisted limbs, a one-sided development and strengthening of certain muscles, etc., make you more capable of working (more productive), then your crooked spine, your twisted limbs, your one-sided muscular movement are a productive force. (Marx 1975)

As we shall see below, Marx's identification of the industrial dis-cipline necessary for creating a globally competitive working class pertained to his day, and to ours. Moreover, the damaging effects on the working class of industrialization were part of an associated process of geo-political expansion and inter-imperialist rivalry.

Protection and Imperialism

List's presentation of tariffs as a means of 'infant industry' protection against superior external competition gives his work an anti-imperialist touch that has been taken up and popularized by writers within the SPE tradition. But he also argued that industrializing countries should strive for colonies. However, his portrayal of the benign effects of colonization on colonized nations was drawn at the level of exchange relations (based on a similar logic to Ricardo's theory of comparative advantage), and he did not enquire into the transformation of social relations necessary for such expansion of free trade (Cowen and Shenton 1996). While he praises England's conquest (in 1655) of Jamaica 'and with it the possession of the trade in sugar' (List 1856, 115), he ignores the English state's role in facilitating the expansion of slavery in the Caribbean, and other forms of bonded labour elsewhere (Schwartz 2000). On this subject Marx wrote:

> The treatment of the indigenous population was . . . at its most frightful in plantation colonies set up exclusively for the export trade, such as the West Indies . . . The colonial system ripened trade and navigation as in a hothouse . . . The treasures captured outside Europe by undisguised looting, enslavement and murder flowed back to the mother-country and were turned into capital there. (1990, 917, 918)

This side of List's thinking has been whitewashed by adherents of SPE as they attempt to transform him into an anti-imperialist figure. But the question remains whether it is possible to dissociate these two aspects of List's political economy? Put differently, are there potentially interconnections between 'protective' tariffs and the necessarily aggressive search for colonial possessions, territorial expansion and potentially war between industrialized (and industrializing) countries? After all, in List's favoured example, the United States, protective tariffs and state assistance to industry had been combined with territorial integration via an expansionary foreign policy disguised under the banner of liberty and Monroe. Marx, recognized the interconnections between internal and international relations:

> We regard such a [protective] system much more as the organization of a state of war in time of peace, a state of war which, aimed in the first place against foreign countries, necessarily turns in its implementation against the country which organizes it . . . (Marx 1842)

Later Marxists illustrated how these possibilities were reinforced by the inner tendencies of capitalism – towards the concentration and centralization of capital within and beyond national boundaries. By the early twentieth century Rudolf Hilferding, argued that tariffs had been functionally transformed: 'From being a means of defence against the conquest of the domestic market by foreign industries it has become a means for the conquest of foreign markets by domestic industry' (Hilferding 1981 [1910], 310). He also warned how prospects of peaceful co-existence between advanced and advancing countries were likely to be undermined by the very processes of capitalist geo-economic competition that the latter advocated:

The demand for an expansionist policy revolutionizes the whole world view of the bourgeoisie, which ceases to be peace-loving and humanitarian. . . . In place of the idea of humanity there emerges a glorification of the greatness and power of the state [hence *Staatswissenschaften*/statecraft] . . . The ideal now is to secure for one's own nation the domination of the world. (1981, 106)

List certainly favoured the territorial expansion of Germany, and his ideas represent the transfer of the Monroe doctrine back to the old world, and prefigure the *Weltpolitik* (World Policy) of the emerging German state which sought its 'place in the sun'. Szporluk (1988, 125, 131) argues that he 'may . . . be viewed as one of the supporters of the *Lebensraum* doctrine', as he favoured German colonization of South-Eastern Europe and Central and South America. List's ideal of harmonious and cosmopolitan relations between advanced countries, once they had industrialized, was thus undermined by the very process of state-guided industrialization and territorial integration. Protection at home and imperialism abroad were thus two sides of the same coin, as implied by a British prime minister's response to the French ambassador in 1897: 'If you were not such persistent protectionists, you would not find us so keen to annex territories' (cited in Hobsbawm 1989, 67). Kees van der Pijl's (2006) concept of 'contender state' captures these geo-political elements of catch-up development – where economic and political power resides in the state class, with little potential for 'free' trade, thus generating highly politicized (and potentially militarized) external economic relations.

Contemporary statist political economists have stripped away List's imperialist tendencies and have attempted to transform the infant industry argument into a progressive vision of development. They have produced an impressive body of literature that undermines the core precepts of neo-classical economics – that free trade is the most assured way for poor countries to achieve economic growth and meaningful human development. However, even with their critiques of liberal economics and their refinements of List's arguments, they cannot escape from Marx's essential critique, that catch-up development requires heightened exploitation, and hence labour repression.

State Capitalism

At this point it might be expected that statist political economists would respond that, yes, while capitalist development has its fair share of disruption, violence and structured inequality, it is, on balance, better than the experiments in catch-up development associated with the centrally planned economies of the Soviet Union and its satellite states. While they would be correct to highlight the high levels of oppression and exploitation associated with these countries (as well as their fair share of economic inefficiency, despite fast growth rates), does this constitute a valid counter-argument? I don't think it does. This is because of the interconnections between SPE's favoured (East Asian) developmental states, and the ideologically excluded 'Soviet' or 'communist' states. For example, in a somewhat surprised tone, Kohli (2004, 384) observes the 'uncanny resemblance between how communist and cohesive-capitalist states generate power resources to accomplish their respective goals'. Why is Kohli surprised and why do followers of List draw a distinct line in the sand between their favoured examples of late development and the communist countries? The principal reason appears to be ideological. While the latter proclaimed their anti-capitalism and commitment to building socialism, the former, conversely, proclaimed their anti-socialism and commitment to building strong capitalist states. However, behind ideological differences lie fundamental similarities. As noted in chapter 1, writers such as Tony Cliff (1974), described Stalinist Russia and other 'communist' states as 'state capitalist'. Hence, despite their ideological proclamations to the contrary, the 'communist' countries of the twentieth century represented variants of, rather than divergences from, the capitalist nation state within a competitive world system.

The concept of state capitalism has been used to refer to wide-ranging attempts by nationalist Third World leaders to pursue late development through varying degrees of state ownership and control over productive resources. Pfeiffer (1979, 10) details the (familiar) characteristics of state capitalism: it exists as a strategy to achieve development in newly independent, post-colonial regimes, in the context of modern capitalism, through rapid economic growth; there exists a domestic capitalist sector which is initially small and weak but is nurtured by the state; enterprises are allocated resources partially based upon their previous profitability; the military officers and bureaucrats who control the state represent a distinctly new nationalist middle class; workers are not represented and are not allowed to form independent organizations (trade unions and political parties); the dominant ideology is radical nationalist. Pfeiffer (1979, 11) continues:

> Many of the characteristics of 'state capitalism' were evident in some of the now advanced countries – Russia, Germany and Japan – in the late nineteenth century, and can be seen in the 'Third World' countries

at a certain stage in their histories – Turkey in the 1920–1930s, Egypt under Nasser, India in the 1950–1960s, Algeria since 1965 and Peru since 1968.

The concept of state capitalism highlights, despite varying ideologies, the existence of the capital–labour relation and the role of the state in reproducing these relations. While SPE emphasizes the effectiveness of state-led resource allocation within developmental states, such effectiveness is analytically secondary to the essential (exploitative) relations between capital and the state on the one hand and labour on the other hand.

The pitfalls of Listian, Stalinist, and, for that matter, neoliberal catch-up strategies are neatly summarized by Burkett and Hart-Landsberg (2003, 148, 156, 157), who argue that 'the catch-up vision . . . simply presumes that the primary role of working people and their material and social conditions is to serve as instruments and vehicles of capital accumulation and economic growth'. They note further that such conceptions limit 'development possibilities to the kinds of capitalist development that have actually occurred historically' and that they offer no space 'for any positive developmental contribution by popular anti-capitalist and anti-imperialist struggles'. The latter movements are conceived of as potentially disrupting the accumulation process, hence the necessity for a strong and, more often than not, repressive state.

Conclusions

Friedrich List formulated his statist political economy in response, and in contradistinction to the cosmopolitan political economy dominant in mid-nineteenth-century Britain. The latter, for List, represented an attempt by the leading industrial power of the day to conflate its interests (rapid economic growth based on an international division of labour with an industrial core and agricultural periphery) with the interests of all countries. For List, cosmopolitanism represented the political economy of imperialism. His critique of English imperialism, if read out of context, appears to suggest that List was an anti-imperialist. But List was committed to a political economy where states in late-industrializing countries would combine industrial protection at home with imperial expansion abroad, and in so doing, generate the same industrial/agricultural division of labour as enjoyed by Britain. Furthermore, List's concept of productive power sought to obfuscate the centrality of the exploitation of labour necessary for late industrialistion. List's political economy, in its totality, is therefore reactionary.

Contemporary statist political economy rejects List's arguments for colonial possessions, and builds on his critique of core capitalist power's tendencies to express their interests in cosmopolitan terms. For these reasons they appear to be more progressive than neoliberal economists. However, their admiration for and advocacy of constructing strong, bureaucratically autonomous states that are able to rationally and effectively generate and allocate resources cannot hide the fact that the these states are involved in overseeing and reproducing highly exploitative labour regimes where workers are regarded as fuel for the accumulation of capital. Contemporary SPE therefore shares many of the same reactionary elements with its founding father and should not be viewed as representing a progressive strategy for development.

— 3 —

KARL MARX, CLASS STRUGGLE AND SOCIAL DEVELOPMENT

The History of all hitherto existing society is the history of class struggle. (Marx and Engels 1848)

The emancipation of the working classes must be conquered by the working classes themselves. (Marx 1867a)

The collapse, in 1989 and 1991, of the Eastern European and Russian regimes signified for many the end of socialism, the end of history, the irrelevance of Marx's critique of capitalism and his conception of a post-capitalist alternative. But Marx did not disappear. Instead he was adopted, by many on left and right, as a prophet of capitalist globalization. For example, *Financial Times* columnist and neoliberal cheerleader Martin Wolf (2004, 174) describes Marx's analysis of global capitalist expansion as 'forward looking', and contrasts it to 'reactionary' movements opposed to global institutions such as the World Trade Organization.

There are sections of Marx's writing that portray capitalism in glowing and progressive terms. Some aspects of his work were taken up and formalized by traditions of Marxism (ranging from the Second to the ossified Third International under Stalin) that explained human history in mechanistic, linear terms.

More than these political and intellectual traditions, the history of Stalinism and Maoism – the deaths of tens of millions of people as Russia and China respectively attempted to achieve 'socialist' industrialization and catch-up with the West – represent developmental dead ends, never, hopefully, to be repeated. That these regimes proclaimed themselves as 'Marxist', 'communist' and 'socialist' repels many from investigating Marx's writings and their implications for contemporary and potentially post-capitalist development (but see this book's introduction for an identification and analysis of these countries as 'state capitalist'). That Marx can be read as an apologist and cheerleader for capitalist expansion represents, however, an inversion of his life's work. As the above epigraph suggests, his central objective was to illuminate processes of class formation, struggle and transformation, and to provide intellectual and political tools to the labouring classes of his day in their struggles against exploitation and oppression.

In contrast to the elite-led understandings of development discussed in this book, including state capitalist variants, this chapter argues that Marx's work provides the basis for comprehending an alternative, labour-centred conception of human development. Labouring classes and their struggles against exploitation by capital are politically prioritized, and are conceptualized as 'developmental' because they can deliver improvements to workers' (and their families' and communities') livelihoods. Marx conceptually connected struggles by workers against oppression and exploitation under capitalism to immediate developmental gains, and to the potential transformation of capitalism into socialism.

Marx and Engels were committed to a vision of human development and the flourishing of individual and collective abilities. They drew on earlier conceptions of socialism to advance their own vision of human development. Pre-Marxist French socialists such as Saint-Simon argued that a socialist society would provide to its members 'the greatest possible opportunity for the development of their faculties'. And for Louis Blanc, in such a society everyone would have 'the power to develop and exercise his faculties in order to really be free' (cited in Lebowitz 2010, 12). In a similar vein, in the Communist Manifesto Marx and Engels wrote how 'Communism deprives no man of the power to appropriate the products of society; all that it does is to deprive him of the power to subjugate the labour of others by means of such appropriations' (Marx and Engels 1967 [1848], 99).

However, as Hal Draper noted, Marx was the first socialist to link these visions to the activities of labouring classes themselves (see below). While Marx and Engels understood that a communist or socialist society would require a revolution against existing capitalist society, they did not limit themselves to speculating about human development in a hypothetical socialist future. They also enquired into what kinds of struggles by labouring classes could better their conditions under capitalism. Marx's intellectual formation developed through his early experiences of state censorship and oppression, and later his witness to the rise of industrial capitalism and the emergence of militant working-class movements.

Marx was born, in 1818, into a middle-class family in Trier, Prussia. After completing his studies at the universities of Bonn and Berlin he became a journalist for the radical newspaper the *Rheinische Zeitung*, where he became increasingly critical, simultaneously of the autocratic Prussian government and the iniquitous laws and practices that underpinned emerging capitalist social relations in the country. Because of his continual and vocal critique of the government he was expelled from Prussia in 1843, living in Paris and Belgium, and then finally settling permanently in London in 1849 (Wheen 2005). Living and working in Victorian London, Marx stood at the epicentre of the first phase of capitalist industrialization and the concomitant rise of the industrial proletariat. Here he developed his understanding and critique of capitalism and his socialist internationalism. As Mandel (1994) notes, Marx drew upon, critiqued and surpassed the highest forms of bourgeois thought – German philosophy, French politics and British political economy. Marx's life was enmeshed within the dynamics of class struggle in Europe. When the struggle was rising he was active politically, writing the Communist Manifesto with Engels in 1848, and founding and leading the First International in 1864. When struggles subsided, he devoted himself to writing, in particular his monumental *Capital*. His identification and political championing of labouring classes as agents of social change distinguishes him, fundamentally, from other theorists of development.

Throughout this book we shall discuss how varying authors understood socialism – Schumpeter as a process of 'socialization' of the economy by large firms and states, Gerschenkron as an ideology to mobilize populations behind the great push of catch-up development and Polanyi as a process where the state 'embeds' the market for the benefit of society. Marx's conception, by contrast, represented what Hal Draper calls 'socialism from below':

> What unites the many different forms of Socialism-from-Above is the conception that socialism (or a reasonable facsimile thereof) must be *handed down* to the grateful masses in one form or another, by a ruling elite which is not subject to their control ... The heart of Socialism-from-Below is its view that socialism can be realized only through the self-emancipation of activized masses in motion, reaching out for freedom with their own hands, mobilized 'from below' in a struggle to take charge of their own destiny, as actors (not merely subjects) on the stage of history. (Draper 1966, original emphasis)

Marx's conception of socialism from below is captured in the first principle of the First International: 'The emancipation of the working classes must be conquered by the working classes themselves' (Marx 1867a).

Eurocentrism and Economic Determinism[1]

Marx and Marxism have been associated with Eurocentrism and economic determinism, where economic 'laws' determine the course of human history and where 'the economy' determines other spheres of human life such as politics, ideas and state actions. Once such a starting point is accepted other precepts can logically follow: a comprehension of capitalism as operating according to its essential 'laws of motion' that cannot be disregarded (or contravened); a linear (straight line) view of history, where all countries follow the same path, for example, through the five stages of human history (primitive communism, slavery, feudalism, capitalism, socialism); and a form of Eurocentrism, where the economically dynamic West 'delivers' development to the stagnant East.

Criticizing such an approach, Edward Said highlights Marx's early writings on India, arguing that 'every writer on the Orient [including Marx] saw [it] as a locale requiring Western attention, reconstruction and even redemption' (2003, 206) and that 'Marx succumbed to thoughts of the changeless Asiatic village' (Said 1993, 183). Similarly, Shlomo Eisenstadt (2000, 1) writes that Marx (and Durkheim and Weber) 'assumed . . . that the cultural program of modernity as it developed in modern Europe and the basic institutional constellations that emerged there would ultimately take over in all modernizing and modern societies'. And John Hobson (2011, 155) argues that 'the Eurocentric cue in Marx's work emerges in his belief that European societies self-generate through an *endogenously determined linear development path* according to their own *exceptional properties . . .*' (original emphasis).

There are indeed writings by Marx that can be construed as embodying the above approach. Far more damaging, however, such formulations were subsequently adopted and formalized by latter-day Marxists. Thus in early twentieth-century Russia for example, Georgi Plekhanov argued that '[t]he organization of any given society

---

[1] Kiely (1995, ch. 2) provides an excellent account of the limitations of economic reductionist Marxism in the study of development.

is determined by the state of its productive forces', and that 'technical progress constitutes the basis of the entire development of humankind' (Plekhanov 1976, 33, cited in Kiely 1995, 17). In the same vein, an official (1963) Soviet text, 'Fundamentals of Marxism' (cited in Kiely 1995, 14) , states that:

> All peoples travel what is basically the same path . . . The development of society proceeds through the consecutive replacement, according to definite laws, of one socio-economic function by another.

In his analysis of English colonialism in India, Marx appears to suggest that advanced nations' actions can assist 'backward' countries emerge from stagnation. And it is here that he is sharply criticized by Said and others, as embodying Eurocentrism. For example, Marx wrote how:

> English interference.... dissolved these small semi-barbarian, semi-civilized communities, by blowing up their economical basis, and thus produced the greatest, and to speak the truth, the only social revolution ever heard of in Asia. (Marx 1853)

Further, and most notoriously:

> England has to fulfil a double mission in India: one destructive, the other regenerating – the annihilation of old Asiatic society, and the laying of the material foundations of Western society in Asia. (Marx 1853)

And again, in the Communist Manifesto, Marx and Engels highlight the differences between capitalism's dynamism and pre-capitalist economic formations: 'The bourgeoisie cannot exist without constantly revolutionizing the instruments of production, and thereby the relations of production, and with them the whole relations of society (Marx and Engels 1967[1848], 83). And, '[t]he bourgeoisie has through its exploitation of the world market given a cosmopolitan character to production and consumption in every country' (Marx and Engels 1967[1848]).

If the above quotes genuinely represent Marx's conception of human development, then turning away from Marx would represent a minimal loss. Ray Kiely identifies this kind of Marxism as a dogma, and notes that it 'has rightly been identified as an example of the worst kind of Eurocentric, modernist arrogance, in which the 'superior' west looks at the 'inferior' Rest as a backward, stagnant and incomprehensible 'other'' (Kiely 1995, 23). Kiely also argues, however, that Marx himself provides an alternative comprehension of human development, which, I shall argue in the following sections, was based on class struggles, and how they interacted with and co-constituted global processes of (contested) capitalist expansion.

An Alternative Reading

While the previous section suggests how Marx's thinking might be interpreted in determinist, Eurocentric and historically linear ways, this represents just one (bad) reading of his work. This section outlines an alternative approach to Marx's conception of human development in four steps. First, through discussing how primitive accumulation and the rise of capitalism was an intrinsically global process. Second, how primitive accumulation generated a distinctive North–South divide, and how combined, third, these processes precluded any linear conception of capitalist development. It also suggests, fourth, how global capitalism generated a global labouring class, and how capitalism's continued reproduction generated rival politics – of divide and rule by capital, and of international solidarity by labour.

Primitive Accumulation and the Rise of Capitalism

Perhaps the most prominent contemporary Marxist explanations of the rise of capitalism are by Robert Brenner (1977 and 1986) and Ellen Wood (1991 and 2003). They argue that in the fourteenth-century European feudalism entered a deep crisis, exacerbated by the Black Death and depopulation. In response to this crisis a series of class struggles between serfs and lords ensued across the continent, and their differentiated outcomes had profound consequences for the emergence of capitalism. In Eastern Europe the class struggle was decisively won by the old feudal lords, resulting in the 'second-serfdom' – a harsher version of the previous form of feudalism, where peasants were re-subjected to harsh, bonded forms of labour. In France agrarian struggles resulted in a relative stalemate, with the peasantry maintaining its independence against the lords, while the French state evolved towards an absolutist form.

Only in England did the class struggle result in the rise of capitalism. There the initial peasant uprisings shattered the feudal structure, giving rise to a free peasantry for a century or more up until the late fifteenth and early sixteenth centuries. From then on, however, and in response to the stimulus of the European market for wool, land was increasingly concentrated in the hands of a new landlord class, at the expense of the peasantry. The latter were expelled through private land seizures and state-sponsored enclosures, and became proletarianized. Simultaneously, the new landlord class rented land to tenant farmers – giving rise to the triumvirate of free wage labourer, tenant farmer and absentee landowner. In this context, competitive markets for land and labour gave rise to capitalist social relations.

Brenner's and Wood's focus on class struggle and its outcomes is a necessary part of comprehending the emergence of capitalism in Western Europe. However, and unlike Marx, they present European class struggles as the core determinant of capitalism's emergence, rather than as a co-determining factor existing within a broader world-historical process. In their account primitive accumulation consisted principally of (a) the separation of the peasantry from the land and (b) concentration of land in the hands of a new landowning class. However, this is to miss other moments of primitive accumulation not necessarily arising from (a) and (b), in particular (c) the amassing of large holdings of wealth in the hands of the emerging capitalist class (Harman 1989; Heller 2011) which was, (d) often based on violence, organized through the exploitation and expansion of pre-capitalist social relations, in particular slavery and colonial plunder. Rather than a single determinant – of differential outcomes to class struggles – these processes existed in a broader, world-wide process, as described by Marx:

> The discovery of gold and silver in America, the extirpation, enslavement and entombment in mines of the aboriginal population, the beginning of the conquest and looting of the East Indies, the turning of Africa into a warren for the commercial hunting of black-skins, signalled the rosy dawn of the era of capitalist production. These idyllic proceedings are the chief momenta of primitive accumulation. (Marx 1990, 915)

Primitive accumulation was a globally integrated process, rather than one specific to a particular country or region, and contrary to Hobson's claim, the emergence of capitalism in Europe generally and in England particularly, was *co-determined* by the existence and reconstitution of an international division of labour.

Moreover, the eventual emergence of England at the heart of the emerging capitalist system was dependent upon the relative balance of power within Europe. As Davidson argues, in relation to the wars of Spanish succession (1701–14) and the possible unity (and hence European and world hegemony) of Spanish and French states under the Bourbon monarchy: 'The English ruling class faced the prospect of its greatest rival presiding over a world empire that stretched from the manufactories of Flanders to the gold mines of the Americas, and which was positioned to seize the English colonies and so cut off one of the main sources of English ruling-class wealth' (Davidson 2010, 350). Without favourable outcomes to these conflicts, emerging capitalism in England might have been reversed.

However, if processes (a) to (d) were necessary for the emergence of capitalist social relations they were still not sufficient. What was essential was that the propertyless producers (the newly established working classes formed out of the disposessed peasantries) be institutionally organized so as to be 'compelled to sell themselves voluntarily' (Marx 1990, 899) – that is, that alternatives to the sale of labour power, such as the renting out of land for private production, or access to other means of production, were eliminated or at least closed off to labouring classes. Such a process was neither instantaneous, nor did it flow automatically from processes (a) to (d). 'Centuries are required', argued Marx,

> Before the 'free' worker, owing to the greater development of the capitalist mode of production, makes a voluntary agreement, that is, is compelled by social conditions to sell the whole of his active life, his very capacity for labour, in return for the price of his customary means of subsistence, to sell his birthright for a mess of pottage. (Marx 1990, 382)

States played a key role in securing these conditions (see below). During this centuries-long transitional phase, from the sixteenth century until the nineteenth and in some parts of the world the twentieth century, capitalism was neither secure, nor its continued expansion inevitable. As Michael Lebowitz argues, the expansion of capitalist social relations takes place simultaneously with the contraction of pre-capitalist social relations, but this is a drawn-out process of historical rupture, during which neither fully developed capitalism nor fully functioning pre-capitalist social formations exist. Far from capitalism sweeping all in its wake, as suggested in the Communist Manifesto and by economic determinist conceptions of Marxism, the struggle to establish capitalist social relations in Old and New Worlds represented a situation characterized by the 'contested reproduction' of capitalist and non-capitalist social forms (Lebowitz 2010, 98). State power was crucial to capitalist expansion: '[S]tate compulsion to confine the struggle between capital and labour within the limits convenient for capital' administered through 'bloody discipline' constituted key actions contributing to the establishment of capitalism (Marx 1990, 904, 905). Such actions were necessary because 'If there is neither the specifically capitalist mode of production nor a mode of regulation that ensures the reproduction of wage labourers who are dependent upon capital, then . . . capitalism is not irreversible' (Lebowitz 2010, 102).

The non-inevitability, and the variety of pre-capitalist social forms, modes and timings of integration into the expanding world system, meant that primitive accumulation would take varying forms and have radically different consequences across the globe. Against those who wanted to turn Marx's insights into historical dogma, he insisted in *Capital* that the expropriation of the peasantry 'in different countries, assumes different aspects, and runs through its various phases in different orders of succession, and at different periods' (Marx 1990, 876). And towards the end of his life he wrote how his treatment of primitive accumulation in *Capital* 'claims no more than to trace the path by which, in Western Europe, the capitalist economic order emerged from the womb of the feudal economic order' (Marx, cited in Shanin 1983, 135).

Primitive Accumulation and the Origins of the North–South Divide

It was these different forms, timings and international relations of primitive accumulation that gave rise to the original North–South divide as well as generating and exacerbating class differentiation in the emerging capitalist core. As Prabhat Patnaik (2005, 65) puts it: 'Economies at whose expense [primitive accumulation] occurs become impoverished by the process; their chances of developing an autonomous capitalism become slimmer on account of their being accumulated *from*' (original emphasis). And while primitive accumulation transferred resources from South to North, it did not benefit northern workers. Thus, 'Holland, which first brought the colonial system to its full development, already stood at the zenith of its commercial greatness by 1648' by which time its working class was 'more overworked, poorer, and more brutally oppressed than those of all the rest of Europe put together' (Marx 1990, 918). Marx's understanding of the processes of global primitive accumulation is far from any conception of expanding Western economic and political power bringing progress in its wake. If it reflects the delivery of modernization to the 'rest' it is a reflection that modernization, like capitalism, is profoundly unequal, uneven and contradictory.

That global capitalist expansion entails (and rests upon) processes of domestic and international uneven development is further elucidated by processes of concentration and centralization of capital:

Capital grows in one place to a huge mass in a single hand, because it has in another place been lost by many. . . . with the development of the capitalist mode of production, there is an increase in the minimum amount of individual capital necessary to carry on a business under its normal conditions. The smaller capitals, therefore, crowd into spheres of production which Modern Industry has only sporadically or incompletely got hold of. Here competition rages. . . . It always ends in the ruin of many small capitalists, whose capitals partly pass into the hands of their conquerors, partly vanish. (Marx 1990, 777)

The consequences of global concentration and centralization of capital is that, unless the state intervenes in ways described by List and Gerschenkron (see next chapter) firms in already established capitalist countries will generally be larger and more competitive than those in newly established capitalist countries, with the larger, more advanced firms eliminating the less advanced firms (Weeks 1997). Firms in less advanced countries are subsequently confined to economic activities and markets characterized by low profitability, that are unattractive to more powerful firms (Patnaik 2005, 66). (These issues are discussed in greater depth in chapters 4 and 5). The global dimensions of primitive accumulation and concentration and centralization of capital shed light on the original North–South divide characteristic of global capitalism. Under such conditions it would be inconceivable to realistically expect late-developing countries to 'follow' a 'path' already established by the first capitalist states. And yet so much Marxism expected exactly this.

Against Unilinearity

The critique of Marx as adhering to a unilinear and Eurocentric view of history rests upon statements such as 'The industrially more developed country shows the less developed only the image of its own future' (Marx, cited in Trotsky 1997, 1219). This unilinear conception of capitalist development was indeed criticized by later writers within and without the Marxist tradition (see chapter 4 on Trotsky and Gerschenkron). However, not only did Marx modify his views as he matured (Anderson 2010), but further, his masterwork, *Capital*, was based upon a comprehension of a capitalist system, comprising a rapidly evolving international division of labour which discounted, *a priori*, a stagist process of human development (Pradella 2010). In fact, even prior to writing the Communist Manifesto with Engels, Marx hinted at the impossibilities of individual states passing through the same stage of development as other states. For example, in his consideration of possible transitions beyond capitalism Marx wrote that 'To hold that every nation goes through this development [beyond capitalism] internally would be as absurd as the idea that every nation is bound to go through the political development of France or the philosophical development of Germany' (Marx 1846). Such observations were expanded into a more cogent theoretical and empirically based comprehension of the evolving world system as Marx matured.

As we have seen, in his early writings on India Marx (1853) wrote of England's 'double mission': 'one destructive, the other regenerating'. This is where Said (2003) concentrates his fire, accusing Marx of Orientalism. But not only does he downplay Marx's analysis of the possibilities of the Indians throwing off England's yoke, but he also misses Marx's later writings on Indian and broader Eurasian development. For example, Marx noted how the English colonialists were motivated 'only by the vilest interests', but were simultaneously transforming India into a national economy, that itself generated the material conditions for a unified anti-colonial revolt (Ahmad 1994). This meant that:

> The Indians will not reap the fruits of the new elements of society scattered among them by the British bourgeoisie, till in Great Britain itself the . . . ruling classes shall have been supplanted by the industrial proletariat, or till the Hindoos *themselves* shall have grown strong enough to throw off the English yoke altogether. (1853, emphasis added)

Even here, at his most 'orientalist', Marx recognizes Indians' agency, denied to colonized peoples by most bourgeois thinkers. He leaves as an open-ended question what kind of society (capitalist or post-capitalist) would emerge from a successful Indian uprising. And several years later when such an uprising did materialize (the Sepoy 'mutiny' of 1857), he wholeheartedly supported it, propounding a solid anti-imperialism, remarking to Engels that 'India is now our best ally' (Marx and Engels 1975). He similarly supported the Taiping rebellion in China, interpreting it as part of a broader uprising by the Asiatic nations against British colonialism. As Pradella (2011) notes, Marx understood how these anti-colonial movements impacted upon the capitalist core and elsewhere in the world system provoking crises for the bourgeoisie and giving an 'impulse to a number of social movements: in Russia for the suppression of servitude; in the United States for the abolition of slavery; while in Europe . . . workers began to mobilize again at syndicalist and political levels.'

International Labouring-Class Politics

For Marx, because labouring classes in different countries were being formed as part of a global process – that is they were in effect different segments of a single global labouring class – their politics *required* solidarity between different sections of that class (regardless of geography, 'race', creed or gender). Such politics sought to counter the divide-and-rule politics of ruling classes. Put differently, and in contemporary parlance, Marx was acutely aware of capitalist strategies of using real and potential differences within and between working classes to attempt to generate a 'race-to-the-bottom' in wages and conditions, thus increasing the rate of exploitation of all sections of labour and minimizing possible and actual resistance to capital.

For example, in his discussion of (eventual) European opposition to the slave trade and its support for the North against the South in the American Civil War, Marx noted how:

> It was not the wisdom of the ruling classes, but the heroic resistance to their criminal folly by the working classes of England, that saved the west of Europe from plunging headlong into an infamous crusade for the perpetuation and propagation of slavery on the other side of the Atlantic. (Marx 1864)

The logic of these politics applies simultaneously within and between countries. In his analysis of working-class politics in England, Marx warned of the dangers of employers' attempts to divide workers along ethnic English and Irish lines, and argued instead for the need for solidarity and in particular an opposition to Irish workers' oppression by the English state:

> All English industrial and commercial centres now possess a working class split into two hostile camps: English proletarians and Irish proletarians. The English worker hates the Irish worker because he sees in him a competitor who lowers his standard of life. This antagonism is artificially sustained and intensified by the press, the pulpit, the comic papers, in short by all the means at the disposal of the ruling classes. This antagonism is the secret of the impotence of the English working class. (Marx to Engels in 1870, in Marx and Engels 1975, 220–4)

Marx's response to the divide-and-rule tactics of the English ruling class, and its acceptance by much of the workers' movement was decisive:

> To hasten the social revolution in England is the most important object of the [First International]. The sole means of doing so is to make

Ireland independent. It is therefore, the task of the 'International' to bring the conflict between England and Ireland to the forefront everywhere, and to side with Ireland publically everywhere. (Marx and Engels 1975)

Marx applied the same logic to white workers in the northern United States and their movements' often fraught relations with the question of emancipation in the slave states of the South. He wrote how 'in the United States of North America, every independent movement of the workers was paralysed so long as slavery disfigured a part of the Republic. Labour cannot emancipate itself in the white skin when in the black it is branded' (Marx 1990, 414).

These brief examples suggest that Marx was keenly aware of the international determinants of capitalist exploitation. As we shall discuss further in chapter 5, Marx was quick to understand ways in which capitalist classes sought to divide in order to rule labouring classes and drive down their wages (what I label a process of 'hyper-babbagization'), but that these efforts also required, and often met, resistance nationally and internationally.

Class Struggles and Human Development: Within, Against, Outside and Beyond Capitalism

An economic determinist reading of Marx would suggest that he viewed economic growth and the development of the productive forces as the core determinant of human development. But, he argues more often than not against such conceptions. Rather, he demonstrated how class relations and struggles, their relation to the state and how they are articulated within and through the world system generate myriad forms and trajectories of human development. Situating class relations and struggles at the core of our analysis therefore provides a key vector along which to analyse divergent and differentiating forms of human development.

This section highlights four examples of Marx's thoughts about the diversity of class structures and struggles across the globe and their human developmental impacts. It highlights how he conceptualized these examples as embodying struggles against capitalism but not for socialism (in the Australian colonies), for improvements to workers' conditions under capitalism (industrial England), within and against capitalism (the Commune in France) and outside and potentially beyond capitalism (in rural Russia) (table 3.1).

Table 3.1   Class Struggles and Divergent Human Development

(1) Anti-Capitalism in the Free Colonies (Australia)	(3) Communism (France)
(2) The Political Economy of Labour (England)	(4) Non-Industrial Transitions to Socialism (Russia)

As we shall see, Marx thought that socialist development on a world scale was already possible in his time. This implies strongly that, for him, the development of the productive forces was already sufficient for socialist transformation, and that the key issue was *not* their further development under capitalism (as dogmatic forms of Marxism argued) but how a future, non-capitalist society would make use of capitalism's legacy of productive dynamism. He also recognized that not all struggles by labouring classes were struggles against capitalism and for socialism. This did not reduce their importance to him. Rather, he analysed them in their specific context and in relation to the evolving world system, attempting to discern their developmental consequences for the labouring classes of his day.

Australia: Anti-Capitalism in the Free Colonies[2]

The protracted and contested process of primitive accumulation was particularly complicated in the so-called 'free colonies' – where the indigenous population had been dispossessed of the land (usually through extermination) but did not constitute the emerging wage labour force for capitalist production. This labour force was imported from the 'mother country' or from its colonies. One such colony was Australia, where Marx observed how on the one hand colonial capital experienced severe difficulties in establishing capitalist social relations, and on the other hand, struggles against capitalist social relations took an anti-capitalist but not socialist form.

Marx notes how the fundamental difference between 'mother country' and 'free colony' is that while capitalist social relations have been established in the former by the 'expropriation of the mass of the people from the soil' in the latter, 'the bulk of the soil is still public property, and every settler on it can therefore turn part of it into his private property and individual means of production' (Marx 1990, 934). The implications of such opportunities for land acquisition by settlers are profound. In the 'mother country' capitalist production

---

[2] I am indebted to Gavin Capps in thinking through this question.

'constantly reproduces the wage worker as wage worker . . . [and] . . . produces always . . . a relatively surplus-population of wage workers' (Marx 1990, 935). In the 'free colonies' however:

> On the one hand, the old world constantly throws in capital, thirst-ing after exploitation and 'abstinence'; on the other, the regular reproduction of wage-labour as wage-labour comes into collision with impediments the most impertinent and in part invincible . . . the wage-worker of today is tomorrow an independent peasant, an artisan, working for himself. He vanishes from the labour-market, but not into the workhouse.

Consequently, Marx commented sardonically:

> This constant transformation of the wage-workers into independ-ent producers, who work for themselves instead of for capital, and enrich themselves instead of the capitalist gentry, reacts in its turn very perversely on the conditions of the labour-market. Not only does the degree of exploitation of the wage-labourer remain indecently low. The wage-labourer loses into the bargain, along with the relation of depend-ence, also the sentiment of dependence on the abstemious capitalist. (Marx 1990, 936)

Attempts by dominant capitalist powers to extend capitalist social relations through territorial expansion thus generated new tensions and forms of class conflict, including attempts by newly imported workers to resist capitalist exploitation through escaping over the frontier. The latters' lack of real or felt sentiment of dependence upon capital represents for Marx the *anti-capitalist cancer* of the colonies' (1990, 938, emphasis added). He quotes Edward Gibbon Wakefield, an English politician and leading figure in the colonization of Australia, lamenting such sentiments and actions:

> Where land is very cheap and all men are free, where every one who so pleases can easily obtain a piece of land for himself, not only is labour very dear, as respects the labourer's share of the produce, but the dif-ficulty is to obtain combined labour at any price. (Wakefield, cited in Marx 1990, 934–5).

The solution to the difficulties of establishing a fully functioning capitalist labour market where wage workers are compelled to sell themselves to the capitalist is to cut off their access to the land through the state putting 'upon the virgin soil an artificial price, independent of the laws of supply and demand, a price that compels the immigrant to work a long time for wages before he can earn enough money to buy land, and turn himself into an independent peasant' (Marx 1990,

938). In addition to pricing wage-labourers out of the land market the colonial state played a significant role in pushing down wages in the urban industrial centres in order to strengthen the dependence of workers on the labour market (Cowen and Shenton 1996). As Gavin Capps notes in relation to the Australian case, but with broader historical relevance: 'The creation of a fully proletarianized working-class, regulated autonomously by the "dull compulsion" of market forces, is . . . a volatile, uncertain and historically protracted process, and one that is constantly violated by . . . political interventions' (Capps 2010, 81). This then raises the question of what kinds of workers' struggles could come forth where capitalist socialist relations had been firmly established?

England: The Political Economy of Labour[3]

In his analysis of the English industrial working class Marx formulated his conception of the political economy of labour – introduced in his 1864 Inaugural Address to the First International. Here he reveals a rival political economy to that of capital. He began his address by critiquing the then (and now) commonly held assumption of the causal relationship between economic growth and enhanced human wellbeing. Speaking about the English experience, he argued that:

> It is a great fact that the misery of the working masses has not diminished from 1848 to 1864, and yet this period is unrivalled for the development of its industry and the growth of commerce. (Marx 1864)

Rather than capital accumulation generating trickle-down mechanisms leading to distribution of wealth among workers, Marx argues that capitalist growth and expansion represents the continued and deepening subordination of labour to its (re)productive requirements. As Lebowitz argues '[C]apital does not merely seek the realization of its own goal, valorization; it also must seek to suspend the realization of the goals of wage-labour' and that a 'necessary condition for the existence of capital is its ability to divide and separate workers – in order to defeat them' (Lebowitz 1992, 85). In an ideal world for capital:

> What the lot of the labouring population would be if everything were left to isolated, individual bargaining, may be easily foreseen. The iron

---

[3] The foremost theorist of the political economy of labour is Michael Lebowitz (1992).

68

rule of supply and demand, if left unchecked, would speedily reduce the producers of all wealth to a starvation diet. (Marx 1867b)

However, workers' organizations contradict these rules and potentially represent an alternative political economy. Collective gains against capital are won through 'negating competition, [and] infringing on the 'sacred' law of supply and demand and engaging in 'planned co-operation' (Lebowitz 1992, 67, citing Marx).

Marx provides two examples of the political economy of labour in his inaugural address to the first International. The first example, the Ten-Hours Act (introduced in England in 1847 which legally reduced the working day to a maximum of ten hours), was the first time that 'in broad daylight the political economy of the [capitalist] class succumbed to the political economy of the working class' (Marx 1864). The second example was the creation of worker-run cooperative factories. The latter were of great significance because '[b]y deed instead of by argument.. [such organizations] . . . have shown that production on a large scale, and in accord with the behests of modern science, may be carried on without the existence of a class of masters employing a class of hands' (Marx 1864). While capitalists always need workers the reverse is not the case. Barker (2006, 68) notes that other principles of the political economy of labour include negating competition between workers (for example, between workers of different 'race', ethnicity or gender, or in geographically separated workplaces), restricting capital's coercive control in the workplace, maintaining the 'normal' working day and reducing the rate of surplus value extraction.

Marx demonstrated how workers' struggles are developmental in that by ameliorating their present conditions through their own actions they do not have to wait for an unspecified time in the future for benefits to trickle down to them. However, while these examples still pre-supposed the existence of capitalism, in his discussion of the Paris Commune Marx observed a movement that he identified as having the potential to transcend capitalism altogether.

France: Communism

Within Marx's lifetime labour's greatest victory over capital was achieved through the Paris Commune of 1871. The Commune emerged within a context of a political crisis in France. Napoleon III had suffered a catastrophic defeat at the hands of Bismarck's Prussian army with most of his army taken captive. He was subsequently overthrown. With neither political cohesion nor available military force the French state encountered a situation of rapidly diminishing authority (Gluckstein 2006).

The working class of Paris represented the majority of the city's population, and laboured in a mass of tiny workshops: 'Sixty percent of economic units consisted of just two workers, while only 7 percent had more than ten' (Gluckstein 2011, 35; Gaillard 1977). David Harvey describes the distinct form that capitalist development took in Paris:

> Many small firms were nothing more than subcontracting units for larger forms of organization . . . [B]y keeping these units perpetually in competition for work, the employers could force down labour costs and maximize their own profits. Workers, even though nominally independent, were forced into subservience and into patterns of self-exploitation that could be as savage and as degrading as anything to be found in the factory system. (Harvey 2003, 160)

Harvey also describes how the proliferation of small businesses partially determined the mode of Parisian worker's resistance to capitalism: 'They continued to exercise collective pressure on labour markets, largely by staying put in their traditional quarters . . . Industries that needed their skills had to go to them' (Harvey 2003, 174).

The fragmentation of the Parisian working class, however, was transformed into political concentration in response to the Prussian army's siege of the city. In the context of rapidly deteriorating economic conditions, the government armed the workers who quickly constituted the majority of the National Guard. As Gluckstein puts it '[t]hus the Parisian working class acquired a collective organization, even if by a highly peculiar route' (Gluckstein 2011, 35). Their neighbourhood-based forms of class action constituted the core of the Commune.

National Guard officers were elected and rank-and-file soldiers enjoyed unprecedented democratic control. Once the French government had agreed a peace with Prussia, however, the government saw the Guard as representing a mortal threat to its rule and attempted, in March 1871, to disarm it. But this sparked a revolt by the Guard and the wider working-class population of Paris, leading to the establishment of the Commune.

The day after the rising a French newspaper described it as:

> Without example in history. Your revolution has a special character that distinguishes it from others. Its . . . greatness is that it is made entirely by the people as a collective communal revolutionary undertaking . . .

70

for the first time without leaders . . . This is a natural power, spontaneous, not false; born from the public conscience of the 'vile multitude'
which has been provided and attacked and now legitimately defends
itself. (La Commune 1871, cited in Gluckstein 2011, 35)

During the Commune's brief two-month life the standing army was
abolished, municipal councillors, public servants, magistrates and
judges were elected and subject to recall, the police were 'stripped of
its political attributes, and turned into the responsible, and at all times
revocable, agents of the Commune'. The Commune's civil servants
received worker's wages. The commitment to human development
was perhaps most evident in the Commune's education policy:

> The whole of the educational institutions were opened to the people
> gratuitously, and . . . cleared of all interference of church and state [and]
> . . . science [was] itself freed from the fetters which class prejudice and
> governmental force had imposed upon it. (Marx 1871)

Marx did not believe that the Commune represented the imminent
transformation of an exploitative class-based society, with its extreme
economic and political unevenness, directly into a non-class, communist utopia. On the contrary, he viewed it as potentially only the
beginning of a long and protracted transitional process:

> The working class did not expect miracles from the Commune . . .
> They know that in order to work out their own emancipation . . . they
> will have to pass through long struggles, through a series of historic
> processes, transforming circumstances and men. (Marx 1871)

The transformative possibilities of the Commune were not lost on
the French and other European ruling classes. As Benedict Anderson
(2004, 94) writes:

> In March 1871 the Commune took power in the abandoned city and
> held it for two months. Then Versailles seized the moment to attack
> and, in one horrifying week, executed roughly 20,000 Communards or
> suspected sympathizers, a number higher than those killed in the recent
> war or during Robespierre's 'Terror' of 1793–94.

Bismarck, presiding over his newly established German state following the previous year's victory against France, put aside international
rivalries and freed thousands of French prisoners of war to join the
Versailles-led destruction of the Commune (Harman 1999). The
defeat of the Commune pushed Marx to consider other sources of
socialism, geographically beyond Europe and potentially achieved by
actors other than industrial working classes.

Russia: Non-Industrial Transitions to Socialism

In his commentaries on non-Western societies discussed above, Marx viewed revolt in India and China as leading to a number of possible outcomes. These included the possibilities of national unification under Indian and Chinese rule respectively, and subsequent 'national' capitalist development, or their revolts acting as sparks to light the fires of further, greater revolutionary upheavals in Europe, which in turn might signal the beginnings of the world-wide development of socialism. In these observations, Marx still posits industrial(izing) Europe as the potential starting point for socialism. If these represented his most mature considerations, then the argument that he privileged the Western European proletariat in a Eurocentric manner might have some traction. But he went significantly further than this. Towards the end of his life in his writings on Russia, he raised an altogether new possibility of human development.

Marx became interested in the pattern of Russian development after the publication of *Capital* in Russian (in 1872) and the intense interest it generated among agrarian populists (Shanin 1983). Their leading figures such as Herzen and Chernyshevsky argued that the specifically cooperative nature of the Russian commune (*Obschina* or *Mir*) rendered it fit for laying the basis for a post-capitalist society in Russia, despite the country's very low level of capitalist development.[4] In 1881 Vera Zasulich (also a populist and a member of Russia's socialist party) wrote to Marx asking whether 'the rural commune, free of exorbitant tax demands, payment to the nobility and arbitrary administration, is capable of developing in a socialist direction' or whether 'the commune is destined to perish' (in Shanin 1983, 98), and whether socialists needed to wait for the full development of Russian capitalism before attempting socialist revolution. The latter position was held by most of Marx's Russian followers (Day and Gaido 2011, 24–32). Marx's response demonstrates his dialectical view of world history and class struggle, and his recognition of the potential agency of labouring classes in the periphery:

> If Russia were isolated in the world, it would have to develop on its own account the economic conquests which Western Europe only acquired through a long series of evolutions from its primitive communities to its present situation . . . There would be no doubt . . . that Russia's communities are fated to perish. (Marx, cited in Shanin 1983, 102)

---

[4] Kitching (1989) provides an excellent discussion of these early populist writers.

But:

> [T]he situation of the Russian commune is absolutely different from that of the primitive communities in the West. . . . . Russia is the only European country in which communal property has maintained itself on a vast, nationwide scale. But at the same time Russia exists in a modern historical context [international capitalism]. . . . Thanks to the unique combination of circumstances in Russia, the rural commune . . . may gradually shake off its primitive characteristics and directly develop as an element of collective production on a national scale. (Marx, cited in Shanin 1983, 102)

Marx identified how the rural commune contained an internal tension. On the one hand communal landownership held it together, while on the other hand individual (family) ownership of the house and yard combined with small-plot farming and the 'private appropriation of its fruits' maintaining a level of individualism potentially incompatible with communal life. Marx saw this tension as containing a potential contradiction as eventually this tension 'could turn into a seed of [the Commune's] disintegration'. Of additional importance was the existence of 'fragmented labour as the source of private appropriation' not subject to communal control and open to individual exchange. Marx observed that 'This was what dissolved primitive economic and social equality' (Marx, cited in Shanin 1983, 120).

The dissolution of the commune was possible but not inevitable. The outcome depended on struggles within and beyond the commune and Russia. 'What threatens the life of the Russian commune is neither an historical inevitability nor a theory; it is oppression by the state and exploitation by the capitalist intruders made powerful, at the expense of the peasantry by this same state' (Marx, in Shanin 1983, 104–5). To save the Russian commune, Marx argued

> [T]here must be a Russian revolution . . . If the revolution takes place in time . . . to ensure the unfettered rise of the rural commune, the latter will soon develop as a regenerating element of Russian society and an element of superiority over the countries enslaved by the capitalist regime. (Marx, cited in Shanin 1983, 116–17)

This revolution could not stop at the Russian border however. It had to extend beyond it and required revolution by workers of the advanced capitalist countries. Indeed, Marx hoped that such a revolution in Russia would *stimulate* revolution in the west, thus unleashing a new form of human development, communism, emerging from combinations of industrially organized workers in the west and agrarian communes in the east:

If the Russian revolution becomes the signal for a proletarian revolution in the West, so that the two complement each other, then Russia's peasant communal landownership may serve as the point of departure for a communist development. (Marx, cited in Shanin 1983, 139)

Here Marx recognizes the agency of labouring classes east and west to transform their own forms and trajectories of human development, with no presupposition that either must follow an already established path or schema of events. Significantly, Marx considered socialism emerging as a consequence of combinations of (at least) agrarian and industrial-based movements by very differently constituted labouring classes. This shows that Marx did not think that only Western industrial workers could breach capitalist social relations, and how he conceived the emergence of socialism as a global moment of world history, based upon the interacting struggles of global labouring classes.

Conclusions

We have seen how within Marx's work there are elements of an economic determinist, Eurocentric and linear comprehension of history. Much worse still is the way these elements have been elevated into a seemingly coherent orthodox dogma that leaves little or no room for the labouring classes of the global south to determine their own fate. If Marx is interpreted as an economic determinist then the intellectual mediocrities of the past century – from Stalinists to neoliberals – have won the day, and an immensely powerful tool for struggling for, and achieving, alternative forms of human development will be lost.

The purpose of this chapter has been, however, to suggest that a reading of Marx centred upon his understanding of evolving and continually dynamic class relations and struggles, and their global interactions, renders untenable the above critique.

In his writings on non-Western societies Marx showed how their interconnections with the imperial centres ushered in a new phase of human history whereby the actions of labouring classes in the periphery could impact upon the forms of social development in the global core. The struggles against imperialism in China and India, Marx argued, could lead to intensification of class struggles in the global core, and/or to the potential establishment of capitalist states in these countries. Marx's analysis of Australian colonization demonstrated how the colonial state was essential in establishing capitalist social

74

relations there. Without state control over the labour market the newly established working classes could escape their subordination to capital and establish themselves as independent peasantries beyond the frontier. Moreover, the persistence of the commune in Russia generated the possibility of a leap to socialism initiated by non-industrial labouring classes, and their playing the leading role in broader European revolutions against capitalism.

Marx's writings on the political economy of labour and on the Paris Commune are of potentially even greater importance under contemporary global capitalism. In the former, Marx highlighted how workers could generate movements that would substantially improve their livelihoods under capitalism. And in the organization of the Commune, he argued that workers had finally found the political-economic structure through which to liberate themselves from the chains of capital.

The examples of struggles in England and Paris are arguably more relevant today than those of colonial Australia or rural Russia because global capitalism has created a global labouring class of billions (compared to the few millions of Marx's day) whose livelihoods are much closer to those of the Manchester textile workers or the Parisian Communards than to the non-capitalist Russian commune or the Australian frontier. However, Marx's discussions of agrarian social formations and movements during his lifetime alert us to the importance of continuing struggles by labouring classes in the contemporary rural world, and raises questions of how sustainable they are on their own terms, what kinds of alliances can be built between them and other labouring classes (in urban settings and/or internationally), and of course, what kinds of contradictions arise in these, as in all, class struggles.

Marx is the key figure who saw class struggles as constitutive of the development process and who demonstrated how the outcomes of struggles between dominant and labouring classes conditioned subsequent historical development. Moreover, he identified with and politically prioritized labouring classes in their attempts to rid themselves of capitalist exploitation.

— 4 —

TROTSKY, GERSCHENKRON AND THE CLASH OF MARXISM AND STATIST POLITICAL ECONOMY

The privilege of historic backwardness ... compels, the adoption of whatever is ready in advance of any specified date, skipping a whole series of intermediate stages. ... The development of historically backward nations leads necessarily to a peculiar combination of different stages in the historic process. (Trotsky 1997, 26)

[I]ndustrialization processes, when launched at length in a backward country, showed considerable differences, as compared with the more advanced countries, not only with regard to the speed of the development (the rate of industrial growth) but also with regard to the productive and organizational structures of industry which emerged from these processes. (Gerschenkron 1962, 7)

This chapter discusses the work of Leon Trotsky and Alexander Gerschenkron. The two men advanced the insights and theories formulated by Karl Marx and Friedrich List respectively. As this chapter's epigraphs suggest, both men understood that late-developing countries potentially possessed a 'privilege' of backwardness which enabled them, under certain circumstances, to leap over more advanced nations. This understanding, which was not explicitly theorized by either List or Marx, enabled Trotsky and Gerschenkron to make further, important contributions to development thinking.

Their work provides a profound analysis of how state-led catch-up development rests upon, and requires, a reshaping of class relations and how those relations impact back upon and can sometimes subvert states' developmental efforts. The chapter shows how Trotsky formulated a more advanced understanding of international relations than Marx, in his concept of uneven and combined development, simultaneously incorporating domestic class relations and international economic relations. Gerschenkron also continued and deepened List's observations about state-led industrialization, demonstrating how international economic relations (competition) impose continually evolving pressures on late developers, requiring the latter to generate *innovative* institutional responses (institutional innovations) if they are to benefit from the advantages of backwardness. It is noteworthy that Gerschenkron drew heavily upon and in some ways contributed to Trotsky's work, while also transforming its political content.

On the one hand, Trotsky's conception of uneven and combined development represents a contribution to and extension of Marxism. On the other hand, Gerschenkron's identification of institutional innovations represents a *theoretical* contribution to statist political economy (SPE). However, it simultaneously undermines SPE's *policy* relevance. This is because if something innovative is required to achieve catch-up development, then that innovation cannot, logically, be predicted or formulated in a prior policy. This observation does not represent a weakness on Gerschenkron's part. On the contrary, it reflects a problem and limitation with the historically based (inductive) methodology employed by List and much of the statist political economy tradition, that does not rest upon a dynamic, transformative comprehension of capitalist social relations. Such a comprehension is present in Gerschenkron (implicitly) and in Trotsky (explicitly), and for these reasons, as we shall discuss, it means that Gerschenkron represents something of a theoretical highpoint for SPE.

In their careers, Trotsky and Gerschenkron could not have been more different. Gerschenkron was a distinguished and highly influential academic who rose to prominence at Harvard (Dawidoff 2002), while Trotsky represented the 'sword' of the Russian Revolution of 1917 and was the theorist of international 'permanent revolution' (Cliff 1990). Gerschenkron's contribution to understanding the rationale for and numerous cases of state-led development is widely appreciated within development studies (Amsden 1990; Kohli 2004; Roxborough 1979), and has been used in combination with List's emphasis on infant industry protection to produce a large number of important works on late development. Trotsky's conceptual framework of uneven and combined development has experienced renewed interest recently in the field of international relations[1] but is still quite marginal in development studies.[2] Despite this disjuncture in their respective popularity within development studies, there are several good reasons to consider their work in tandem. They shared a common problematic that can be summarized as an understanding of:

(1) how the 'advantages of backwardness' generate possibilities for poor countries to skip developmental 'stages' and achieve rapid industrialization and capitalist development;

(2) how even when successful, late industrialization would unleash great social tensions that might undermine industrialization attempts; and

(3) the non-inevitability of industrialization (and, for Trotsky at least, an understanding of the world system as a differentiating mechanism, generating both economic advance and retardation).

While there have been numerous recent references to the commonalities of the two men's work (Ashman 2009; Davidson 2006; Rosenberg 2008; Van der Linden 2007), these have not yet been expanded into a more systematic comparison. For example, and in a somewhat chronologically challenged manner, Roxborough (1979, 24–5) refers to Trotsky's work as 'the Marxist equivalent of Gerschenkron's theory of the advantages of backwardness' but does not investigate the similarities further. More to the point, and despite Fishlow's (2003) claim that Gerschenkron's approach was anti-Marxist, perhaps what connects them most is not just their joint Russian(Ukrainian)/Jewish heritage, but that Gerschenkron was familiar with the work of Trotsky, and that his work bears many uncanny similarities to that of the joint-leader of the Russian revolution.[3] Van der Linden (2007, 2013) notes how, in the 1920s and

---

[1] Justin Rosenberg (e.g. 1996) has been at the forefront of this renewed interest.

[2] During the late 1970s and early 1980s some work came close to using Trotsky's framework for investigating and comprehending processes of late capitalist development. See, for example, Dunkerley (1988) and Post (1978). Cardoso and Faletto's (1979) approach was contributed to by Roxborough's (1984) sympathetic critique. Lowy (1981) was, of course, the most explicit in attempting to theorize and apply Trotsky's framework.

[3] When I contacted Gerschenkron's grandson and biographer Nicholas Dawidoff, and enquired whether Gerschenkron knew about Trotsky's writings, he responded with the following: 'Of course my grandfather read Trotsky, but what specifically he read, when he read it and what he thought of it I cannot say' (email received 17 May 2008).

1930s, Gerschenkron was an Austro-Marxist and critical supporter of the Soviet Union.

Part of the argument in this chapter is that Gerschenkron's more techno-industrial focus enables him to make quite detailed and precise predictions about processes of industrialization (although not the precise institutions necessary to achieve it), while Trotsky's more sociological framework, painted on a much broader canvas, enables him to identify the central importance of class relations in processes of late development. Despite his insights, Gerschenkron has a relatively weak understanding of the barriers to late development and the processes that propel countries even further backward (relatively and absolutely). A better approach to how the totality of units (states) within the global system are subject to two contradictory tendencies – simultaneous economic divergence and economic convergence – is necessary, and can be comprehended through Trotsky's conception of uneven and combined development. These insights are developed further in the following chapter, on creative destruction and global inequality.

The remainder of this chapter is organized as follows. The second section discusses how Trotsky and Gerschenkron reject linear conceptions of development. The third section highlights Gerschenkron's major insights into late industrialization – the necessity of institutional innovations in enabling states to achieve catch-up development. The next section outlines Trotsky's concept of uneven and combined development. The fifth section considers Trotsky's comprehension of international relations and suggests how this provides valuable pathways into studying late capitalist development. The sixth section discusses the role and position of labour in late development.

Against Linear Concepts of Development

In comprehending the possibilities of economically backward countries achieving catch-up development, both Trotsky and Gerschenkron began by rejecting unilinear conceptions of development. For Gerschenkron, writing in the United States academy of the 1950s and 1960s Rostow's (1960) five-stage modernization approach (traditional society, pre-conditions to take-off, take-off, drive to maturity, age of high mass consumption) dominated mainstream thinking about development. Trotsky also opposed crude versions of the stageist Marxist theory of history (primitive communism, slavery, feudalism, capitalism, socialism) that prevailed at the turn of the

79

twentieth century within the Second International and from the mid-1920s within the increasingly Stalinized Third International.

Both authors reject abstract and deductive methods associated with modern liberal economics (predictions based upon a theory), but also concrete and inductive methods associated with Listian political economy (predictions based on past historical patterns). Rather, they utilize a dialectical approach to international development, implying a comprehension of a dynamic, transformative system (capitalism), combined with a conception of how the unequal units of the system are internally constituted and externally connected (cf. Rees 1998, 262–89) This approach, which is explicit in Trotsky and, I argue, implicit in Gerschenkron, strives to account for (1) the evolving world system, (2) the timing of backward economies' catch-up attempts and (3) how domestic social structures interact with international forces to influence a country's developmental trajectory.

Both take as their point of departure a soft disagreement with Marx's statement that 'the industrially more developed country presents to the less developed country a picture of the latter's future' (Marx, quoted in Gerschenkron 1962, 6). Both accept that capitalism (Trotsky) and industrialization (Gerschenkron) impart certain basic similarities to all countries, such as the establishment of an urban wage-labour force (hence their soft criticism of Marx), but both also assert that this represents only half the story. The timing and nature of earlier developers impact upon late-comers, introducing new and different elements to the development puzzle. Against what we can label the pessimism of the late starter's thesis, Trotsky and Gerschenkron highlighted the potential advantages of backwardness. Trotsky formulated how late arrivals on the world capitalist stage enjoyed potential advantages:

> A backward country assimilates the material and intellectual conquests of the advanced countries. But this does not mean that it follows them slavishly, reproduces all the stages of their past . . . Although compelled to follow after the advanced countries, a backward country does not take things in the same order. The privilege of historical backwardness – and such a privilege exists – permits, or rather compels, the adoption of whatever is ready in advance of any specified date, skipping a whole series of intermediate stages. (Trotsky 1997, 26)

Gerschenkron noted that:

> In a number of important historical instances industrialization processes, when launched at length in a backward country, showed considerable differences, as compared with the more advanced coun-

tries, not only with regard to the speed of the development (the rate of industrial growth) but also with regard to the productive and organizational structures of industry which emerged from these processes. (Gerschenkron 1962, 7)

Further:

> Industrialization always seemed the more promising the greater the backlog of technological innovations which the backward country could take over from the more advanced country. Borrowed technology ... was one of the primary factors assuring a high speed of development in a backward country entering the stage of industrialization. (Gerschenkron 1962, 8)

The benefits of technology transfers' contribution to development are widely recognized and constitute an important aspect of liberal (Ricardian) political economy. Here technological diffusion enables poorer countries to avoid having to re-invent the wheel. Within this liberal framework such diffusion occurs most rapidly within a world economy based upon mutually beneficial national-level specialization and markets open to foreign direct investment.[4] But for Gerschenkron specialization and openness to world markets did not determine successful adoption of new technologies. Radical institutional innovation did. Similarly, Trotsky analysed the role of the (Russian) state in facilitating such diffusion and adaptation but he also investigated and conceptualized the sociological impacts of late development – what he would label 'combined development' (see below).

Trotsky and Gerschenkron were not making original points in their recognition of the advantages of backwardness. For example, in 1915 the American economist Thorsten Veblen claimed that while in the 1870s Germany was economically and politically 250 years behind Great Britain, it had overcome this gap by the time of the First World War (Veblen 1939). The benefits of late development had been recognized by the Russian populist Herzen as early as the 1850s when he noted that '[h]uman development is a form of chronological unfairness, since late comers are able to profit by the labours of their

---

[4] Lipsey and Sjöholm (2005) note, however, that developing countries' hopes of benefiting from spillover effects from foreign direct investment are often thwarted when the technology gap between foreign and national firms is too big, or when the developing countries' absorptive capacity is below a certain threshold, again pinpointing the centrality of the institutional variable in comprehending why similar forms of market integration may lead to differing national-level developmental outcomes.

predecessors without paying the same price' (cited in Berlin 1960). However, as Davidson (2006, 20) notes, for Herzen and his fellow populists this analysis meant that Russia could avoid the traumas of capitalist development. Trotsky and Gerschenkron's originality lay in recognizing its necessarily difficult and disruptive nature, arising from the new socio-political 'combinations' brought about by such attempts at catch-up development.

Gerschenkron on Late Industrialization

By identifying the role of institutions in realizing the advantages of backwardness, Gerschenkron stood in a tradition of political economy going back at least as far as Friedrich List. List had provided detailed analyses of the role of states in facilitating industrialization and achieving international competitiveness. But he was still a theorist of absolute late industrialization, where backwardness necessitated the use of strategies such as infant industry protection. However, the extent and relations of backwardness, for example the technological lag and its impacts on catch-up strategies, were not considered by List in any great detail. What he could not predict, given his inductive methodology, was the progressive upward curve of state activity in economically backward countries as they attempted catch-up development within a dynamic world system. While the late developers of the Victorian age (Germany, Japan, Russia, the United States) played a relatively 'simple' role of protection and subsidy provision, the 'developmental' states of the twentieth century extended their activities to the regulation and monitoring of investments by private firms and undertook directly major investments in infrastructure and industry (Chibber 2005).

The changing roles of late-developing states in the twentieth century within a dynamic capitalist world system generated pressing new issues requiring modifications of theory, attempted by an emerging number of development economists, including Gerschenkron. It is only a small exaggeration therefore to suggest, as Diana Hunt does (1989, 46), that Gerschenkron and his peers' analyses of late development emerged within the context of 'pre-paradigm' science, in which 'every individual scientist starts over again from the beginning'.

Gerschenkron and his peers were stimulated to understand processes of economic development and stagnation by the specific world historical processes of their time. These included the rapid rise and expansion of Soviet power under state planning and the positive example this set for many contemporary poor countries (many of the new development economists were, like Gerschenkron, of Central/ Eastern European origins, and were acutely aware of the influence of the Soviet model – for example, Rosenstein-Rodan [Austria], Nurske [Estonia], Hirschman [Germany], Kaldor [Hungary]); following the Keynesian revolution, the increased role of the state in the core economies; rising anti-colonial movement and the proliferation of independent sovereign states; the promotion by the United States of its own (modernization) development theory; and continuing economic divergence between rich and poor countries. Moreover, the new development economics, as it later became known (Hunt 1989), was reacting against the methodology and expectations of the evolving liberal orthodoxy (Solow 1956) which were perceived by it as methodologically deductive and based upon unrealistic assumptions (including for example regarding technology as a freely available public good, the existence of 'perfect competition' and full employment, and diminishing, or at least constant, returns). Based upon these assumptions liberal models of development expected economic convergence between poor and rich countries as long as markets were free from distortions.

The emerging development economists aimed to deal with real-world processes of development and underdevelopment. For example, Paul Rosenstein-Rodan's (1943) concept of the 'big push' emphasized how for investments to lead to productivity increases they needed to be of a relatively high minimum in order to generate external economies and the conditions for (virtuous) cumulative causation (see below). Similarly, Ragnar Nurske (1953) argued that states needed to engage in coordinated and wide-ranging industrial investment and resource mobilization to break their countries out of vicious circles of poverty. Against these approaches Albert Hirschman's (1958) theory of unbalanced growth addressed the issue of how to overcome limits to entrepreneurial ability. He stressed the need for concentrated and targeted investments in strategic sectors, in particularly manufacturing where the most capable entrepreneurs operate, which in turn would generate forward and backward linkages and encourage further investments by less capable entrepreneurs. Nicholas Kaldor (1972) emphasized how rapid investments created possibilities for 'learning by doing', a rising curve of productivity and competitiveness and increasing returns. In another influential contribution W. Arthur Lewis (1954) theorized the benefits of growth with 'unlimited supplies of labour' in his dual sector model – where surplus labour in the subsistence sector represents a source of cheap labour for the advanced capitalist sector (see the 'Labour in Late Development' section below for Gerschenkron's understanding of the transfer of labour from agrarian to industrial sectors).

Gerschenkron and his co-thinkers drew on Schumpeter's (1934) understanding of the strategic role of (entrepreneurial) innovation, supported by bank-provided finance. They envisioned the state playing a role analogous to that of banks in conditions of economic backwardness, and thus rejected Hayek's (2010 [1944]) arguments that state planning would undermine human freedom. Rather, they saw such intervention as essential for realizing rapid industrialization. While most of these thinkers were generally optimistic about the possibilities of states playing a positive developmental role, Gunnar Myrdal's (1956) concept of cumulative causation also illustrated the dangers of economic backwardness, and argued that, if not aggressively tackled, backwardness would beget further backwardness (we shall return to this concept below).

All of these thinkers were engaged in an attempt, from the perspective of development economics, and encapsulated at the most general level by Karl Polanyi (2001), to illustrate the importance and possibility of states guiding, controlling and subordinating capitalist markets to societal development objectives. These contributions both stood in and extended the tradition of the infant industry argument formulated by Friedrich List.

While many of the above insights could be incorporated into Gerschenkron's framework, he suggested that even though such policies might be *necessary* for states attempting catch-up development, they were not *sufficient*. This was because with each case of successful late development not only was the bar raised to future states attempting the leap, but the nature of the playing field (the world economy and the political economic interactions between nations) was transformed. This in turn required something new. Therefore '[t]he very concept of substitution is premised upon creative innovating activity ... upon *something that is inherently unpredictable*' (Gerschenkron 1962, 359–60, emphasis added). In this way Gerschenkron was able to identify aspects that were necessary to late industrialization, while leaving as open-ended and unpredictable the processes that would contribute to the all-important institutional innovation.

Most of these insights, while constituting the core of the emerging discipline of development economics, missed out a single, vital, factor: how did all of this technology transfer and industrial upgrading, in the context of an evolving world system, impact upon social relations within poor countries and their relations with other states?

While Gerschenkron shares much of the techno-industrial focus of his peers, because of his intellectual debt to Trotsky, he does have significantly more to say about social relations, as we shall see below. For now, however, the argument is that Gerschenkron supersedes not only List, but also many of his own contemporaries, in his identification of the relationship between the extent of a countries' backwardness (i.e. its developmental or technological gap) and its institutional response: the further behind economically, the greater (in size and extent) the institutional response. Hence, his 'general rule' of late industrialization:

> The more backward a country, the *more likely* its industrialization was to proceed under some organized direction; depending on the degree of backwardness, the seat of such direction could be found in investment banks, in investment banks acting under the aegis of the state, or in bureaucratic controls. So viewed, the industrial history of Europe appears not as a series of mere repetitions of the 'first' industrialization but as an orderly system of *graduated deviations*. (Gerschenkron 1962, 44, emphasis in original)

For both Trotsky and Gerschenkron the UK represented the first and only case of 'early' industrialization. All subsequent cases therefore were considered 'late' and, as we shall see below, their novel institutional responses also had profound consequences for the form and content of their developmental trajectories and external relations. Again, there is no sense here of repetition (and hence linearity) but rather of continual divergence from earlier cases of industrialization.

Because Gerschenkron's general rule enables him to make certain predictions about future cases of late development, Justin Rosenberg argues that he 'imparted a social scientific rigour to ideas which Trotsky had expressed rather impressionistically' (2008, 19). His analysis identifies (a) the systemic effects of the international system on late industrializers, and how (b) this gives rise to a pattern of domestic social structural differentiation between countries as they industrialize (Rosenberg 2008, 20). Rosenberg is certainly correct about Gerschenkron's social scientific rigour if we consider only the industrialization process. But, if we extend our view to the broader canvas of late capitalist development, Trotsky's approach and emphasis on social classes is as rigorous as Gerschenkron's (see below).

Following Gerschenkron's lead in identifying the scale of institutional response as a key determinant in successful late development, Chandrasekhar notes that '[o]ne set of distinctive features of late industrialization . . . relates to the size, technological level, sequence,

Table 4.1 Gerschenkronian Institutional Innovations and Late Industrialization

Temporality	Country and Institutional Innovation
Mid-1880s 'Area of Extreme Backwardness'	**Russia** State + Banks + Factories = Militarily orientated state 'assumed the role of primary agent propelling the economic progress in the country' (Chandrasekhar 2005, 17) via large-scale direct industrial investments.
1870s 'Area of Moderate Backwardness'	**Germany** Banks + Factories = Highly centralized, state-directed industrially orientated banks engaged in 'cartelization and amalgamation of industrial enterprises' (Gerschenkron 1962, 15).
1860s 'Area of Moderate Backwardness'	**France** Banks + Factories = Industrial banking providing long-term loans to finance heavy industry.
1780s 'Advanced Area'	**Britain** Factories = Use of 'primitive' technology by an 'enterprising, not particularly well-educated or subtle, not particularly wealthy body of businessmen and artisans' (Hobsbawm 1969, 60). No role for banks in providing long-term loans (Gershenkron: 1962, 14).

Source: Adapted from Gershenkron (1962)

and variety of new industries that are created in the course of the industrial transformation of a country' (Chandrasekhar 2005, 182). These cumulative dynamics are illustrated in table 4.1.

Gerschenkron (1962, 353–4) identified how the later industrialization commenced, the greater the 'stress on bigness' in the industrializing country, and therefore the more likely that the following four 'syndromes' would characterize the country's political economy:[5]

---

[5] Actually he identifies six features but, following Schwartz (2000, 85), I have compressed them into four.

(1) the more likely that it would be characterized by very fast initial growth, with a stress on large-scale capital (as opposed to consumer) goods production;

(2) the greater the pressure upon consumption levels of the population (to be kept low) and, by extension, the greater the need for the 'disciplining' of the working class and peasantry;

(3) the greater the need for increasingly coercive 'special institutional factors' to supply capital to emerging industries, to provide them with centralized and highly skilled entrepreneurial guidance and to ensure they adopt the latest hard and soft technologies (machinery and management techniques);

(4) the less likely that its agricultural sector would be able to act as a domestic market for industrial outputs.

Rapidity was deemed necessary because the construction of new industrial sectors generated significant opportunity costs (output forgone) within the existing economy via taxes and other forms of resource transfer to fund new industries. And there are economic (and political) limits to the extent to which the existing economy can support an industrialization drive before it begins to decline due to excessive financial extraction without compensation via growth.

The history of late development as illustrated by Gerschenkron, and more recently, by those writing about the East Asian experience, suggests that the above observations do appear to be general features characterizing late industrializers. The latter writers observe, for example, large-scale state investments in R&D, state-directed upgrading projects from low- to higher-value industrial production, harsh repression of labour, low rates of pay and very long working hours (Wade, 2003). However, as Byres (1991) and Kay (2002) illustrate vis-à-vis point 4 above, just as state-level institutional innovations can overcome problems of late industrialization, so they can potentially contribute to addressing the agrarian question in ways conducive to rapid industrialization. Crucially, points 2 and 3 highlight the disruptive, tension-laden and high-risk nature of late development, which constitutes one of Trotsky's central focuses (discussed further below).

As noted, Gerschenkron's approach fits closely with the most advanced authors within the classical development economics tradition. But his approach stands out because of his recognition of (a) the impact of the timing of attempted catch-up upon latecomers' institutional innovations and strategies, and (b) the sociologically disruptive nature of late development. It was Trotsky, however, who more fully captured this sociology.

87

Uneven and Combined Development

We have noted that Trotsky and Gerschenkron were not the first to identify the advantages of backwardness. Gerschenkron's conception of late development focused upon industrialization, in particular overcoming barriers to productivity growth, presented the analysis in more techno-industrial terms than Trotsky, and was therefore able to make both precise observations and predictions (or 'predictabilities') about future courses of industrialization (Gerschenkron 1962, 359). However, Trotsky was acutely aware of the disruptive impulses engendered by catch-up strategies, and identified how these could be turned into opportunities, not for capitalist industrialization but for socialist revolution. He also understood how late development processes were co-determined by the constitution of social classes.

Trotsky's conception of uneven and combined development emerged over a thirty-year period, during which he was engaged in two major political struggles. The first was within the Second International in the decade and a half prior to 1917 and concerned the possibilities of revolution in an economically backward country (Trotsky 1969). The orthodoxy then was that workers' revolutions could take place only in advanced countries. The second debate, with uncanny similarities to the first, took place from the mid-1920s to early 1930s and was against Stalin's conception of 'socialism in one country'. Stalin and his followers argued that since countries develop at their own, uneven tempos, they must advance through a series of stages, including socialism, at their own pace. In both debates Trotsky argued against simple conceptions of uneven development. He drew on Parvus' (Alexander Israel Helphand) conception of world totality to illustrate the intrinsically interconnected nature of the world economy and hence the impossibility of individual 'stages' of development (Lowy 1981).

Trotsky began his analysis of late development by re-stating the advantages of backwardness thesis, but then transcended and transformed the concept altogether:

> Unevenness, the most general law of the historic process, reveals itself most sharply and complexly in the destiny of the backward country. Under the whip of external necessity their backward culture is compelled to make leaps. From the universal law of unevenness thus derives another law which for want of a better name, we may call the law of combined development – by which we mean a drawing together of the different stages in the journey, a combining of separate steps, an amalgam of archaic with more contemporary forms. (Trotsky 1997, 27)

Hence, not only do countries enjoy advantages (and disadvantages) of backwardness, but through integrating themselves into the world system under the 'whip of external necessity' they also generate combinations of new and old social forms, melded together at high speed and unrecognizable from the lens of unilinear conceptions of development.

Gerschenkron too understood these combining processes: 'In every instance of industrialization, imitation of the evolution in advanced countries appears in combination with different, indigenously determined elements' (1962, 26). For example, in *Bread and Democracy in Germany* (1943) Gerschenkron documents how rapid industrialization occurred under the very illiberal domination of the landed Junker elite, which protected itself through tariffs from competitive pressures exerted by new non-European centres of agrarian accumulation. The unequal alliance between industrialists and Junkers was characterized by Gerschenkron (1943) as the 'compromise between iron and rye'. The obverse of this process was the creation of a huge industrial working class, organized largely by the German Social Democratic Party. The conflicts between the emerging working class and the Junkers' attempts to maintain their 'traditional' role in German society, backed up and supported by the German state, reflecting the fact that 'the Prussian landowning class was more solidly at one with its state than any other in Europe' (Anderson 1974, 265), constituted a fault line in German society that was first overcome by the Nazi accession to power in 1933 (when working-class organizations were smashed) but only finally resolved in 1945 (when German society was re-formed from outside, Junker political and economic power being eliminated in the process). And following Gerschenkron, Barrington Moore (1967, 448), argued that the basic elements of Nazi ideology were present in the Junkers' attempts at winning hegemony over the peasantry in part to counter-balance the emerging power of the working class.

Trotsky and Gerschenkron thus recognized how late development generated its own specific pressures via the creation of new social forces that were not present for earlier industrializers, and that these in turn generated new threats to states attempting late industrialization and, potentially, to the entire international system. Thus it seems incorrect, as Davidson (2006, 2010) does, to argue that Gerschenkron did not appreciate the impacts of technological change and late development strategies upon wider society. It is, rather, precisely because Gerschenkron drew so heavily on Trotsky's work that he was able, quite uniquely among the emerging development economists of the 1940s and 1950s, to understand the combined nature of late development.

The existence of already industrialized countries and an increasingly competitive world market constitutes a 'whip of external necessity' which forces latecomers to adapt to radically new circumstances. While this adaptation may entail industrialization ('development') it may also entail the re-enforcement of social forces inimical to liberal capitalism and democracy. These forces may exercise a determining social and political role inside the later developing country, and their subsequent domestic dominance may also impact upon those countries' international political and economic relations, in turn transforming the nature of the international system itself. The histories of Russia and Germany prior to the Second World War provide ample confirmation of this prognosis.

It is perhaps worth spending some more effort in thinking through why late development = combined (rather than just simply uneven) development, and why, therefore, capitalist development is highly unpredictable. Again, Tsarist Russia constitutes our case study. Two novel implications arise from Trotsky's framework (cf. Davidson 2006, 20). First, it is not the case that modern and archaic simply coexist, side by side. Rather, combined development implies a melding and fusing of modern and archaic social forms in new and unstable ways: 'The backward nation, moreover, not infrequently debases the achievements borrowed from outside in the process of adapting them to its own more primitive culture' (Trotsky 1997, 27). For example, Tsarism utilized the most advanced industrial machinery to construct a powerful manufacturing base with which to supply its national army to defend Russian absolutism. And, as Rosenberg notes, 'the more Russia was integrated externally into the international system ... the more its internal social structure was being twisted into a shape that actually prevented it from developing along the path taken by the liberal states of Western Europe' (1996, 8).

The effort of catch-up development implies, as Gerschenkron recognized, huge downward pressures upon the population's consumption. Trotsky observed how large surpluses were extracted from the Russian countryside to fund industrialization and repay foreign loans: the Tsarist state 'converted the peasant into a tributary of the stock exchange of the world' (Trotsky 1969 [1906], 49). Such high rates of exploitation could not but generate resentment and resistance – which contributed to the second half of Trotsky's conceptual innovation. These new combinations and instabilities give rise to social conflicts unknown in prior cases of capitalist development.

For Trotsky, this observation gave him the confidence to predict a worker–peasant alliance in the simultaneous overthrow of Tsarism (the bourgeois phase of the revolution) and the establishment of socialist state (the proletarian phase), in turn igniting the spark of international revolution – in short his theory of permanent revolution. Of great importance here, however, is how contending social classes shape and respond to development processes (in order to maximize advantages and displace disadvantages). The outcomes of these struggles impact significantly upon processes and outcomes of late development. And, because the outcomes of these struggles cannot be predicted in advance, neither can the process of uneven and combined development.

We noted previously, following Rosenberg (2008), how Gerschenkron provided a social scientific rigour to his analysis of late industrialization – in particular his comprehension of how the greater the developmental gap between advanced and backward countries the larger-scale the latter's institutional response needed to be if the advantages of late development were to be realized. While Gerschenkron's rigour extended to his analysis of late industrialization, Trotsky imparted a rigour of his own to the concept of uneven and combined development. And here we find a significant weakness in Gerschenkron's conception of late development. While he assumes that late development is a distinct possibility, he fails to incorporate satisfactorily into his considerations broader political processes. Trotsky by comparison does incorporate these considerations into his schema.

In Gerschenkron's interpretation (table 4.1) there is no recognition of how class relations contextualize attempts at and outcomes of late industrialization. While France, Germany and Russia were posited by Gerschenkron as following the British industrial revolution, he does not discuss how they attempted also to follow the British political bourgeois revolution and its broader repercussions, from the mid- to late seventeenth century onwards. Once this question is posed we can point to 1789 in France and 1871 in Germany – two essentially bourgeois revolutions, the first from below, the second from above (Callinicos 1993; Davidson 2005). These revolutions contextualized their respective, successful, late industrialization and economic catch-up attempts with more economically advanced countries. The Russian bourgeoisie, by contrast, did not have its revolution – either from above or below. While the Russian state forced high-speed industrialization upon its population, without a legitimating bourgeois revolution which would bind together a new class alliance

91

behind the industrialization drive, it was politically weakened from the beginning and ultimately succumbed to a joint worker–peasant revolution from below. It is not just that Gerschenkron focuses on industrialization and Trotsky on politics. Trotsky's placing of class dynamics at the centre of his framework of uneven and combined development means that his approach is analytically prior to that of Gerschenkron's. To comprehend the possibilities of state-led development, based upon a successful institutional innovation, it is necessary to identify the class relations within and through which, states pursue such development strategies. But because these class relations are continually evolving, it is very difficult to predict what sets of relations are more favourable to institutional innovations and state development strategies.

In *Results and Prospects* (1969 [1906]) Trotsky, following Marx, discussed the uneven rise of the bourgeoisie across Europe. He contrasted the relative fearlessness of the French bourgeoisie in 1789 with the more timid German bourgeoisie in 1848 and 1871, and explained this difference as a consequence of the presence and greater political and economic strength of an industrial proletariat in the latter case. The reasons for the German bourgeoisie's timidity was its understanding of its contradictory position – nominally fighting for liberal rights (liberty, equality, fraternity) while simultaneously representing a new exploiting class. This situation was magnified all the more in Tsarist Russia because:

> The proletariat immediately found itself concentrated in tremendous masses, while between these masses and the autocracy there stood a capitalist bourgeoisie, very small in numbers, isolated from the 'people', half foreign, without historical traditions, and inspired only by the greed of gain. (Trotsky 1969 [1906], 51)

Here then is one of Trotsky's great observations: the later the attempt at industrialization and the larger the proletariat, the more fearful, and hence less ambitious, audacious and competent the bourgeoisie. This in turn means that the latter will be more likely to align with old feudal classes, thus generating ever-greater strains (between bourgeoisie and old feudal classes, on the one hand, and between the state and the proletariat, on the other) in the process of late development, which then generate new opportunities for other forces (such as worker and peasant organizations) to push for revolutionary change. And in 1905 and 1917 the Russian proletariat showed its ability to unleash historically unprecedented forms of social struggles, by establishing the Soviets (workers' councils) which first Trotsky (in 1905) and later Lenin (after April 1917) recognized as potential pillars of a new post-capitalist society. It found itself in such a position, in part at least, because of the extreme timidity of the weak Russian bourgeoisie, which, while relatively against Tsarist absolutism, was absolutely more fearful of the proletariat's capacity to unleash mass struggles from below.

To delve deeper into Trotsky and Gerschenkron's understanding of uneven and combined development we turn next to the question of international relations and of labour. And it is here that their perspectives begin to diverge significantly.

International Economic Relations and Late Development

Gerschenkron's framework enabled him to comprehend processes of differentiated late industrialization in European countries. However, while the structure of the international system is implicit in his framework, Rosenberg notes that 'Gerschenkron builds his model around the effects of this structure . . . without fully conceptualizing the structure itself' (2008, 22). A major problem for any Gerschenkronian analysis immediately becomes evident: where do international economic and political relations fit into the theory? For example, Gerschenkron's framework did not include an analysis of the role of empires in the processes of late (or no) development (Chandrasekhar 2005). He did not consider how modern imperialism complicated processes of late development or engage with authors who did (Hilferding, 1981; Lenin 1917). Nor did he consider how early developers' successful industrialization was interlinked with their imperial expansion and 'underdevelopment' of other societies (see Byres 2005; Wolf 1980). Why is this important? Because in Gerschenkron's model the principal barriers to be surmounted for countries attempting catch-up development were the mobilization, transfer and investment of resources, and the solving of myriad collective action problems through radical institutional innovations in order to attain international competitiveness. All this, he assumed, took place under conditions of political sovereignty. What happens, however, when states are unable to make decisions necessary to achieve (or even attempt) such resource allocations? It is not difficult to identify situations where control by an outside power not only denies a 'state' the opportunity to pursue catch-up development, but also generates mechanisms of anti-developmental path-dependence, which, even after political independence, places considerable new

93

barriers in front of any attempts at rational resource allocation (For example, see Kohli 2004, 291–366 on Nigeria). Gerschenkron's almost exclusive focus upon the European experience (bar a few comments here and there) magnifies these weaknesses.

Trotsky did not develop a theory of imperialism like Lenin, and also Bukharin (1973), but he did conceptualize the relationships between states in the global system as organized within an imperialist chain (Ashman 2006, 96). This enabled him to connect, conceptually and empirically, domestic economic development and a country's international relations, recognizing that there was no clear and unproblematic division between internal and external within the global system of his time. For example, while Gerschenkron focused on the domestic institutional innovations that enabled latecomers, including Tsarist (and later Stalinist) Russia, to achieve high rates of industrial growth, Trotsky comprehended these innovations from the perspective of the imperial chain within which Russia played a subordinate role. As Knei-Paz puts it:

> Having no independent economic base . . . the propertied classes had no capital of their own . . . so [they] did the only thing possible: [they] turned to the European bourgeoisie. Thus began the era of the direct intervention of European business interests in the internal economy of Russia. (Knei-Paz 1978, 71–2)

Catch-up industrialization generated significant results by the turn of the century. For example, Russia produced 10 million poods of pig iron (1 pood = 16.3 kilograms) in 1767, 19 million in 1866, 98 million in 1896 and 180 million in 1904 (Knei-Paz 1978, 74) and industry doubled in size between 1905 and 1917 (Murphy 2005,11).

Trotsky recognized the external influence in Russia's internal development, but connected it, following Lenin and Hilferding, to the stage of capitalist development in Europe: 'The new Russia acquired its absolutely specific character because it received its capitalist baptism in the latter half of the nineteenth century from European capital which by then had reached its most concentrated and abstract form, that of finance capital' (cited in Ticktin 2006, 37). As the Russian state financed much of its investment by raising money on the international bond market, this strategy further tied it to external political, economic and military imperatives. For example, when in 1887 Bismarck prohibited the sale of Russian bonds on the German money market, they were bought enthusiastically by French financial interests, leading to closer economic and politico-military relations between the two countries, in turn contributing to the Franco-Russian alliance of 1894 (Von Laue 1969, 25–6), which endured until 1917 and partly precipitated the outbreak of the Great War.

Trotsky's comprehension of the imperialist chain, comprising more and less dominant powers, enabled him to identify how the structure of the chain would have a differential impact on how its units interacted with each other, through economic and military competition. When in 1914 Russia entered the First World War under pressure from its more economically developed Western allies, the industrialization effort of the previous three decades gave the Tsar's government confidence that the country could wage war on an equal footing with her more advanced neighbours. A more geo-politically and socio-economically realistic picture was painted by Trotsky:

> India participated in the war both essentially and formally as a colony of England. The participation of China, though in a formal sense 'voluntary', was in reality the interference of a slave in the fight of his masters. The participation of Russia falls somewhere halfway between the participation of France and that of China. (Trotsky 1997, 38)

Russia paid the price of its failure to catch up with the great powers and its intimate involvement with their geo-political manoeuvres. During the first ten months of the war around 300,000 of Russia's men a month were killed, maimed or captured (Pares 1941, 88–9, cited in Haynes 1997). And these losses and the actions of the Russian state to maintain itself in the war raised domestic social tensions. Murphy (2005, 11) notes how Russia constituted an intensely unstable social formation based upon the concentration of very militant workers in huge enterprises, a lack of political reforms and intense state persecution. These factors, underpinned by the country's rapid integration into the world system, combined with disastrous military adventuring to tip Russia from a state of intense domestic and international contradictions into one of disintegration and revolution.

International Capitalism and Barriers to Industrialization

Gerschenkron was certainly interested in factors that prevented late industrialization, even though he did not attempt to theorize them. He discussed Bulgaria's and Italy's failed industrialization and referred to the former's 'missed opportunity' (Gerschenkron 1962, 362) and the latter's 'ill advised economic policies which persisted in favouring less promising branches of industrial endeavour'. He also noted how the 'intensification of labour conflicts' exercised a dampening effect upon

Italy's growth (Gerschenkron 1962, 363). He proposed that a partial explanation of Denmark's non-industrialization in the nineteenth century was its proximity to England's vast urban industrial market, which presumably he understood to exert international pressures pushing countries such as Denmark to specialize in export agriculture (Gerschenkron 1962, 16).

Here Gerschenkron comes closest to positing the disadvantages of backwardness: the 'accumulation of 'advantages of backwardness' can, at least at times, be paralleled by an accumulation of disadvantages of backwardness' (Gerschenkron 1962, 363–4). This recognition perhaps represents what might be termed a Gerschenkronian counter-tendency. While he did not pursue this further, two of his contemporaries, Kaldor and Myrdal, did, and in potentially complementary ways. Kaldor's (1972) understanding of increasing returns and learning by doing (building on Verdoorn's earlier work [1980]) led him, like Myrdal, to a concept of cumulative causation – where improvements (usually in industry) lead to further improvements in industry and more broadly in economy and society. This observation constitutes a pillar of a Gerschenkronian catch-up strategy. However, the obverse is also, obviously, a possibility – that economic sectors and entire economies that fail to generate increasing returns fall further behind.

Kaldor's technologically focused analysis of cumulative causation was preceded, and framed in a wider, socio-political context, by Myrdal (1956) who showed how economic sectors in poor regions of the world economy were likely to suffer from lower rates of technological change and productivity growth than those in richer regions. These tendencies might be counter-balanced by radical state action, but if such action did not take place or failed in its objectives, Myrdal suggested that these regions would experience a sequence of worsening conditions of (a) low incomes leading to (b) limited consumer markets leading to (c) fewer incentives or resources for capitalists to invest in new products and technologies, in turn further depressing employment generation, leading to (d) a relatively small tax base and (e) hence fewer possibilities of state action to kick-start industrialization, generating a downward spiral of poverty. Berger argues that Myrdal's and Kaldor's conception of cumulative causation 'is not a doctrine of hopelessness because vicious circles can be broken' (2008, 358), and it is precisely Gerschenkron's emphasis on institutional innovation that suggests how these circles are broken. But processes of cumulative causation suggest that such institutional innovations become increasingly difficult to achieve under conditions of increasing relative backwardness. These differentiating dynamics – of simultaneous and co-dependent growth and stagnation – are examined in more detail in the following chapter.

These observations add to Trotsky's conception of the capitalist world system.

> By drawing countries economically close to one another and levelling out their stages of development, capitalism operates by . . . anarchistic methods which constantly undermine its own work, set one country against another, one branch of industry against another, developing some parts of the world economy while hampering and throwing back the development of others. (Trotsky, 1957, 19–20)

Complementing Trotsky, Weeks uses the concept of the 'stratification of capitals' to denote a process of uneven capitalist development, whereby 'the process of accumulation has within it the devaluation of existing capitals' (1981, 204–5): capitalism's internal dynamics consist of two counter-tendencies – accumulation and centralization on the one hand, devaluation and marginalization on the other. Or, to put it another way, the strong rise while the weak fall, establishing a stratified chain of capitals. As Weeks elaborates:

> Far from establishing a harmonious equilibrium, capitalist competition disrupts, eliminates the weak, challenges the strong, to force upon industry a new standard of efficiency and cost. The movement of capital to equalize profits across industries is the process of generating uneven development: equilibrium in exchange (a single price in the market) hides the generation of uneven development in production. (Weeks 1997, 105)

While competition acts as a leveller, via establishing a single price in the market, it also punishes those capitals that cannot realize their profits through sale at that single price. Technical efficiency in production equates to superior competitiveness in exchange (the market) (Ashman 2006, 2009). However, simultaneous accumulation and devaluation does not imply a state of constant change. Just as countries and firms may benefit from the advantages or disadvantages of backwardness, so too can they benefit from first-mover advantage. Leadership in hard and soft technologies (machineries and management systems) make firms more competitive than their rivals, enables them to capture super-profits and yields to them greater funds from which to re-invest and potentially extend their technological lead (see next chapter). This leads to further differentiation between capitals, and ultimately the states within which those capitals operate. Smith argues that '[t]he drive to appropriate surplus profits through technological innovation . . . tends to systematically reproduce and exacerbate tremendous economic disparities in the world market over time' (2004, 233). In his regression analysis (of 22 countries which were rich in 1870) and survey of processes of global convergence and divergence De Long concludes thus: 'The forces making for 'convergence' . . . appear little stronger than the forces making for 'divergence' . . . the absence of convergence among nations relatively rich in 1870 forces us to take seriously arguments . . . that the relative income gap between rich and poor may tend to widen' (1988, 1148).

How then do weaker firms and countries begin competing in such ruthless conditions? This is where Gerschenkron's emphasis on institutional innovations constitutes such an important contribution to development economics. And the work of numerous authors on East Asian industrialization is instructive here (see chapter 2). Rigorous agrarian reforms to capture economic surpluses to part-finance industrialization, tariffs to protect young industries, a bank-based state-directed financial system to channel funds into chosen economic sectors, establishment of new firms through direct state investments, state subsidies for industry based on performance requirements, disciplining and training of new labour forces, the provision through state-funded agencies of research and development – all these strategies fall within Gerschenkron's approach to late industrialization. However, none of these processes can be comprehended fully without acknowledging the role of labour repression in late development.

Labour in Late Development

We discussed above Gerschenkron's analysis of the predicaments facing latecomers and their need for innovative institutional arrangements to facilitate rapid industrialization. However, Gerschenkron also identified the importance of 'the labour question'. In doing so he broke away from a techno-economic analysis and fleetingly engaged with the issue that was Trotsky's central focus. For Gerschenkron, at least in his discussion of labour, catch-up development is necessarily bound up with large-scale transformative sociological processes. Industrialization is not simply a technological issue but requires the re-ordering of society. He emphasizes the immense difficulties of establishing a skilled, disciplined and reliable labour force that 'has cut the umbilical cord connecting it with the land and has become suitable for utilization in factories' (1962, 9).

This understanding is perfectly compatible with and gains value when used in conjunction with Trotsky's concept of uneven and combined development. Moreover, Trotsky's and Gerschenkron's approach to labour within the context of late capitalist development provides a potential bridge to a political economy of develop-ment associated with writers such as Brenner (1977), Byres (1991), Kay (2002), and Moore (1967), which in turn feeds back into Gerschenkron's concern with institutional innovations. These writers, discussing processes as wide-ranging as the transition to capitalism (Brenner and Byres), political forms of modern societies (Moore) and differentiated capitalist development in the twentieth century (Kay), have convincingly identified how class struggles and their outcomes become institutionalized, thus constituting one of the core variables determining a country's developmental trajectory.

For Gerschenkron, institutional innovations are not simply of the techno-industrial form (for example, the provision and channelling of industrial finance), but are also deeply sociological. He notes how a necessary corollary of the aforementioned institutional innovations is the ability of states and firms to establish a well-educated, hard-working and, above all, disciplined labour force. He compares the earlier successes of English industrialists in achieving these objectives to their later, German competitors:

> Many a German industrial labourer of the nineteenth century had been raised in the strict discipline of a Junker estate which presumably made him more amenable to accept the rigours of factory rules. And yet the difficulties were great, and one may recall the admiring and envious glances which, towards the very end of the century, German writers . . . kept casting across the channel at the English industrial worker, 'the man of the future . . . born and educated for the machine . . . [who] does not find his equal in the past'. In our time, reports from industries in India repeat in a still more exaggerated form the past predicaments of European industrialization in the field of labour supply. (Gerschenkron 1962, 9)

While Gerschenkron did not detail the mechanisms of achieving such sociological upheavals and securing a pliant and capable source of labour, he was familiar with Marx's *Capital* which detailed processes of state-sponsored primitive accumulation (the removal of the direct producers from the land), the establishment of a pool of surplus population (the reserve army of labour available for employment at low wages by capital) and the mechanisms by which early industrial-ists sought to maximize surplus value extraction via, for example, observation, piece-rate systems and industrial discipline. This also suggests that, as a partial qualification of Lewis's (1954) assumption that plentiful supplies of labour in economically backward countries would contribute to late industrialization, for Gerschenkron such possibilities depended upon states to generate, discipline and deploy new industrial working classes. In short, the 'labour question' was not a technical but a highly political issue.

Trotsky viewed the labour question from a diametrically opposed position. He understood as clearly as Gerschenkron the requirements of Russian state and capital for a disciplined workforce in the country's attempts to catch up with the West, but he also understood that to achieve such objectives, the Russian state would have to use significant force and that consequently the potential for resistance and revolution was heightened.

As contemporary observers of Tsarist industrialization were aware, Russian industrialization gave rise to a small, concentrated and relatively homogeneous and politically powerful working class. In the early twentieth century over 40 per cent of industrial workers were employed in only 453 enterprises of 1000 workers or more compared, for example, to the much more economically advanced Germany of 1895 where only 296 enterprises employed more than 1000 workers (Knei-Paz 1978, 74). And the formation of the Russian working class had been particularly disturbing. Workers were 'thrown into the factory cauldron snatched directly from the plough' (Trotsky 1997, 476).

Working conditions were harsh. Twelve-hour days were the norm with discipline meted out by factory managers and repression by the police of any political opposition. While Russia experienced fast economic progress this was not matched by political progress. For example, between 1906 and 1908, during the years of Tsarist reaction following the military loss to Japan and the 1905 revolution, over 60,000 political detainees, most of whom were industrial workers, were 'exiled, sentenced to penal servitude, or executed without trial' (Murphy 2005, 17–18). Parallels can be drawn between these descriptions and both recent and present examples of labour repression in East Asia, where independent trade unions were and still are something of a rarity, and where violence against striking or protesting workers would shock Western observers accustomed to the relatively peaceful coexistence of labour and capital in the advanced capitalist countries.

Trotsky's analysis of the living and working conditions and strategic importance of the emerging working class in Russia gave him the intellectual confidence to overthrow established stage-ist thinking, predominant within most Marxist circles, that argued that Russia was destined to follow behind the more advanced capitalist countries of Western Europe, and that the most the working class could aspire to (according to the Bolsheviks prior to Lenin's 1917 April thesis) was to play the leading role in a bourgeois revolution in Russia. Against these orthodoxies Trotsky argued that the working class in Russia was in a sufficiently strong position to (a) lead and win both the bourgeois stage (abolition of feudalism and establishment of a liberal democracy) and the socialist stage (working-class political and economic power) of a forthcoming revolution, and that (b), due to the integrative effects of global capitalism, this would light the spark of international revolution – in short, his theory of permanent revolution:

> Binding all countries together with its mode of production and its commerce, capitalism has converted the whole world into a single economic and political organism ... This immediately gives the events now unfolding an international character, and opens up a wide horizon. The political emancipation of Russia led by the working class ... will make it the initiator of the liquidation of world capitalism, for which history has created the objective condition. (Trotsky, cited in Lowy 2006, 32)

The 'privilege of backwardness' for Trotsky is simultaneously about states' capacities to pursue catch-up development (which is where Gerschenkron stops) and, within that inevitably tension-generating context, the ability of emerging working classes to exercise their economic and political power in order to reshape society. Hence, when we look at the 'labour question' in Trotsky's and Gerschenkron's considerations of the 'advantages of backwardness' we see diametrically opposed visions of human development.

Conclusion

Trotsky and Gerschenkron undermine unilinear, stagiest, conceptions of development. However, and perhaps ironically given Statist Political Economy's intellectual debts to Gerschenkron, his work, while theoretically advancing SPE, simultaneously undermines its policy relevance. This is because by utilizing an inductive, historical methodology, SPE can identify institutional and state practices that have worked in the past, and can then posit these as necessary strategies and practices for contemporary developing countries. In

101

this way SPE potentially identifies what is necessary for future states' catch-up attempts. But it cannot identify what is sufficient for these states. Its 'policy' advice, therefore, becomes a set of codified, generic suggestions, which constitute only part of the answer to the catch-up development challenge (see for example, Wade 2004, chapter 11, and Chang and Grabel 2004, part 2). There is no guarantee of success for a contemporary state bureaucracy that attempted catch-up development were it to follow SPE's policy.

In making such generic proposals, authors in the SPE tradition run the risk of replicating the fallacy of composition – that what is good for one country is good for all countries – so prevalent within mainstream liberal development discourse. Liberal development policy suffers from such a weakness because of its deductive methodology, where theoretical assumptions apply equally to all units of analysis and cannot readily take into account dynamic transformations over time and space.

With each case of successful late development the international field for economically backward countries is transformed (with the developmental gap increasing further between advanced and backward countries), which then requires institutional innovations and novel state and social practices within poor countries if they are to achieve catch-up development. Strategies and practices from past cases are only part of the puzzle; the other part depends to a large degree on the social (class) structures prevailing in any given society on the eve of their catch-up attempt, and how they influence processes of institutional formation and innovation. Necessary policies for late development, induced from the past, are not, therefore, sufficient for the present. And what are sufficient are the institutional innovations that, by definition, cannot be predicted in advance. Once this dilemma is grasped, SPE's development policy enters a new and much less coherent realm of understanding and action, which explains why contemporary SPE practitioners have not been able to supersede Gerschenkron's key insight and theory.

While Trotsky and Gerschenkron often complement each other, Trotsky's conception of late development is ultimately superior to Gerschenkron's because he recognizes how attempts at achieving late development exist within an analytically prior (although once in motion, mutually interactive) class context. Without class analysis the combined aspect of late, uneven development is lost. And it is this aspect that contributes so fundamentally to the non-linear and unintended nature of late capitalist development. In short, if those influenced by Gerschenkron adopt Trotsky's framework, their understanding of late development is strengthened, but simultaneously their ability confidently to suggest policy for contemporary poor countries is weakened.

Even if the previous points are accepted, there remains a fundamental tension in trying to synthesize Trotsky's and Gerschenkron's thoughts. The former was the theorist and instigator of world revolution and international socialism, the latter the theorist and advocate of late capitalist industrialization. These objectives are incompatible (unless one adopts a stage-ist view of historical development, rejected by both men).

For followers of Gerschenkron the disciplining and repression of labour in late-developing countries in the twentieth century was a necessary (but not sufficient) condition for successful industrialization. The conflicts that were subsequently generated were thus viewed as potentially detracting from the autonomy of states to pursue rational economic policies. Labour repression was thus normatively and prescriptively advocated.

For followers of Trotsky, while labour repression was a predictable ingredient of late industrialization, an understanding derived from their analysis of intra-capitalist competition and the 'whip of external necessity', such repression also generated resistance and provided the opportunity to organize workers and peasants into potentially revolutionary movements that could pursue an alternative form of development.

Gerschenkron's identification of the institutional innovations required to engender successful late development represents a theoretical high-point for SPE. His insight uncovers the indeterminacy of late development, but does not provide the tools for explaining how to successfully achieve such development, because, as he also shows, it would be impossible to do so. While the tradition of SPE has evolved, by illustrating how states have pursued industrialization in countries such as South Korea and Taiwan, it has not been able to approximate the theoretical heights scaled by Gerschenkron. Marxist traditions, following Trotsky's insights, have continued to stress the self-activity of labouring classes in their struggles against oppression and exploitation and for real human development (Cliff 1999). While combining the insights of Trotsky and Gerschenkron provides significant benefits in our investigation and understanding of the complexities of the analysis of late development, the politics of the two men represent opposed visions and strategies for advancing human development.

— 5 —

CREATIVE DESTRUCTION AND GLOBAL INEQUALITY: FROM MARX TO SCHUMPETER, AND BACK

Economic progress in capitalist society means turmoil. (Schumpeter 1987, 32)

[T]he problem that is usually . . . visualized is how capitalism administers existing structures, whereas the relevant problem is how it creates and destroys them. (Schumpeter 1987, 84)

Joseph Schumpeter's concept of creative destruction, captured in this chapter's epigraphs, explains how industrial innovations continually reshape capitalism. It elucidates how capitalist economies undergo internally driven transformations, generating turmoil and, in the process, raising a minority of firms and individuals into positions of economic and political power. It suggests that it is myopic to expect that capitalism can ever be stabilized or regulated so as to remove its 'destructive' elements (such as recessions and unemployment). These are part and parcel of capitalist expansion.

Schumpeter's objectives in formulating the concept of creative destruction was to explain capitalism's malaise (he published *Capitalism, Socialism and Democracy*, where the concept is most fully developed, in 1943). He predicted that processes inherent to the capitalist economy – monopolization, the growing size of firms, and the increasing role of the state in the economy – signalled the demise of capitalism and the rise of a bureaucratic top-down form of socialism. While he was wrong about socialism, he was undoubtedly correct about the internal dynamics of the capitalist system (monopolization of the economy by increasingly large-scale firms).

The concept of creative destruction also represents a significant, although two-sided, intellectual debt by Schumpeter to Marx. On the one hand he praises Marx's brilliance in comprehending capitalism's internally driven transformative drive. On the other hand, however, his conception of capitalism seeks to justify its hierarchical and exploitative structures and processes, the better to undercut Marx's arguments for socialism from below. This intellectual debt merits a close examination of the similarities and differences between the two men's conceptions of capitalism. In this chapter I argue that Schumpeter's attempts to justify the capitalist system mean that, while superior to liberal conceptions of the functioning of the capitalist economy, his concept of creative destruction is ultimately inferior to Marx's understanding of capitalist competition. This is because, in the process of re-formulating the process of creative destruction as a celebration of the capitalist entrepreneur, he strips away two of Marx's core concerns: (a) how capitalism is constituted by exploitative class relations, and (b) how 'national' economies exist in and operate through the capitalist world system. That is, Schumpeter's limited appropriation of Marx led him to present the capitalist economy in relatively a-social and methodological nationalist terms. If, however, we can reformulate the concept of creative destruction to encompass these socio-spatial dynamics – of class and international economic relations – then we are in a position to utilize it to examine the dynamics of capitalist competition on a global scale, and potentially, to comprehend processes of global stratification and inequality – between and within nation states.[1]

This chapter is structured as follows. The remainder of the introduction discusses two comprehensions of the relationship between industrialization and capitalist development as a means of setting up the chapter's core concern – of how industrial innovation generates socio-spatial inequalities. The next section provides a brief background to Schumpeter's intellectual evolution and his conception of the capitalist economy. The third and fourth sections explain Schumpeter's conception of creative destruction but show how, despite its strengths, it is based upon weak conceptual foundations – its blindness to socio-spatial dynamics. The next section shows how once these weaknesses are remedied, through an engagement with Marx, the concept of creative destruction provides us with a conceptual basis for understanding global socio-spatial inequality. The final section applies this framework to the creative destruction dynamics of the contemporary world system.

---

[1] In this endeavour I draw upon the World Systems Theory and the Global Commodity Chains literatures (Wallerstein 1974, Gereffi 1994; Selwyn 2012).

The Lure of Industrialization

For much development thinking, for example in the work of List and Gerschenkron and the schools of thought influenced by them, industrialization is analogous to development. Schumpeter certainly viewed industrial innovations and the more general spread of industry as representing the essence of capitalist development. As we shall see, however, his understanding of technological innovation and diffusion suggested that gains from industrialization would not spread equally. Rather, a small minority of firms would win spectacular profits leaving the majority with quite average, if any, profits. Schumpeter identifies innovations with both capitalist expansion and development, but also with inequality and hierarchy.

The long-held conviction of a positive relationship between industrialization and development was reformulated most eloquently by Nigel Harris (1987) in his analysis of the rise of the 'global manufacturing system'. For Harris, with the emergence of this system the previous international division of labour, of a minority of rich/core industrial economies and a majority of poor/peripheral agricultural economies, no longer existed. Instead, countries of the previous agricultural periphery were experiencing rapid industrialization. Consequently:

> The conception of an interdependent, interacting, global manufacturing system cuts across the old view of a world consisting of nation-states as well as one of groups of countries, more and less developed . . . The process of dispersal of manufacturing capacity brings enormous hope to areas where poverty has hitherto appeared immovable, and makes possible new divisions of labour and specializations which will vastly enhance the capacity of the world to feed everyone. (Harris 1987, 200, 202)

From Harris's perspective globalization of industrial production is a levelling process, which offers hope to previously poor countries and raises the potential for a more equal world system. Industrialization is analogous to development, with the added bonus that globalizing capital is facilitating its rapid spread across the globe.

This chapter argues that equating industrialization with development (or at least the possibilities of meaningful development) rests upon a one-sided understanding of capitalist expansion. It ignores the intrinsic socio-spatial inequalities upon which such expansion is based, and which it reproduces and generates anew. A conception of creative destruction that is sensitive to class and spatial relations, potentially illuminates the double-sided nature of industrialization and capitalist development.

106

Table 5.1 GNP per capita for a Region as a Percentage of the Core's GNP per capita

REGION	1960	1980	1999
Sub-Saharan Africa	5	4	2
Latin America	20	18	12
West Asia and North Africa	9	9	7
South Asia	2	1	2
East Asia (without China and Japan)	6	8	13
China	1	1	3
SOUTH	5	4	5
North America	124	100	101
Western Europe	111	104	98
Southern Europe	52	60	60
Australia and New Zealand	95	75	73
Japan	79	134	145
NORTH (= core)	100	100	100

Source: Arrighi, Silver and Brewer (2003). Figures are rounded.

In their response to Harris's argument, Arrighi, Silver and Brewer (ASB) (2003), who operate within the World Systems perspective (Wallerstein 1974, 1980, 1989), illustrate how, despite decades of developmental effort and industrial transformation, the income and developmental gap between the countries of the global south and global north have been reproduced (table 5.1). On the one hand the global south as a whole has 'converged' and in some cases overtaken the global north in its percentage of GDP in manufacturing as a percentage of the global north's – from 74.6 per cent in 1960 to 118 per cent in 1998, providing the basis for Harris's optimism. On the other hand, as a proportion of national incomes of the global north, national incomes of the global south as a whole have remained more or less stagnant – at about 5 per cent of northern GNP per capita (ASB 2003, 12, 13). ASB note the 'bifurcation' within the global south, both in terms of industrialization and national incomes, with East Asia and in particular China taking a significant share of rises in both. Nevertheless, as a whole the global south has not experienced income convergence with the global north, despite industrial convergence.

ASB draw on Schumpeter's concept of creative destruction to contradict Harris's optimism. They suggest that the global spread of industry is bound up with and generates new hierarchical structures. This chapter builds on and extends ASB's insights by illustrating how these hierarchical structures are purposefully managed by TNCs, and that they rest upon and operate through systems of global class relations. In order to undertake this endeavour, however, it is necessary to delve into Schumpeter's political economy, in particular his relationship to Marx, so that we can generate an alternative, socio-spatially aware conception of creative destruction.

Schumpeter's Social Economics

This section discusses Schumpeter's intellectual formation and interactions with the main currents of thought that predominated during his early years. It focuses on his engagements with the increasingly dominant neoclassical (marginalist) school of economics, and with Marxism.

Joseph Alois Schumpeter (1883–1950) was born in Moravia, part of the Austro-Hungarian Empire. In 1901 he began his study of law and economics in Vienna under one of the chief theorists of the 'Austrian School' Eugen Böhm-Bawerk. At this time the long-emerging but increasingly dominant school of economics was the neoclassical variant, formulated above all by William Jevons, Léon Walras and Carl Menger during the late nineteenth century (of which the Austrian school was a branch) (see Blaug 1973). The transformation of classical political economy into the much narrower field of economics by the neoclassical practitioners was stimulated by two events in particular. First, the publication of Marx's *Capital* Vol. 1 in 1867, and second, the Paris Commune of 1871 (Perelman 2011). These events signalled the dangers faced in bourgeois civilization by emerging labouring classes and their potential to draw on Marx's political economy to explain their experiences of exploitation under a 'free' market system.

While certainly not homogenous, this troika of thinkers and their emerging framework rested upon four principles, that, combined, represented a concerted attack upon core elements of the previously dominant tradition of classical political economy of the late eighteenth and early nineteenth centuries, as practised by Smith and Ricardo (and of course the critical political economy of Marx). Together, their new approach constituted what would become known as the 'marginalist revolution'. Its four pillars were:

(a) the rejection of the labour theory of value (which had been adhered to in one way or another by Smith, Ricardo and Marx); and as its alternative;

(b) an embrace of ulilitarianism (subjective preference theory based on supply and demand) to explain prices;

(c) an abstract and deductive (non-historical) method

(d) a form of 'methodological individualism' as opposed to collectivist or organicist conceptions of society (Milonakis and Fine 2009).

As Milonakis and Fine (2009, 97) put it, with the marginalist revolution 'the subject matter of economic science shifted from the investigation of the causes of wealth and its distribution, to the interrogation of the economic behaviour of individuals, especially in the form of the principle of (utility) maximization.'

Many of these features are present in Schumpeter's political economy in one way or another – most notably his rejection of Marx's labour theory of value and his embrace of the individual entrepreneur as the driver of economic development. Schumpeter thought of Walras, a key figure in the marginalist revolution and the founder of general equilibrium theory, as the greatest economist of his generation (Bottomore 1992).

However, while Schumpeter admired the achievements of marginalism, and began his intellectual career working within its framework, he was also knowledgeable about Marxism. This was in part because of the presence of strong Marxist-inspired political movements across Europe. As importantly, however, his economics teacher Böhm-Bawerk led seminars where rival schools – representing Marxism (including Rudolf Hilferding and Otto Bauer) and proponents of marginal utility theory (including Ludwig von Mises and Böhm-Bawerk himself) would debate their respective positions (Bottomore 1992).

At first blush Schumpeter's engagement with both marginalism and Marxism might appear to be eclectic if not downright contradictory. Hence, while Robert Heilbroner (1968) considers Schumpeter to be a 'worldly philosopher', he also highlights the contradictions of the man and his work. However, Milonakis and Fine (2009) argue that along with Max Weber (who also embraced many core tenets of neoclassical theory), Schumpeter can be considered one of the founders of economic sociology or social economics (*Sozialökonomik*). Social economics rejected sole reliance on the abstract and deductive methodology propounded by marginalism and instead held that economics

109

needed to include historical and social considerations. Schumpeter described *Sozialökonomik* as 'the description and interpretation of economically relevant institutions, including habits and all forms of behaviour in general, such as government, property, private enterprise, customary or 'rational' behaviour' (Schumpeter 1949a, 293, cited in Milonakis and Fine 2009, 196). *Sozialökonomik* was thus a world removed from the emerging neo-classical orthodoxy.

Schumpeter's Critique of Neoclassical Economics

So, despite his admiration for marginalism, Schumpeter understood its limitations. For example, in his *Theory of Economic Development* (1961 [1934]) he starts by describing a central pillar of marginalist thinking, the 'circular flow of economic life'. This represented a static model, as proposed by Walras, which 'does not change 'of itself'', and which 'describes economic life from the standpoint of the economic system's tendency towards an equilibrium position' (1961, 9, 62–5 in Milonakis and Fine 2009, 210, 211). As Bellamy Foster (1984, 15) puts it '[t]he stream of economic activity is viewed as flowing incessantly through the same channels . . . all economic action in the circular flow is repetitive and based on prior experience. As in all theories of stationary equilibrium . . . the aggregate quantities of supply and demand, expenditures and receipts, tend towards equality.' Swedberg notes how Schumpeter's intention was to use the circular flow model in order to illustrate its intrinsic limitations, enabling him, in turn, to create a dynamic model of the economy, and thus account for economic change. However, while his dynamic theory may have originally been intended to complement Walras's static conception of the circular flow, 'as the analysis progresses . . . it increasingly came to replace it'.

The intellectual and political conservatism of neoclassical economics' static conception of the economy is apparent in a number of ways. Schumpeter recounts how, in a conversation with Léon Walras, the most eloquent advocate of general equilibrium theory, the latter told him:

> Of course life is essentially passive and merely adapts itself to the natural and social influences which may be acting on it, so that *the theory of a stationary process constitutes really the whole of theoretical economics* and that as economic theorists we cannot say much about the factors that account for historical change, but we must simply register them. (cited in Rosenberg 1996, 49, emphasis added)

As noted in chapter 1, Albert Hirschman (1981) labels the neo-classical approach as representing 'monoeconomics' because, theoretically, it allows only one mode of economic governance. This one-size-fits-all approach was encapsulated by a leader of the Austrian school, Carl Menger:

> [If] economic humans under given conditions want to assure the satisfaction of their needs as completely as possible, *only one road* prescribed exactly by the economic situation leads from the strictly determined starting point to the just as strictly determined goal of economy. (cited in Meek 1972, 509, emphasis added)

The socially regressive nature of the neoclassical approach is high-lighted by Pareto's 'law of optimality' – which posits that redistributive acts are acceptable only where they make one or more persons better off, without making anyone else worse off. Such situations are rare, thus redistribution as a socio-economic policy is strictly limited. Instead, neoclassical approaches hold that maximizing the efficiency of resource allocation benefits all economic actors through increasing general output (which in turn cheapens goods and enables an increase in general consumption).

Neoclassical economics is a system of thought predicated upon a simplified conception of, and complete ideological commitment to, endless economic growth (Panayotakis 2011, and see chapter 1). It does not allow for alternative ways of thinking about resource generation and allocation, let alone alternative forms of ownership and control in the economy.

His realization of the above-mentioned limitations led Schumpeter to radically different theoretical and political conclusions about economic development under capitalism:

> Our position may be characterized by three corresponding pairs of opposites. First, by the opposition of two real processes: the circular flow or the tendency towards equilibrium ... [against] a change in the channels of economic routine or a spontaneous change in the economic data arising from within the system ... Secondly, by the opposition of two theoretical apparatuses: statics and dynamics. Thirdly, by the opposition of two types of conduct, which, following reality, we can picture as two types of individuals: mere managers and entrepreneurs. (1961, 82–3)

In distinguishing himself from neoclassical economics, Schumpeter drew on Marx.[2]

Schumpeter's Intellectual Relationship to Marx: Debts and Divergences

Schumpeter's intellectual debt to Marx is revealed by a passage from the Communist Manifesto:

> The bourgeoisie cannot exist without constantly revolutionizing the instruments of production, and with them the whole relations of society ... Constant revolutionizing of production, uninterrupted disturbance of all social conditions, everlasting uncertainty and agitation distinguish the bourgeois epoch from all earlier ones. (Marx and Engels 1967 [1848], 83)

Schumpeter wrote of the opening pages of the Manifesto as 'a panegyric [tribute] upon bourgeois achievement that has no equal in economic literature' (1949a, 209). He praised Marx's economic interpretation of history as 'one of the greatest intellectual achievements of sociology to this day' (cited in Milonakis and Fine 2009, 197). Yet his interpretation of Marx was devoid of the latter's careful attention to the conflictual social (class) relations, that characterize capitalism. Rather, the above quote from the Communist Manifesto provides Schumpeter with a basis for placing the bourgeois entrepreneur at the heart of his system while sidelining any serious consideration of capital–labour relations. For Schumpeter, the entrepreneur is responsible for industrial innovations, which propel forward the capitalist system. He identified four to five forms of entrepreneur-driven innovations entailing introductions of (a) new methods of production and/or new forms of industrial organization, (b) new commodities, (c) new sources of supply, and (d) new trade routes and markets (Schumpeter 1954, and see below).

Schumpeter's interpretation of Marx leads Catephores (1994) to characterize him as a 'bourgeois Marxist' not only because of (a) his intellectual debt to Marx, but also (b) because of his opposition to the latter's foundational critique of and opposition to capitalism. For Schumpeter, Marx:

---

[2] While Paul Samuelson denies this debt, most commentators recognize it (Bottomore 1992; Elliot 1980; Rahim 2009), so much so that authors such as Nathan Rosenberg and William Lazonik (both 2011) argue that he should be considered a quasi-Marxist (but see Galambos 2011 for a response).

[h]ad gone too far. Led astray by youthful romanticism, he had taken sides with the poor, the underprivileged, the weak who deserved to be downtrodden [sic], all those unable to stand up for themselves . . . [Marx] had abused his genius by putting it to the service of the crowd . . . This potent weapon had to be wrested from the hands of the masses, it had to be restored to its rightful owners; the few who by sheer force of personality shaped the destinies of mankind. The imperious Austrian [Schumpeter] . . . made it his task to co-opt Marx's ideas to the service of the masters. (Catephores 1994, 8)

At the core of Schumpeter's attempts to re-politicize Marx was his rejection of the latter's labour theory of value (which identified the mechanisms of exploitation of labour by capital), which he described as 'dead and burried' (cited in Milonakis and Fine 2009, 210). Delinking Marx's conception of capitalism from the labour theory of value enabled him to employ concepts utilized by Marx, but in ways designed to ideologically celebrate the entrepreneur's activities as the lifeblood of capitalist development.

For example, and of central importance to this chapter, his concepts of entrepreneurial profits and rents (Schumpeter 1987 [1943],) have many similarities to Marx's conception of surplus or super profits, which derive, in part, from capitalists' abilities to raise the rate of relative surplus value extraction (explained below). In *Capital* Marx demonstrated how firms derive super or surplus profits from (a) being technologically more advanced than other firms, enabling them to operate at above the average rate of productivity and profitability, and/or (b) enjoying monopolies in technologies and resources. Both aspects are compatible with Schumpeter's conception of entrepreneurial innovations and rents. However, while Schumpeter insists that profits were either 'wages to management' or rewards to entrepreneurs derived from innovation, for Marx by contrast, both average profits (of non-innovating firms) and super profits were rooted in the exploitation of labour by capital. This is the central divergence between the two political economists.

While Marx analysed technological and managerial innovations in detail (for example, Marx 1990, chapter 15), his political economy is distinguished by its focus on strategies pursued by capitalists to increase the rate of exploitation of labour. And unlike Schumpeter, he demonstrated how these strategies are intrinsically interlinked with entrepreneurial innovations. Capitalists pursue objectives of increasing labour's exploitation through combinations of raising the rate of *absolute surplus value* (through lengthening and intensifying the working day) and the rate of *relative surplus value* (through technological innovations). Importantly, increasing relative surplus value extraction makes labour more productive and reduces the socially necessary labour time (or average unit labour costs) to produce the same good as previously.[3] Marx also identified a third strategy for increasing the rate of labour exploitation, *immiseration*, achieved through pushing down wages. Capitalists often attempt to pursue all three strategies simultaneously, but the extent that they are able to achieve one or the other depends, in part at least, on their level of technological innovation (which is itself dependent on their position in the innovation cycle, see figures 5.1 and 5.2), and the balance of class power between capital and labour.

In addition to technological innovation (making labour more productive), increasing the rate of relative surplus value extraction could also be achieved through reducing labour costs by getting access to cheaper inputs, enabling capitalist to (a) cut the costs of wage goods (such as basic foodstuffs) and of (b) capital goods (such as machinery), through the innovations identified by Schumpeter. Cutting wage and capital goods costs contributes to reducing average unit labour costs. Getting access to these cheaper inputs depends, significantly, on geo-politics and the position of firms within the world market.

For example, In *Capital* Vol. 1, Marx (1990) documents how relative surplus value extraction predominated in northern England's Cotton mills, the epicentre of the first industrial revolution, while strategies and process of absolute surplus value extraction predominated in the slave economies of the Americas, which did not experience the full extent of the industrial revolution's technological dynamism. That managers of slave plantations could increase the rate of exploitation of slaves through absolute surplus value extraction, thus making cotton cheaper, in turn complemented the competitive strategies of managers of industrial cotton mills in England. The interlinking of these relations were actively promoted by the English state as it sought to maintain its control over the world trading system (culminating in the so-called Pax Britannica from 1815 onwards), so as to intensify the global competitiveness of its industries and achieve and maintain its position as the 'workshop of the world'.

Farshad Araghi (2003, 49) notes that the variety of strategies available to capitalists for raising the rate of exploitation are sometimes conceptualized by Marxists (for example those operating with

---

[3] The concepts of socially necessary labour time and average unit labour costs describes a situation where a worker produces a good based on average skill and energy, working with machinery of average productivity.

'stage-ist' conceptions of historical development, as described in chapter 3), as occurring within workplaces or 'national economies'. Such a conception reflects, like Schumpeter, a methodological nationalism, rather than Marx's global conception of capitalism. Araghi argues, instead, that the above-mentioned strategies, and we may add, processes of entrepreneurial innovation, need to be viewed as 'global value relations'. That is, entrepreneurial innovations and strategies for raising the rate of labour exploitation exist, are facilitated and are managed by powerful firms and states across and through the capitalist world system. This observation corresponds with chapter 3's discussion of the global determinants of capitalism's emergence and expansion.

Capitalism, Creative Destruction and Social Classes

In *Capitalism, Socialism and Democracy* Schumpeter wrote how:

> Capitalism . . . is by nature a form or method of economic change and not only never is but never can be stationary. . . . The fundamental impulse that sets and keeps the capitalist engine in motion comes from the new consumers' goods, the new methods of production or transportation, the new markets, the new forms of industrial organization that capitalist enterprise creates. (Schumpeter 1987, 82–3)

In terms diametrically opposed to neoclassical conceptions of static economies, Schumpeter argued that 'Creative destruction is the essential fact about capitalism. It is what capitalism consists in and what every capitalist concern has got to live in' (1987, 83). Creative destruction emanates from industrial innovations, introduced by entrepreneurs. The process of technological innovation and diffusion occurs in two 'acts'.

The first act is the introduction to the market of an innovation. Schumpeter distinguishes between innovating entrepreneurs and non-innovating, normal businessmen. He describes how '[t]he new products and new methods compete with the old products and old methods not on equal terms but at a decisive advantage that may mean *death to the latter*' (Schumpeter 1987, 32, emphasis added).

Innovators win entrepreneurial profits – the 'difference between receipts and outlays' – when the outlays are momentarily 'smaller per unit of product than for other businesses' (Schumpeter 1961, 128, 129, 131) (figure 5.1). Such profits rest, in part at least, upon raising the rate of relative surplus value extraction, through the reduction of

115

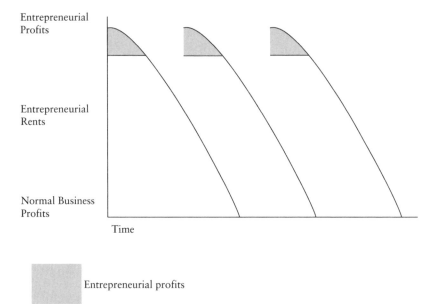

Figure 5.1   Schumpeter's Entrepreneurial Profits, Rents and Normal
Business Profits

what Marx termed socially necessary labour time, or in mainstream economics, average unit labour costs (figure 5.2). Such reductions are achieved through combinations of new technologies and higher labour productivity compared to market-following firms, which potentially enables innovating firms to preside over labour systems characterized by both rising profits and wages (although the rise of the latter usually lags behind the former).

Non-innovators, i.e. 'normal businessmen', risk expulsion from the market due to innovators' greater competitiveness, unless they can compensate for their cost-disadvantages. They can do so by raising the rate of absolute surplus value extraction, through cutting labour costs by lengthening the working day or increasing its intensity, and/ or through immiseration (forcing down wages).

Following the introduction of the innovation a 'second act' occurs in the competitive drama. Industry is completely re-organized and the 'final result must be a new equilibrium position, in which . . . the law of cost again rules' and 'the surplus of the entrepreneur in question and his immediate followers disappears' (Schumpeter 1961, 131–2). Between the introduction of the innovation and its diffusion a time

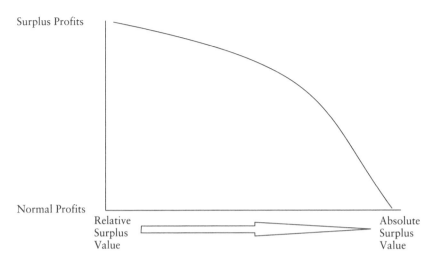

Figure 5.2 Surplus and Normal Profits – Relative and Absolute Surplus Value

lag exists during which innovators and early adaptors of the innovation win 'rents' based on their greater competitiveness compared to firms that have not yet introduced the new way of doing things (figure 5.1)

When innovations cluster together they generate leading sectors which 'create new products with high demand, made with newer, cheaper forms of energy and distributed via newer, cheaper modes of transportation' (Schwartz 2010, 69). Entrepreneurial profits and rents confer cumulative advantages upon market-leading firms, leading to the monopolization of the economy.[4] Schumpeter was scathing about proponents of anti-monopoly policy, who derived their arguments from neoclassical precepts, accusing them of misunderstanding the real dynamics of capitalist competition and yearning for a mythical past of perfect competition:

> Theirs is the ideology of a capitalist economy that would fill its social functions admirably by virtue of the magic wand of pure competition, were it not for the monster of monopoly or oligopoly that casts a shadow on an otherwise bright scene. No argument avails about the performance of largest-scale business, about the inevitability of

---

[4] Schumpeter mistakenly identified these as processes of 'socialization', leading to bureaucratic socialism (see Schumpeter 1987).

its emergence, about the social costs involved in destroying existing structures, about the futility of the hallowed ideal of pure competition. (Schumpeter 1949b, cited in Mason 1951, 142)

According to Schumpeter, creative destruction operates temporally (over short, medium and long cycles or waves) generating economic booms and slumps:

> While these things [innovations] are being initiated we have brisk expenditure and predominating 'prosperity' . . . and while [they] are being completed and their results pour forth we have the elimination of antiquated elements of the industrial structure and predominating 'depression'. (Schumpeter 1954, 68)

Class Relations and Capitalist Innovation

Schumpeter's recognition of the dynamics of capitalist competition and their monopolizing tendencies were not, however, complemented by a similarly dynamic view of class relations. His understanding of class under capitalism was diametrically, and purposefully, opposed to Marx's. This is a central divergence between the two, and represents a weakness in Schumpeter's understanding of capitalist expansion. He argued that:

> Every class . . . has a definite function . . . [T]he position of each class in the total national structure, depends . . . on the *significance that is attributed to that function*, and . . . on the degree to which the class *successfully performs the function*. Changes in relative class position are always explained by changes along these two lines. (Schumpeter 1951a and b, emphasis added)

Schumpeter has two interlinked objectives here. The first is to rebut Marx's exploitation-based understanding of class, which he does through rejecting Marx's labour theory of value and embracing neoclassical economics' subjective preference theory of value. The second objective is to account for class differences/hierarchies and mobility between them. He attempted this by employing a functionalist explanation of class – where different social classes perform distinct roles in a society's division of labour, contributing to societal reproduction, and are rewarded by society according to the value of their contribution. This, following Pareto, is an elite theory of class which justifies the rewards accrued by the capitalist entrepreneur and identifies his actions with capitalist dynamism (see Robinson 1996, 13–72).

118

While Schumpeter's conception of creative destruction illuminates how gains from innovation are distributed unevenly between firms, his elite theory of class excludes considerations of how class relations co-determine processes of technological innovation and diffusion. His attempts to habilitate the capitalist entrepreneur as the dynamic force of capitalist innovation while discounting Marx's class analysis have obvious political objectives. However, they also weaken his understanding of capitalist development. As Angus Maddison argues, 'the main weakness in [his] long-wave theory . . . [is that] he does not provide a persuasive explanation why innovation (and entrepreneurial drive) should come in regular waves rather than in a continuous but irregular stream . . .' (Maddison 1991, 103).

Schumpeter emphasized how entrepreneurs' search for profits and continuous intra-capitalist competition constitutes a key determinant of innovation, of booms and slumps, and of the monopolization of the economy. But Marx identifies a second source of innovation, which was purposefully concealed by Schumpeter: conflicts between capital and labour – where the former struggles for greater profits and the latter for higher wages and better working conditions. It is this second source that helps answer the question posed by Maddison above. Mandel (1980) argues that as workers' struggles intensify, preventing increasing rates of exploitation and challenging the ruling ideologies of the time, capitalists begin seeking out new means of re-asserting their control over labour in order to raise again the rate of exploitation. They do this through industrial innovation – entailing new technologies and new labour processes and labour regimes. Herman Schwartz (2010) draws out a number of synergies between Schumpeter's analysis of leading sectors and Mandel's understanding of their basis in new labour processes, and how they cluster in time, as represented in table 5.2.

Schwartz argues that the overlap between Schumpeter's leading sector and Mandel's labour process is not coincidental:

The sheer scale of investment needed to utilize new technologies usually mandates both new organizational forms and new work practices. Neither innovation can stand alone: new work practices and management systems make little sense unless changes in machinery and power systems accompany them; new machinery cannot be used to its full potential without changes in work practices and the management of production. (Schwartz 2010, 72)

Leading-sector innovations are generated by the capital–labour dialectic as much as through continual competition between firms. And

119

Table 5.2 Industrial Innovations and Class Relations

Time Period		Leading Sector (Schumpeter)	Labour Process (Mandel)	Form of Workers Organization (Mandel)
Schumpeter	Mandel			
1780s–1820s	1789–1848	Cotton, textiles, iron and water power – canals and mills	Craft workers operating water- and steam-powered machinery in small factories	Owenite unionism and Chartism
1840s–1870s	1848–1890s	Steel, steam engines and railways	Industrial production of machines by specialized firms + emergence of specialist machine operators	Skill-based unions
1890s–1920s	1890s–1930s	Industrial chemicals, electricity and intra-urban trams	Taylorist methods of production	Mass unionism
1940s–1970s	1930s–1960s	Internal combustion engine, petroleum and motor vehicles	Assembly lines	Great strike wave of '1968' and beyond
◊1980s–Present	◊1980s–Present	Digitalization, microelectronics and 'information'	Continuous-flow, just-in-time production	In formation . . . (see last section of this chapter)

Derived from Schwartz (2010, 69–72), Mandel (1980) and Schumpeter (1934, 1987).
◊ Schwartz's extrapolation.

120

their emergence and spread is based upon, and works through global relations.

Spatial Dynamics of Creative Destruction

In his schema of creative destruction Schumpeter understands market-leading activities (innovations) and market-following activities (diffusion of innovations) as occurring temporally, generating booms and slumps, within discreet national economies. However, to quote Angus Maddison again, he 'makes no distinction between the lead country and the others, but argues as if they were all operating on a par as far as productivity level and technological opportunity is concerned. Thus his waves of innovation are expected to affect all countries simultaneously' (Maddison 1991, 104–5). This is in contrast to Marx, who 'considered the world market to be the real framework of economic fluctuations' (Mandel 1980, 8) and who raised the problematic of how an international division of labour impacts upon the innovation and developmental trajectories of different national economies. For example:

> If we now conceive this feverish agitation as it operates in the market of the *whole world*, we shall be in a position to comprehend how the growth, accumulation, and concentration of capital bring in their train an *ever more detailed subdivision of labour*, an ever greater improvement of old machines, and a constant application of new machines – a process which goes on uninterruptedly, with feverish haste, and upon an *ever more gigantic scale*. (Marx 1847a, emphasis added)

What are the implications for global inequality of this ever more detailed subdivision of labour? In his study of the Irish and English cotton industries in the late eighteenth and nineteenth centuries, Denis O'Hearn (1994) argues that conceptions of capitalist innovation need to be comprehended globally and geo-politically:

> There is no such thing as a *national* system of innovation because clustered innovations require global strategies to secure raw materials, capture markets for the export of core products, and stifle competition from within and outside the core. (O'Hearn 1994, 595, original emphasis)

O'Hearn's argument is further strengthened by Marx's analysis of the English cotton industry, and his specific focus on what Araghi terms their global value relations:

121

Direct slavery is just as much the pivot of bourgeois industry as machinery, credit, etc. Without slavery you have no cotton; without cotton you have no industry. It is slavery that has given the colonies their value; it is the colonies that have created world trade, and it is world trade that is the pre-condition of large-scale industry. (Marx 1846)

In a similar vein to O'Hearn, Volker Bornschier (1992, 4) refers to a 'world market for protection,' illustrating the role of states as facilitators and/or protectors of innovation. The developmental consequences of such facilitation and protection are significant for different countries and their social classes. Hegemonic powers' abilities to restrict the diffusion of leading-edge technologies can 'consign peripheral firms to use out-moded technologies or previous innovations' (O'Hearn 1994, 594). While such technological diffusion may enable peripheral firms to maintain a presence in industrial sectors, they do so based on 'lower profit rates and lower wage rates' (ibid.) (fig. 5.3). Differential technological generation and diffusion impacts directly on workers' wages and conditions:

Those that do something new make a creative response – they utilize new technologies or forms of organization in ways that allow them to outcompete others. Those that respond by extending their existing practices make an adaptive response, which enables them to compete with innovations for a time by intensifying workers' efforts, reducing wages, and accepting lower rates of profit. (O'Hearn 1994, 593)

O'Hearn observes, in ways that complement Araghi's conception of global value relations and Schwartz's observations about the capital–labour dialectics of innovation, how technological innovations and responses are based upon and reinforce the forms of exploitation that prevail across different countries and the relations between these countries. Firms that generate technological innovations tend to raise their profit rates through relative surplus value extraction (through increasing the efficiency of the production process, and reducing socially necessary labour time or average unit labour costs), while firms that adopt these innovations as technologies diffuse through the system tend to increase their profit rates through absolute surplus value extraction (lengthening the working day) and/or immiseration (pushing down wages).

Complementing O'Hearn's analysis, Arrighi and Drangel (1986) and ASB (2003) show how unequal international economic relations are reproduced through the world market. They highlight three elements of this process. First, costly industrial innovations are more likely to occur in wealthy countries because their *higher incomes* mean

122

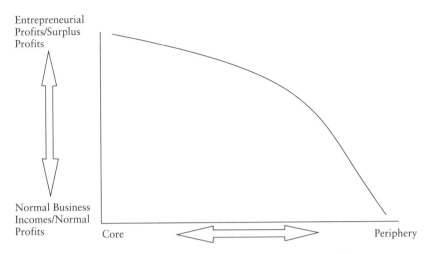

Figure 5.3   Marx and Schumpeter on Core and Periphery

higher aggregate demand and larger actual and potential markets. Higher production costs generate greater pressures for technical innovations (to reduce costs). Cheap and plentiful credit facilitates the financing of innovations (ASB 2003, 18). Market-leading firms that benefit from entrepreneurial profits and rents possess larger sums of re-investible capital than market-following firms, enabling them to re-invest and seek further innovations compared to follower firms. It also enables them to manage the interactions of other firms within their commodity chains to more effectively monopolize entrepreneurial profits and rents (see below).

A second tendency, almost a mirror-image of the first, is generated among follower countries and firms (assuming that they do not benefit from compensating institutional support, discussed by List and Gerschenkron in chapters 2 and 4). ASB (2003, 18) note how the poor countries in which the majority of market-following firms operate 'resemble Schumpeter's "large majority of businessmen," ... who end up with 'very modest compensation or nothing or less than nothing''' (citing Schumpeter 1987, 73–4). Poor countries have industrialized by introducing widely available (codified) industrial technologies which (a) often structurally preclude them from innovating and thus winning entrepreneurial profits and rents, and (b) are subject to quick devaluation, caused by innovations containing much more costly, complicated and hard-to-replicate tacit knowledge in the core of the world system.[5] Poor-country firms compete in world markets, to a significantly greater extent than rich-country firms, based on their ability to raise the rate of absolute surplus extraction, and through immiseration of their workers (see below).

This two-sided dynamic generates yet a third tendency which concerns the destructive sociological aspects of innovation, referred to by Schumpeter as 'the elimination of antiquated elements of the industrial structure' (1954, 68). Such elimination impacts unequally upon wealthy and poor countries, where the former are more easily able to adjust both economically and socially (through welfare policies, for example) than the latter, in part as a consequence of the greater volume of distributed wealth derived from prior entrepreneurial profits and rents, and higher incomes (ASB 2003, 18). Robert Wade (2005a) summarizes the above situation as one where poor and rich states 'are embedded in the same "system," and systemic effects help to explain the divergent outcomes'.

Commodity Chains and Global Stratification

The above conception of global creative destruction, as a dual set of asymmetrical relations – between more and less powerful units of capital, and between capital and labour – represents a useful lens through which to comprehend patterns of global stratification. This section focuses on contemporary TNC strategies of competitive accumulation, and how they pursue these on a global scale within and through the manipulation of these asymmetric relations. These firms' objectives are 'the maintenance or establishment of their position as one of the top two or three companies in the global marketplace' (Nolan 2003, 301, and see table 5.3).

TNCs have pursued their objectives of global leadership since the 1980s, and the rise of the global manufacturing system, through a three-pronged strategy of (a) employing their institutional power to generate a 'world market for protection' through lobbying international institutions and national governments (such as the WTO and the US and EU states) (Gallagher 2005), (b) selling off their non-core businesses and developing their core competencies to attempt to monopolize entrepreneurial profits and rents within the value chain (and in the process extending further the global sub-division of

---

[5] The classic discussion of tacit and codified knowledge is by Michael Polanyi (1966).

124

Table 5.3   Industrial Consolidation within Global Value Chains, 2006–8

	Number of firms	Global market share
Large commercial aircraft		
Engines	3*	100
Braking systems	2	75
Tyres	3	100
Automobiles		
Auto glass	3	75
Constant velocity joints	3	75
Tyres	3	55
Information Technology		
Micro-processors for PCs	2	100
PC operating systems	1	90
Glass for LCD screens	2	78

Source: Nolan and Zhang (2010) *Including GE's joint venture with Snecma

labour, as indicated by Marx above), and (c) cutting wage and input costs, and intensifying the exploitation of labour across the whole chain.

The IPE of Entrepreneurial Profit Monopolization and Inter Capitalist Relations

As argued above, entrepreneurial innovations rarely occur within a pristine national economic sphere. Rather, they exist within a hegemonically organized world system. For example, Sell (2002) and Wade (2005b) have documented how TNCs in the entertainment, pharmaceutical and software industries have promoted both the discourse and the WTO-backed legislation protecting intellectual property rights. The World Bank (2002a) estimates that with a full application of the WTO's Agreement on Trade Related Aspects of Intellectual Property Right (TRIPS), across the globe, US companies would gain an additional US$19 billion a year in royalties, with much of these flows originating in, and constituting a financial drain from, countries of the global south. In a similar vein, as noted in Chapter 2, Linda Weiss (2005) characterizes the WTO as an 'upgrading club' for advanced capitalist countries – where the organization attempts to deny developing countries the 'right' to utilize infant industry protection strategies associated with successful late development, while facilitating developed country governments' support for their own fledgling industries.

And Henderson et al. (2002, 450) note how international financial institutions are part of the struggle for 'value enhancement and capture', where the 'capacity to exercise power to influence the investment and other decisions of lead companies and other firms integrated into [global commodity chains] is inevitably asymmetric'.

TNCs' focus upon developing their core competencies and regulating tightly their supply chains has been pursued through a huge increase in spending on R&D (for example, from around US$160–170 billion by the world's top 300 firms in the early 1990s to US$240 billion in 1998); through increased spending on branding; through 'a massive increase in expenditure by the world's leading firms on IT hardware, software and services', and a 'merger frenzy' where, for example, spending on transnational mergers and acquisitions increased from US$156 billion to US$1,100 billion between 1992 and 1997 (Nolan 2003, 302, 303). A consequence of lead firms' concentration on core competencies is that a 'cascade effect' is operating across industrial sectors, generating intense pressure upon first- and then second-tier suppliers to merge, acquire and themselves follow TNC strategies. Nolan concludes that:

> Large capitalist firms now stand at the centre of a vast network of outsourced businesses which are highly dependent on the core systems integrators for their survival. The systems integrators possess the technology and/or brand name which indirectly provides sales to the supplier firms. They are therefore able to ensure that [they] obtain the lion's share of the profits from the transactions between the two sets of firms. (Nolan 2003, 317–18).

For example, Dedrick, Kraemer and Linden (2008, 20) illustrate how US computer giant Apple 'maintains control over its supply chain by controlling essential elements such as core software, a propriety standard and valuable brand image'. Consequently, 'Apple captures 53 per cent of the measured value from US sales and 47 per cent from sales outside the US.' In these ways TNCs attempt to manage the innovation process to better capture the entrepreneurial profits and rents associated with it. Already in the 1960s Baran and Sweezy (1966), following (and quoting) Schumpeter's arguments about tendencies towards monopolization in the capitalist economy, observed that '[o]nce the 'largest-scale unit of control' has taken over, 'the new commodity, the new technology, the new source of supply, the new organization' all tend to be monopolized by a handful of giant corporations . . .' Consequently, rather than TNCs competing against each other on price, they engaged in non-price competition in order to achieve the 'permanence of monopoly profits and their steady increase over time' (Baran and Sweezy 1966, 73–4). While Baran and Sweezy overstated the monopoly form that capitalism took in the post-war period (see Harman 1984b, 148–54) they did identify strategies that TNCs *sought to engage in,* and which constitute a driving force of the contemporary global business revolution. In centralizing their economic power, Strange and Newton (2006, 184) suggest that monopsonistic buyers are able to 'push down the prices of supplies to marginal cost and thus extract the full profits from the sales of the final goods from a smaller capital stake'. Milberg calls this the 'mark-up effect . . . [through] which the lead firm in the global value chain is able to raise the mark-up over costs, not in the traditional oligopoly fashion of raising product prices, but through the control of input costs' (Milberg 2008, 429).

These strategies are observable across different economic sectors. In the global food industry, for example, retailers impose a range of standards and conditions upon suppliers, generating continuous cost-down pressures. In the United States, between 1986 and 2006, the average annual percentage change in import prices for beverages, fruit, vegetables and nuts, meats and fish fell by 0.41 per cent, 0.58 per cent, 0.62 per cent and 0.91 per cent respectively (Milberg 2008, 432). As Milberg sums up, in the United States, significant import price declines (of over 40 per cent between 1986 and 2006) have benefited US firms engaged in computers, electrical and telecommunications products, clothing, footwear, textiles, furniture, chemicals and miscellaneous manufactures (including toys) (Milberg 2008, 433). Operating under fierce cost-down pressures, TNCs' suppliers experience low profit volumes and limited opportunities for innovations that can generate lucrative entrepreneurial profits and rents (Kaplinsky 2005). These 'mark-up effects' are dialectically related to TNCs' attempts to organize and manage globally diverse labour systems.

Capital–Labour Dimensions of the Global Business Revolution

This chapter has argued, first, that creative destruction needs to be conceptualized as a global process, uniting firms within TNC-governed global commodity chains (GCCs), in asymmetric relations across the world. The second element of this argument is that global creative destruction and stratification must also be understood as an inherently conflictual social process, based upon the exploitation of labour by capital. Class relations cannot be understood only as

127

existing within nation states (or national firms), but must be conceived of as global social relations. That is, just as the most powerful
units of capital (TNCs), with assistance from hegemonic states and
international institutions, seek to organize their relations with subordinate units of capital, so too do they seek, through the governance
of their GCCs, to organize global capital–labour relations. This is
not to argue that TNCs (mostly located in core economies) directly
manage the labour regimes of their supplier firms (mostly located in
peripheral and semi-peripheral economies). Rather, their governance
of global commodity chains enables TNCs to effectively sub-contract
the management of labour to their suppliers. In this way 'local labour
control regimes' exist as sub-regulatory systems within the global
labour regime (Jonas 1996).

The proliferation of GCCs has occurred in tandem with, and based
upon, the expansion of the world's labouring class, which, as noted
in chapter 1, more than tripled in size between the 1980s and the mid
2000s. This expansion was stimulated by waves of depeasantization
across the global south (Araghi 2000). The expansion of the global
labouring class has been managed closely by international financial
institutions in an attempt to facilitate local and global capital accumulation through heightened labour exploitation (Rainnie et al.
2010). For example, Brady and Martin (2007) report how workers
in countries that implemented IMF agreements were 60 per cent less
likely to be in a trade union after the programme, making them easier
to exploit. In a similar vein Paul Cammack argues that the World
Bank's objectives, as formulated in its annual World Development
Reports, are 'to deliver an exploitable global proletariat into the
hands of capital . . . to deny the poor any alternative, and to create
a reserve army of labour that will enforce the disciplines of capitalist
labour-markets across the greater part of humanity' (2002, 125).

While the IFIs have attempted to manage labour relations through
influencing state policies, TNCs have played a complementary role,
through the global restructuring and governance of their supply
chains. They have done this, particularly, through the spatialization
of production, in ways that Schumpeter described as the reorganiza-
tion of industry. Buckley and Ghauri have emphasized how:

> The managers of [Transnational Corporations] are increasingly able to
> segment their activities and to seek the optimal location for increasingly
> specialized slivers of activity. . . . The more precise use of location and
> ownership strategies . . . is the very essence of increasing globalization.
> (2004, 83)

At the heart of this strategy lies the so-called Babbage principle.[6] Charles Babbage (1835) argued that the division of labour could both lead to general productivity increases (as Adam Smith had argued) but also that it could be used to cut wage costs. He observed that skilled workers often undertook unskilled tasks, and argued that it would be possible to allocate skilled tasks only to skilled and higher-paid workers and other tasks to less skilled and lower-paid workers, thus establishing a hierarchy of wages and reducing wage costs.[7] Under contemporary globalization his principle has been pursued with a vengeance by TNCs, and has evolved into what could be termed 'hyper-babbagization', where the spatial disaggregation of production constitutes a strategy by capital to increase labour exploitation on a global scale. Jonas (1996, 326), following Burawoy (1985) notes how 'labour's collective vulnerability to the national and international mobility of capital is the source of capital's power to extract concessions and assert its hegemony in the workplace.'

Hyper-babbagization strategies operate in at least six ways. First, they reflect TNCs ability to benefit from and purposefully structure a system of global labour arbitrage – where they are economically rewarded through their use and manipulation of the international wage hierarchy.[8] Bernard and Ravenhill illustrate the strategic value of this principle to TNCs in 1990s East Asia. A Japanese calculator producer/exporter (Jinbao) sought to benefit from the Babbage principle by creating a hierarchical production network across East Asia that would reduce production costs and boost profitability:

> The innovation behind the product, the brand name, and the marketing are Japanese. All key components for the calculators, such as liquid crystal displays and production equipment in the Thai factory such as insertion equipment, are imported from Japan. All procurement and administration are controlled from Taipei, and the management of the plan is Taiwanese. The labour is Thai. (Bernard and Ravenhill 1995, 186)

---

6 Charles Babbage was a nineteenth-century English mathematician and utilitarian philosopher associated with Bentham, and was concerned with the scientific organization of industrial society (Schaffer 1994). In this way he was a predecessor of Frederick Winslow Taylor's 'scientific management' (see Braverman 1998).

7 Marx viewed Babbage and Bentham, as organic intellectuals for the industrial capitalist class, and their interest in technology as reflecting class interests. He wrote how 'It would be possible . . . to write a whole history of the inventions made since 1830 for the sole purpose of providing capital with weapons against working class revolt' (Marx 1990, 563).

8 See, for example, a discussion in *The Economist* ('Moving back to America': 2011).

By locating production in peripheral regions with supportive states, firms can benefit from low-cost and potentially highly malleable labour, and can combine low wages, long hours and productivity drives, raising rates of absolute surplus value extraction. For example, CAFOD (2004, 30–4) reported how in China electronics workers need to work 15–16 hours per day under very poor conditions in order to earn the minimum wage, while in Thailand sub-contracted workers earn a 'minimum wage' that does not even cover their food and household expenses.

Secondly, TNCs' attempts to increase the rate of labour exploitation are based upon real and imaginary gender divisions of labour. In their classic and still relevant study of export manufacturing factories in the global south Diane Elson and Ruth Pearson (1981) highlighted how women's work is often characterized by employers: 'Women are considered not only to have naturally nimble fingers, but also to be naturally more docile and willing to accept tough work discipline, and naturally more suited to tedious, repetitive, monotonous work' (Elson and Pearson 1981, 93). These ascriptions served a higher and specific purpose for factory managers: 'Female labour must either be cheaper to employ than comparable male labour, or have higher productivity, or some combination of both; the net result being that unit costs of production are lower with female labour' (Elson and Pearson 1981, 92). Elson and Pearson cited evidence that in these factories women received wages between 20 per cent and 50 per cent lower than their male counterparts for comparable tasks (Elson and Pearson 1981, 92).

Sklair (1993) further deconstructs the ideology of 'nimble fingers' as follows:

> The image of the 'ideal' woman worker ... for TNC employment around the world is the image that the transnational capitalist class is gradually developing of the 'ideal' worker, per se. ... Docile, undemanding, nimble-fingered, non-union, and unmilitant workers will be offered the jobs on the global assembly lines, while aggressive, demanding, clumsy, union, and militant workers will not. (Sklair 1993, 172)

He notes how this ideology is not immutable and how it is directed at the global working class as a whole:

> Once the image of the 'ideal' ... worker is institutionalized and accepted by the working class ... the need to employ women in preference to men diminishes, and job opportunities for docile, undemanding, nimble-fingered, non-union and unmilitant men open up. (Sklair 1993, 173)[9]

---

[9] For a complementary account of female (and male) workers in contemporary North East Brazilian export agriculture see Selwyn (2012).

Thirdly, hyper-babbagization draws on much older divide-and-rule strategies of capital to ethnicize and racialize the word's working class. As Wallerstein (1991, 87–9) points out, racism 'provides the only acceptable legitimation of the reality of large-scale collective inequalities within the ideological constraints of the capitalist world economy', and, 'the ethnicization of the work force adds a degree of flexibility to the capitalist system'. He concludes that '[r]acism and underdevelopment . . . are . . . constitutive of the capitalist world-economy as a historical system. They are . . . essential manifestations of the unequal distribution of surplus value' (Wallerstein 1991, 92).

Fourthly, hyper-babbagization facilitates an increase in the rate of relative surplus value extraction of core economy labour. This is achieved by the effective subsidy to core economy capital through reducing the costs of wage and capital goods imported from peripheral and semi-peripheral countries, and thus the costs of labour power, as reflected in Milberg's observations above. In these ways core economy labour can be remunerated at falling pay rates relative to the productivity gains of capital, while maintaining consumption levels necessary to sustain its generational reproduction and the ideological glue that encourages it to identify with core capital. Hence, very low cost production of wage goods in Asia has facilitated simultaneous wage reduction with increased consumption in the advanced countries (Harvey 2005). In the United States, for example, between 1973 and 1988 median wages fell by about 8 per cent (Collins, Hartman and Sklar 1999, 10) and continue to fall into the twenty-first century.

Fifth, hyper-babbagization enables TNCs to attack workers' wages in core economies, as the latter often accept wage cuts through fear of losing their jobs off-shore (Dunn 2009). In her study of eighteen industrialized countries between 1985 and 2000, Guscina (2006) found that the combination of trade openness, FDI and imports from developing countries all contributed to the falling percentage of labour's share in national income.

Finally, Stephen Hymer (1972a, 104) observed a sixth component of TNC's hyper-babbagization strategy in the early 1970s: 'The power at the bottom [among workers] is . . . weakened by the spatial division of labour. Each national or regional labour force performs a specialized function which is only meaningful to the integrated whole [the TNC managers] yet it has no understanding of this whole' (Hymer 1972a). Through spatialization labour 'remains an isolated group whose connections to other groups are matters foreign and external to it'. The potential/danger of labour-unity across the chain is minimized through the spatial disaggregation of production. Hyper-babbagization thus cuts production costs, provides cheaper wage and capital goods the better to further reduce average unit labour costs, divides the workforce along numerous lines and enables an intensification of exploitation of labour across the whole commodity chain.

TNC strategies of profit-maximization are not free from contradiction however. Following our discussion of the synergies between Schumpeter and Mandel's analyses of leading sectors and dominant labour processes (see table 5.2 above) we would be justified to expect that industrial innovations generate responses from labour through new forms of class mobilization and struggle. It is not that surprising, therefore, to note that various authors (Herod 2001; Dunn 2005; Feeley 2008; Selwyn 2007, 2008) illustrate how, while just-in-time systems of production and delivery are designed by firms to enhance their profitability (through flexible sourcing and hyper-babbagization) they simultaneously give workers the ability to disrupt the functioning of commodity chains through short bursts of strike action at strategic 'choke points' of the chain. This is particularly evident in contemporary China, where Applebaum (2008) shows how the emergence of huge factories has *encouraged* labour militancy because workers can understand disruptive effects of their collective action on the global supply chains. These strikes have turned China into the centre of 'world labour unrest' (Silver and Zhang 2009). Barboza (2010) argues that 'soaring labour costs in China could change the cost structure of global supply chains.' These observations suggest that despite TNCs' best efforts to divide, discipline and exploit labour, responses from organized labour will force capital to seek further and continual innovative solutions to its perennial problem of spiralling costs and falling profits.

Conclusions

Schumpeter's concept of creative destruction highlights the internally driven and inherently disruptive nature of capitalism. While much development thinking hails technological innovation and industrialization as processes that contribute to the welfare of poor-country populations, Schumpeter's concept potentially highlights that this is not the case. His explication of the generation of entrepreneurial profits and rents suggests how initial innovations produce longer-term cumulative processes, whereby market-leading firms are able to maintain and extend their dominant position in relation to other firms. However, Schumpeter's concept is founded upon a methodological nationalist conception of the economy, which is understood to operate as a discreet national entity, and so he was unable to draw out the global implications of creative destruction. His formulation also obscures rather than illuminates the social relations upon, and through which, innovations and firm profits are generated.

A Marxist conception of creative destruction is founded upon different precepts. First, that national economies exist within a context of a world system and their economic dynamics cannot be understood in abstraction from that system. Secondly, that capitalist competition in general and technological innovations in particular are generated through a dual relationship – between firms in their never-ending battle of competitive accumulation, and between capital and labour, where the former attempts to raise the rate of exploitation and the latter tries to resist its increase. Class relations are themselves constituted at the global level. From this perspective then, capitalist competition and entrepreneurial innovations cannot be understood as occurring within discreet national economies, but must be comprehended as existing within and through a world system stratified by different-sized units of capital and by exploitative class relations.

The consequences of adopting this revised conception of creative destruction to comprehending the production and reproduction of global inequality are that: (a) technological innovations tend to cluster in richer zones of the world system, conferring repeated entrepreneurial rents to these regions' firms, which in turn generates cumulative processes of innovation and rent appropriation; (b) technological diffusion to parts of the globe in which market-following firms are located enables the latter to participate in the global manufacturing system, but with little opportunity of entrepreneurial innovation and rent appropriation; (c) nation states in which innovations occur and those which depend on technological diffusion tend to be characterized by different labour systems – the former relying more on relative surplus value extraction, the latter on absolute relative surplus value extraction. These dynamics reproduce the tendencies towards innovation on the one hand, and dependence on diffusion on the other hand, as labouring classes in states where the former processes occur tend to have higher incomes and generate higher economy-wide aggregate demand than those in the latter; (d) under contemporary globalization, dynamics (a)–(c) are managed and reproduced through both IFIs' organization of international economic relations and TNCs' attempts to manage their global commodity chains. The global consequences of these dynamics and hierarchical market structures were described by Stephen Hymer as a situation where 'income, status and consumption patterns . . . radiate out from [the major] centres along a declining curve' (Hymer 1972b, 38). These dynamics explain the 'paradox' of the global south's industrial convergence with the global north, but its continual income divergence.

The final section of this chapter introduced the concept of hyper-babbagization to highlight ways in which TNCs use and reproduce spatial difference to preside over a functionally integrated and geo-graphically fragmented global labour force, the better to raise the rate of exploitation across their commodity chains. Geographical frag-mentation breaks potential solidarity between labouring classes and generates and reproduces a hierarchy of wage differentials. Functional integration of product and labour markets through global commodity chains intensifies the competition between labouring classes located within separate nation states. However, TNCs' powers to manage their global commodity chains and the global labour systems upon which they are based are vulnerable to new forms of industrial action by labouring classes, in particular as globally spanning commodity chains generate opportunities for 'bullwhip effects' to reverberate across national boundaries and throughout the chains. These indus-trial actions, if they continue and escalate may contribute to new entrepreneurial innovations that seek to avoid such damaging actions to capital, and may contribute to the generation of a new leading sector, based on new technologies and new sets of capital–labour relations. They may also become more militant and begin to challenge capitalist social relations themselves.

— 6 —

CLASS STRUGGLE OR EMBEDDED MARKETS? MARX, POLANYI AND THE MEANINGS AND POSSIBILITIES OF SOCIALISM

Man's economy is, as a rule, submerged in his social relations. The change from this to a society which was . . . submerged in the economic system was an entirely novel development. (Polanyi 1947, 113)

To allow the market mechanism to be sole director of the fate of human beings and their natural environment . . . would result in the demolition of society . . . (Polanyi 2001 [1944], 76).

To what extent can markets work for society and contribute to human development? Karl Polanyi's ideas, in particular his concept of the embedded market, have influenced social science and social democratic politics since their formulation in the mid-twentieth century. For example, John Ruggie (1982) has argued influentially that the post-war settlement (c. 1945–1970s) represented a case of 'embedded liberalism', a period which Eric Hobsbawm (1994) refers to as the 'golden age' of capitalism. A recent collection (Khan and Christiansen 2011), aptly sub-titled *Market as Means Rather Than Master*, aims to orient development studies' theory and practice towards the instituting of market relations in order to achieve favourable human development.

Polanyi's arguments for subordinating markets to society also have a more popular and political appeal. Joseph Stiglitz (2001), for example, argues that Polanyi's ideas are directly relevant to those concerned with global injustices and reckless financial institutions. And, in the context of continued economic crisis in the UK, leading labour politician John Cruddas has recently argued, in Polanyian language, that '[a]n economic system of shared responsibility will help to re-embed capitalism in society and reassert the practices of democracy and reciprocity' (Cruddas 2012). These positions reflect

135

a deeper resurgence in interest in Polanyi's ideas and their potential relevance for the twenty-first century (Bienefeld 1991; Lacher
1999, 2007; Stiglitz 2001; Sandbrook 2011; Holmes 2012; Silver
and Arrighi 2003; Silver 2003; Munck 2006, 2010; Hann and Hart
2009).

Unlike List, Gerschenkron and Schumpeter, Polanyi did not regard
economic growth as an indicator of social development. As the above
epigraphs make clear, he abhorred the idea that the 'free' market represented a sphere within which such development could occur. Like
Marx, Trotsky and Amartya Sen, he placed a premium upon human
freedom, which he thought was undermined by market economy
and society. Human freedoms could only be realized and protected
if society was able to subordinate the market to its democratically
formed objectives. The principles of a Polanyian political economy
are articulated by Richard Sandbrook, who argues that developing
countries

> [W]ould need to be immersed in such norms and institutions as soli-
> darity, democratic control and . . . ecological protection and shared
> prosperity. Solidarity norms (mutuality, cooperation, trust) appear most
> central. (Sandbrook 2011, 423)

Polanyi's *The Great Transformation (TGT)*, first published in 1944,
remains one of the great critiques of liberal economics. In many ways
it complements Marx's general critique of, and arguments for, transcending capitalism. While *TGT* discusses at length the emergence of
the English industrial revolution, it does so in order to explain the
collapse of nineteenth-century civilization, in particular the end of
the self-regulating market, and the consequent 'institutional transformation' (Polanyi 2001, 30) that Polanyi interpreted as sweeping the
world in the 1930s – socialism in Russia, fascism in Germany and
the New Deal in the United States. As he put it '[i]n order to comprehend German fascism, we must revert to Ricardian England' (Polanyi
2001, 32).

Polanyi's Background and Influences

Marx and Polanyi's lives had much in common. Both were born into
Jewish families, lived in exile and wrote journalistically and more
profoundly about, and attempted to intervene in, contemporary
political debates and events. There were also significant differences
however. In particular, while Marx was establishing what was to
become a new way of understanding and acting upon the world

(historical materialism), Polanyi spent much of his life responding and reacting to Marx's own work and latter-day Marxism, and in doing so constructing an institutional political economy that drew on many sources.

While Polanyi drew on Marx, he was also influenced by the German Historical School (in particular Ferdinand Tönnies) and Max Weber, and owed a significant political debt to Robert Owen. Owen was a landowner and capitalist, but also a major contributor to the early nineteenth-century English labour movement, through his philanthropy, novel industrial relations practices (providing education to workers) and crucially, through advocacy and support for regulation of capital in favour of labour. As will become apparent, Owen's importance for Polanyi was that he represented, through ownership and advocacy, three of the major social classes of nineteenth-century English capitalism – capital, landed property and labour. Most significantly, he advocated socialism for society as a whole and not at the expense of one or other social class, and explicitly rejected 'class hate' (cited in Draper 1966). Importantly, however, Marx described Owen as a 'utopian socialist' because of his inability to conceptualize how workers would achieve their own emancipation from the chains of capital.

While having a Jewish background, Polanyi was also very much influenced by, and participated in, English Christian socialism. One of his objectives was, in the early 1930s at least, to combine Communism and Christianity, arguing that socialist movements required a spiritual/ moral basis. For example, he wrote that ' . . . I have got a long way towards a synthesis of C. and C., both on the philosophical side and . . . on the practical side' (Polanyi, cited in Dale 2010, 41).

As we shall discuss in greater detail below, Polanyi was also influenced by Max Weber's methodology of ideal-type construction. The ideal type represented a 'one-sided accentuation of one or more points of view' and a 'synthesis of a great many diffuse, discrete . . . concrete-individual phenomena, which are arranged according to those one-sidedly emphasized viewpoints into a unified analytical construct' (Weber 1949, 90). The ideal-type methodology was particularly useful in highlighting similarities and differences between societies across space and time, and Polanyi put it to excellent use in comparing and contrasting capitalist England to non-capitalist and non-Western societies.

These influences distinguished Polanyi from Marx in a number of important ways with significant political implications. Nevertheless, both men were advocates of socialism of one sort or another. For example, a few days before his death in 1964 Polanyi stated how '[t]he heart of the feudal nation was privilege; the heart of the bour-geois nation was property; the heart of the socialist nation is the people, where collective existence is the enjoyment of a community culture. I myself have never lived in such a society' (cited in Polanyi-Levitt 2006, 168). His daughter Kari Polanyi-Levitt summarizes how Polanyi's life's work reflected a dedication to 'a civilizational transformation in accord with the fundamental need of people to be sustained by social relations of mutual respect' (Polanyi-Levitt 2006, 179).

In order to compare and contrast their views of socialism, this chapter discusses the differences between Marx's historical material-ism and Polanyi's institutionalism. Its core argument is that the two men differ in their conception of the way capitalism disrupts society – Marx through his theory of class divisions *within society* and, Polanyi's repeated emphasis of how disembedded markets disrupt *society as an organic whole*. This divergence in the two men's thought highlights other differences, outlined in table 6.1.

In stark terms, we can compare and contrast Marx's historical materialism, conception of modes of production, theory of class-based exploitation and how socialism potentially emerges from workers' resistance to, and attempts to overcome exploitation, with Polanyi's institutionalism, ideal-type conception of different economic systems, emphasis on society as an organic whole, the dis-embedding of the economy under capitalism, and the possibilities of 're-embedding' the market through the actions of a societal counter-movement (table 6.1).

Table 6.1 Marx and Polanyi: Key Ideas Concerning Capitalism

	Marx	Polanyi
Mode of analysis	Historical materialism	Institutional political economy
Principle by which societies are articulated	Modes of production	Ideal-type analysis of different economic systems
Unit of analysis	Class	Society as an organic whole
Core problematic in the analysis of capitalism	Exploitation	The disembedding of the economy by the institutions of the self-regulating market
Solutions	Socialism	Re-embedding the market
Mechanism driving social change	Class struggle	Societal 'counter-movement' leading to the re-embedding of economies

These differences have significant implications for understanding the prevalence of poverty under capitalism, struggles against capitalist commodification, and the possibilities of achieving a society where 'collective existence is the enjoyment of a community culture'. This chapter argues that, while Polanyi's institutionalist analysis and sharp critique of liberal economics potentially contributes to the endeavour of creating such a society, it is most effective when completed by Marx's more fundamental critique of capitalism and vision of socialism.

The remainder of this chapter is structured as follows. The second section outlines the differences between Marx's historical materialism and Polanyi's institutionalism, a discussion that runs through the rest of the chapter. Section three highlights Polanyi's critique of the liberal 'economic fallacy', followed by his disussion of his conception of the market. The next section uses Marx to critique Polanyi, in particular his rejection of Marx's argument that capitalism is a fundamentally exploitative system. It discusses how one of Polanyi's central concerns, the prevalence of poverty under capitalism, can better be comprehended by conceptualizing commodification and exploitation as two interrelated, rather than mutually exclusive, processes and relations. Finally, the previous arguments are drawn together and the ambiguities of Polanyi's conception of social(ist) transformation are highlighted.

Historical Materialism and Institutionalism

An important ontological difference between Marx and Polanyi was that while the former established historical materialism, the latter was broadly associated with the tradition of institutionalism. Polanyi employed institutionalism as a methodological contrast to the liberal classical and neoclassical economists of his time and their conception of the market economy as a competitive and self-regulating system which emerged as a result of spontaneous and natural evolution of trade and exchange:

> We must rid ourselves of the ingrained notion that the economy is a field of experience of which human beings have necessarily always been conscious. To employ a metaphor, the facts of the economy were originally embedded in situations that were not in themselves of an economic nature, neither the ends nor the means being primarily material. The crystallization of the concept of economy was a matter of time and history. But neither time nor history have provided us with

139

those conceptual tools required to penetrate the maze of social relationships in which the economy was embedded. This is the task of what we will here call institutional analysis. (Polanyi et al. 1957, 242)

Polanyi's institutional approach is based on the 'substantive' view of the economy, which focuses on 'an instituted process of interaction between man and his environment, which results in a continuous supply of want satisfying material means' (Polanyi 1957, 248). In particular, he focused on 'locational movement' (his term for production and transportation of goods and services) and 'appropriative movement' (referring to distribution and ownership) as ways to illuminate 'the transcending importance of the institutional aspect of the economy'.

The objective of this method was to show that not all forms of society in human history can be reduced to market relations and 'the logic of rational action' (Polanyi 1957, 234). At the same time, because of his commitment to an institutional analysis, and arguably as a consequence of his use of Weber's ideal-type methodology, Polanyi's approach to understanding the economy is overwhelmingly focused on describing and cataloguing the appearances of how goods and services are exchanged or distributed in a given society, *rather than providing a systematic account of social change*. This often led, however, to a somewhat formal and superficial characterizations of economic and social organizations: formal because surface-level differences are equated, and superficial because underlying mechanisms of how wealth is produced and is transformed into a form fit for distribution are not analysed. For example:

> What occurs on the process level between man and soil in hoeing a plot or what on the conveyor belt in the constructing of an automobile is, *prima facie* a mere jig-sawing of human and nonhuman movements. From the institutional point of view it is a mere referent of terms like labour and capital, craft and union, slacking and speeding, the spreading of risks and the other semantic units of the social context. The choice between capitalism and socialism, for instance, refers to two different ways of instituting modern technology in the process of production. (Polanyi 1957, 249)

Following the German Historical School, and in particular Max Weber, Polanyi's institutionalism employs ideal types, which he calls 'forms of integration'. Subsequent sections discuss how Polanyi's conception of the economy is detached from questions of property and power relations. This is in contrast to Marx's historical materialism, which locates the dynamics of social reproduction and change in the way human collectivities simultaneously interact with each other, and with nature:

> The specific economic form, in which unpaid surplus-labour is pumped out of direct producers, determines the relationship of rulers and ruled, as it grows directly out of production itself and, in turn, reacts upon it as a determining element. Upon this, however, is founded the entire formation of the economic community which grows up out of the production relations themselves, thereby simultaneously its specific political form. (Marx 1981, 927)

Polanyi and Marx share much in terms of their analytical focus. For example, both focus on the relations between humans and nature, and the necessity of production and distribution in order to survive in the given ecological condition. Also, they both stress the importance of social relations in understanding different societies, although as discussed below, they had different views on the nature and driving forces of social relations, and consequently, social change.

Marx analysed society from the perspective of class relations, intent upon illustrating the way exploitation has been organized throughout the history of class society, with the goal of illuminating how exploited could ultimately overthrow exploiters. Polanyi's concern was to show how 'economic' activity took various forms and was instituted in different ways across human history, how this undermined liberal economics' conception of *homo economicus* (human beings portrayed as rational, self-seeking actors), and how, consequently, future forms of society could exist and flourish without being subordinated to profit-orientated market systems.

Such differences have significant intellectual and political implications. Sandra Halperin (2004) argues that while Polanyi had a 'top-down' understanding of how societies changed, Marx approached the question of social transformation from the 'bottom-up'. Hence, 'Polanyi begins his analysis [in *TGT*] . . . with the nature of the over-arching international system and then shows how that system shaped the emergence and development of local social institutions' (Halperin 2004).

This 'top-down' approach, Halperin argues, weakens Polanyi's understanding of the post-Second World War transformation towards what he portrayed in *TGT* as a globally re-embedded economy (which is what the book's title alludes to). Within two years of the end of the Second World War, however, Polanyi (1947) was already expressing serious doubts about the extent and possibilities of such a transition. What is at issue here are not Polanyi's predictive powers (a dangerous game for anyone to play), but rather the analytical framework (institutionalism) that led him to make such predictions. Indeed, Ruggie's (1982) concept of embedded liberalism was intended to show how, while the post-war free market and laissez-faire state gave way in varying degrees to regulated markets and interventionist states, contrary to Polanyi's expectations, the liberal international order survived. And as Lacher (2007) and Standing (2007) note, the extent of the regulation of markets within nation states was mixed, and in many cases quite limited, precisely because these regulations did not intervene substantially in the capital–labour relation.

While Polanyi was concerned to show how 'society' organized its social reproduction through distribution of goods, which he identified through their institutional arrangements, Marx was concerned to show how, among other things, particular classes reproduced their rule over others through the appropriation of the latter's surpluses. While Marx represented the crystallization of socialism 'from below', Gareth Dale (2010) suggests, drawing on Hal Draper (1966), that Polanyi embraced a mix of socialist traditions 'from above' and 'from below'. This chapter argues that Polanyi's institutional political economy lent itself to a number of intellectual and political positions: a limited conception of how one form of society changes into another, and, relatedly, of what would constitute the de-commodification of labour; a paternalist concern for labouring classes; and subsequently, a contradictory (at best) conception of the role and potential of labouring classes in identifying and advancing their own interests, and in generating societal transformation.

Against the Economistic Fallacy

Both Polanyi and Marx advanced critiques of the liberal economic precepts commonly accepted during their lifetime and now under neoliberalism. As his subtitle made clear, Marx's *Capital* is a "Critique of Political Economy", directed against the classical political economy of Smith, Ricardo, Bentham and others working in the late eighteenth and early nineteenth century. In *TGT*, Polanyi also criticizes Ricardo, Bentham and Malthus. However, the context during which he formulated the ideas for *TGT*, in the 1930s and early 1940s, was the period of the dominance of marginalist economics, although it was also the period in which Keynes's ideas were formulated and increasingly popularized. Polanyi's critique is thus simultaneously directed against classical political economy and (neoclassical) marginalism.

142

Marginalist economics rested upon a triple reductionism consisting of: an individual reductionism, where the economy is conceptualized as an aggregation of its individual members; an asocial reductionism, where the economy is considered in isolation from other social and political actors and processes; and an anti-historicist reductionism, where economic analysis is divorced from historical considerations (Milonakis and Fine 2009, 109).

Polanyi's critique of marginalism therefore, and not surprisingly, focused on its methodologically individualistic, ahistorical and asocial conception of the 'economy' as the point of departure for his institutional approach. He contrasted the 'formal' conception of the economy by the orthodoxy with its 'substantive' meaning. The 'formal' concept of the economy is based on 'the logic of choice' by individual agents 'induced by an insufficiency of means' (Polanyi 1957, 247). Polanyi's institutional analysis, by contrast, focused on the way in which economies are empirically instituted, identified by structured patterns called 'forms of integration'. He points out that 'formal' economics is contingent on the historical and social contexts, and thus '[o]utside of a system of price-making markets economic analysis loses most of its relevance as a method of inquiry into the working of the economy' (Polanyi 1957, 247). Crucially, for Polanyi, 'mere aggregates of personal behaviours ... do not by themselves produce structures.' He thus focused on institutional conditions that cannot be reduced to individual optimizing behaviour and 'choice' (Polanyi 1957, 250–1).

In *TGT* and other writings such as 'The Economy as Instituted Process' (Polanyi 1957), he formulates this critique through: (a) a statement on the novelty of 'market society' in England, that is, the particular form of integration of market society, (b) an account of society's 'counter-movement' against the ravages of the market and (c) a critique of economic liberalism's anti-historical and anti-sociological understanding of the economy.

The Novelty of Market Society

While *TGT*'s objectives are to explain the collapse of the nineteenth-century civilization, and the emergence of a new form of civilization based on increasingly regulated markets, it deals in some considerable depth with the emergence of industrial capitalism, or what Polanyi called 'market society', with particular focus on the rise and fall of laissez-faire liberalism. Polanyi draws a sharp distinction between societies where markets have existed and 'market society'.

Prior to market society, economic relations were 'embedded' within non-economic relations including kinship, religion and the family: 'The outstanding discovery of recent historical and anthropological research is that man's economy, as a rule, is submerged in his social relationships' (Polanyi 2001, 48). Other ways of organizing economic life than the profit motive have included the principles of 'reciprocity' and 'redistribution' based upon institutional patterns of symmetry and centricity (Polanyi 2001, 51). Polanyi draws upon anthropological studies from writers such as Malinowski and Mauss, of societies where economic activity has been organized around such principles and argues further that such societies exhibit:

> [T]he absence of the motive of gain; the absence of the principle of labouring for remuneration; the absence of the principle of least effort; and especially, the absence of any separate and distinct institution based on economic motives. (Polanyi 2001, 49)

In contrast, market society is defined as a society that is 'somehow subordinated to' the requirements of markets (Polanyi 2001, 74), rather than the other way around. Polanyi exposes the 'familiar assertion that a market economy can function only in a market society' made by liberal political economists of his time, which provided the ideological underpinning for the 'deliberate State action' with the aim to produce such a society (Polanyi 2001, 60, 147). A market economy, in turn, is defined as 'an economic system controlled, regulated and directed by markets alone: order in the production and distribution of goods is entrusted to this self-regulating mechanism' (Polanyi 2001, 71), or more explicitly, 'an economy directed by market prices and nothing but market prices' (Polanyi 2001, 45). Polanyi further maintains that a 'market economy must comprise all elements of industry, including labour, land and money' (Polanyi 2001, 74).

For Polanyi, market society emerged from the late eighteenth century onwards, as a result of two processes, one technical the other ideational. On the one hand the British industrial revolution was based on the development of the factory system, and the underlying widespread technological innovation – the creation of new, advanced, specialized and costly machinery that required a fundamental transformation of the relations of society with technology:

> Industrial production ceased to be an accessory of commerce organized by the merchant as a buying and selling proposition: it now involved long-term investment with corresponding risks. Unless the continuance

of production was reasonably assured, such a risk was not bearable. (Polanyi 2001, 78).

Such risks were acceptable to industrial investors only if all the factors of production (the fictitious commodities of labour, land and money, see below) were readily available for purchase/sale on the market. Only a market society, subordinated to market economy, could ensure the constant availability of such commodities. And once such a market was established in Britain, it generated powerful pressures for its global extension (Silver and Arrighi 2003).

On the other hand, however, Polanyi argued that such a powerful economic and social transformation also required an ideational offensive in order to promote the merits of the new system, and banish pre-existing remnants of moral economy. Here Ricardo and Bentham's exposition of and parliament's support for the proposition of 'man's secular salvation through the self-regulating market' was the second element contributing to the rise of market economy (Polanyi 2001, 141). From the 1830s onwards parliamentary legislation facilitated the emergence of the self-regulating market: the amendment of the Poor Law in 1834, subordinating the working class to the market's price-mechanism for labour, Peel's Bank Act of 1844, which subjected domestic money supply to the Gold Standard, and the Anti-Corn Law bill of 1846, which dismantled protection, opening up free imports of corn to the UK from anywhere in the world, thus formed a coherent whole (Polanyi 1947; Silver and Arrighi 2003, 330).

However, despite technological requirements, and ideational offensives by parliament and the industrial bourgeoisie, Polanyi argued that the self-regulating market rested upon an impossible fiction:

> Labour, land and money are obviously *not* commodities . . . Labour is only another name for a human activity which goes with life itself . . . land is only another name for nature . . . actual money . . . is merely a token of purchasing power which . . . comes into being through the mechanism of banking or state finance. None of them is produced for sale. The commodity description of labour, land and money is entirely fictitious. (Polanyi 2001, 75)

The 'fictitious' commodification of labour, land and money is problematic for Polanyi for two reasons. First, he accepts that the market has a self-regulating mechanism for commodities produced for sale, but because labour, land and money are not originally produced to be sold on a market, he argues that the price mechanism cannot effectively adjust their supply and demand. Put differently, he postulates that the supply of labour (or in Marx's terms 'labour power'), land and money cannot be readily increased or decreased. This leads to Polanyi's second objection to the fictitious commodities, which is based on his moral condemnation of laissez-faire liberalism. Not only is the modern market economy historically unprecedented, without roots in prior historical forms of exchange, but because it requires the transformation of labour, nature and means of exchange into commodities, it also threatens the very basis of society:

> To allow the market mechanism to be sole director of the fate of human beings and their natural environment, indeed, even of the amount and use of purchasing power, would result in the demolition of society . . .
> (Polanyi 2001, 76)

While capitalist market imperatives centre around fear of hunger (by workers) and love of gain (by capitalists), such organizing principles of economic life are ultimately unsustainable because they violate 'the fundamental requirements of people to be sustained by family, community and other social relations' (Polanyi-Levitt 2005, 178). In response to these de-humanizing processes Polanyi asserts that society engages in a 'counter-movement' designed to restrict the extent of commodification.

The Counter-Movement

The unleashing of the market generated a response by English society, reacting against its subordination to the market economy and generating novel forms of social protection. Importantly, while Polanyi recognized that society was constituted by different social classes – workers, landlords and capitalists – he portrayed the generalized reaction against the free market as representing a social, supra-class, interest. Here he draws heavily upon Tönnies' organic conception of society (Dale 2008). For example, he argues that in a crisis brought on by the subjection of society to market fluctuations (such as trade cycles leading to growing unemployment), 'the *unity of society* asserted itself through the medium of intervention' (Polanyi 2001, 216, emphasis added). While different classes seek to protect their interests, these are in turn bound up with the interests of society as a whole. Workers established trade unions and campaigned for the state to institute laws governing the buying and selling of labour power (such as minimum wages), as well as establishing welfare states to provide non-commodified services such as health and housing

146

provision. Landlords sought protection via limiting competitive food imports. Central banks sought to regulate the supply of money. Even some capitalists sought state legislation against monopolization of the economy. Polanyi interprets these moves as expressions of a broader societal response to the onslaught of the market.

He argues explicitly that the mobilization of 'narrow class interest' (i.e. by workers, or capitalists, or landlords alone) will not generate their intended outcomes, and that such mobilizations therefore need to occur in relative concert and collaboration with each other (Polanyi 2001, 156). It is here, then, that Polanyi's vision of cross-class resistance to the deleterious effects of the market system were, in part, derived from his admiration for Robert Owen's brand of paternalist socialism. Owen had argued, for example, that a future socialist society 'must and will be accomplished by the rich and powerful. There are no other parties to do it . . . it is a waste of time, talent and pecuniary means for the poor to contend in opposition to the rich and powerful . . .' (cited in Draper 1966). While, unlike Owen, Polanyi recognizes that workers would play a part in the construction of an alternative society, he explicitly rejects Marx's arguments that their emancipation from capital was to be achieved by their own struggles.

However, Polanyi's conception of the double movement, and in particular his explication of how workers resist the onslaught of the market system, is problematic for at least two reasons. First, Polanyi appears to believe that workers will spontaneously resist such disruptions. As Michael Burawoy argues, he holds to a notion of class formation where worker initial disorganization in the face of the market onslaught 'miraculously leads to organization' (Burawoy 2003, 221). Here perhaps, there is more than an element of religious-like hope in the prevalence of justice, derived from his Christian socialism. Thus, secondly, Burawoy (2003, 229) charges Polanyi with naivety in his failure to comprehend the ability of the capitalist state to side with dominant social classes in its repression of workers' struggles. These weaknesses in Polanyi's conception of society and the double movement are rooted, partially at least, in his rejection of Marx's arguments about the inherently exploitative nature of capitalism and the class struggles that it potentially generated.

The Economistic Fallacy

For Polanyi, economic analysis that focused solely on the 'market', as formalized by the marginalists, represented an economistic fallacy. Because other 'forms of integration', such as reciprocity and redistribution, were more prevalent in human history than exchange, Polanyi argued that the assumptions of marginalist economics – that the rule of individual choice based on conditions of scarcity necessarily involved market exchange – did not hold. Moreover, he contested the widely held assumption of self-regulating markets as a natural consequence of the market mechanism, by emphasizing the role of the state and ideology in the emergence of market society.

The intellectual representatives of the English industrial bourgeoisie (including Ricardo, Bentham and Malthus) steered political economy in a new direction, rooting the discipline in naturalistic foundations. For example, Polanyi castigates Townsend, one of the lesser political economists of the time: 'Hobbes had argued the need for a despot because men were *like* beasts; Townsend insisted that they were *actually* beasts, and that, precisely for that reason, only a minimum of government was required' (Polanyi 2001, 119, original emphasis). The consequences of the 'discovery' of natural laws of human interaction and the elevation of these laws into governing principles of economy and society, Polanyi argued, were dehumanizing theoretically and politically (by discounting alternative forms of human interaction) and socially (by condemning a major part of the population to poverty).

He characterized economic liberalism as a fanatic 'religion' borne of the 'result of the sudden aggravation of the task it found itself committed to: the magnitude of the sufferings that were to be inflicted on innocent persons' (Polanyi 2001, 145, 141). The promise of human freedom under market society 'thus degenerates into a mere advocacy of free enterprise' which means 'the fullness of freedom for those whose income, leisure and security need no enhancing, and a mere pittance of liberty for the people' (Polanyi 2001, 265). Earl Gammon argues, in a vein complementary to Polanyi's critique, that liberal economists' elevation of the market as a self-organizing redistributive mechanism, operating objectively and 'above' society, was an 'expression of a desire to punish and objectify those who resisted or stood in the way of the creation of a new technological utopia that was supplanting conceptions of a natural moral economy' (Gammon 2008, 255).

While economic liberals preached the doctrine of laissez-faire, Polanyi exposed their inconsistency, showing how the English state had played an essential role in establishing a market society:

> The road to the free market was opened and kept open by an enormous increase in continuous, centrally organized and controlled

interventionism. . . . the introduction of free markets, far from doing away with the need for control, regulation and intervention, enormously increased their range. (Polanyi 2001, 146–7)

And, like all non-scientific, religious belief, economic liberalism made itself immune from falsification:

> Its apologists are repeating in endless variations that but for the poli-
> cies advocated by its critics, liberalism would have delivered the goods;
> that not the competitive system and the self regulating market, but
> interference with that system and interventions with that market are
> responsible for our ills. (Polanyi 2001, 150)

In his critique of the liberal utopia *TGT* represents a tour de force. But when we turn to Polanyi's explanation of what kind of socio-economic system capitalism is, how it functions, why it requires the transformation of labour into a fictitious commodity and why this, in turn, contributes to the simultaneous widespread poverty across society and the accumulation of wealth in the hands of a few, Polanyi encounters significant difficulties.

Polanyi's Conception of the Market

As we have seen Polanyi had a particular understanding of the nature of the market economy, as an economic system 'controlled, regulated and directed by markets alone' (2001, 71) where all elements of industry (including labour, land and money) are commodified and subject to the dynamics of supply and demand. He writes that '[a] self-regulating market demands nothing less than the *institutional separation of society into an economic and political sphere* . . . [a] market economy must comprise all elements of industry, including labour, land, and money' and '[to] include them in the market mechanism means to subordinate the *substance of society* itself to the laws of the market' (Polanyi 2001, 74–5, emphasis added). Polanyi also notes that although the self-regulating market demands the above-mentioned institutional separation, it cannot achieve this, precisely because of the fictitious nature of labour, land and money. Hence, the notion of a 'market economy' actually operating according to the self-regulating market mechanism implies 'a stark utopia' (Polanyi 2001, 3). This was especially so with the emergence and persistence of institutions designed by society for self-protection from harmful effects of the market. As Polanyi noted:

149

Though the new protective institutions, such as trade union and factory laws, were adapted, as far as possible, to the requirements of the economic mechanism, they nevertheless interfered with its self-regulation and, ultimately, destroyed the system. (Polanyi 2001, 81)

Interference with the self-regulating market disrupts its laws and thus undermines it. Ironically, such sentiments were held by the very liberals against whom Polanyi was so vehemently opposed. For example, Lionel Robbins argued that 'It is not capitalism, it is interventionism and monetary uncertainty which are responsible for the persistence of the slump' (cited in Polanyi-Levitt 2006, 165). The difference is that while laissez-faire liberalism (and in turn neoclassical economics) promoted the removal of these institutions (to remove impediments to the markets' self-regulation) the same understanding of institutional interference with the market mechanism led Polanyi to postulate that 'no market economy separated from the political sphere is possible' (Polanyi 2001, 205) and to stress the necessary role of the state for market economy to sustain itself. In contrast to the assumption of the marginalist economists, Polanyi maintained that market society cannot emerge spontaneously or sustain itself within its inner logic of 'self-regulation' without state intervention.

And yet, despite his opposition to the laissez-faire liberalism, and his claim that the spheres of economy and society cannot be fully or really separated, Polanyi ultimately failed to go beyond an asocial technical conception of the market, as shared by the liberal classical political economists and marginalists. As noted previously, for Polanyi, market, along with 'reciprocity' and 'redistribution', is simply another 'form of integration' or an 'instituted process' that characterizes how resources are exchanged and circulated in a particular society. Each 'form of integration' represents a distinctive logic and mechanism for resource allocation and circulation, while being subjected to moral, cultural and social processes and institutions.

Polanyi employs 'forms of integration' as Weberian ideal types, which describe and classify patterns of economic behaviour and social organizations across human history, and as a conceptual tool to 'penetrate the maze of social relations in which the economy was embedded' (Polanyi et al. 1957, 242). But what kind of social relations is he examining? Polanyi's objective is to depict the social relations and institutions that govern how goods are circulated and distributed, rather than to explain the relations of exploitation within these societies. Consequently, his concept of the market is an empirical one: of a technical mechanism that moves goods and services from one individual to another.

Ultimately, Polanyi's conception of the market is detached from what Marxists call the social relations of production, which underpin how surplus is produced, controlled and distributed within the particular mode of production. This under-socialized conception of the market has important implications for his analysis of capitalism and his vision for the socialism.

Capitalism and Exploitation

Polanyi's rejection of one of the central tenets of Marxist political economy, the labour theory of value, enables him to construct an image of society as a potentially organic whole – one that, in its attempts to protect itself from the market can potentially overcome any systematic form of exploitation. Polanyi suggested that exploitation should not be 'defined strictly in economic terms as a permanent inadequacy of rations of exchange' (2001, 166) but instead emphasized social, cultural and moral degradations as consequences of 'disembedded markets'. Thus, first, Polanyi understood 'economic' exploitation under capitalism as being based on unequal exchange (for example, under-payment for commodified goods and services, including labour). Secondly, exploitation is to be understood as a consequence of society's inability to sufficiently regulate or modify the effect of the 'market' under capitalism. Thus, exploitation can, hypothetically, be eliminated by re-embedding the 'market' within non-market institutions.

Polanyi's distinctive conception of exploitation reflects the dichotomy in his thinking between society and economy. It also hinders his ability to understand the origins and nature of capitalist, market society in particular. His organic conception of society, rooted in his institutionalist political economy, disables him from viewing a central determinant of social (re)production and transformation: exploitation and resistance to exploitation. This means that as Burawoy (2003) has observed, despite his counter-posing of 'society' against 'the market', Polanyi has a strangely weak understanding of society itself.

The Emergence of Capitalism

In certain passages of his writing in *TGT*, Polanyi appreciates the role of technological change, particularly the development of the factory system, as constituting the underlying historical process that necessitated the establishment of the 'fictitious' and 'instituted' commodification of labour, land and money, and the social disembodiment of the market economy. Where this technological dynamism came from, however, is never explained by Polanyi. Elsewhere in *TGT*, the 'fictional' nature of commodification is promoted by the ideational offensive by the emerging industrial bourgeoisie. Once again, the material basis of such ideational movement is never explored. Polanyi's narrative of institutional change and transition to capitalism is thus based upon a combination of technological (rather than 'economic') determinism and ideological voluntarism. He finds it hard to explain the processes giving rise to either initial technological change or ideational offensive, that is, he lacks a conception of how social relations determine socio-economic change.

Polanyi depicts society as a (semi-autonomous) sphere of political contestation, class alliances, and state actions in support of different social groups. It is relatively distinct from, and can potentially regulate, the economy (but not when the economy has been disembedded). Put differently, Polanyi does not adequately show how economic processes generate social classes within society that then seek to reproduce these economic processes. This relatively de-socialized conception of market economy is particularly evident in his concept of 'fictitious commodities', where he fails to offer a coherent theory of the commodification of labour, land and money, and the role of this process in the rise of capitalism. Polanyi's argument that these are not originally 'produced for sale' is based on his 'empirical definition of a commodity' (2001, 75), as opposed to Marx's conception of the commodity as a product of social relations. This leads Polanyi to contrast 'fictitious commodities' to 'normal' commodities, implying that 'generalized commodity production could exist in the absence of commodified labour-power' (Dale 2010, 77). As Hüseyin Özel (1997, 182) notes, Polanyi

> [uses] the term 'commodity' in its 'empirical' sense; that is, a commodity is a thing which is bought and sold at the market. [He] . . . forget[s] the fact that a commodity, being a social relation, is not simply a thing.

Sandra Halperin (2004, 13) argues in a complementary vein that for Polanyi land, labour and money are the basic substances of societal reproduction 'rather than bases of class formation and class interest' and that consequently 'protection of them is a general, social interest.' Further, as Lie (1991, 225) suggests, Polanyi's concept of fictitious commodities rests on a moral condemnation 'against treating people as means rather than ends'. Consequently, '[b]y elevating the moral criticism at the expense of the analytical, he discloses neither the institution nor the process of market exchange' (Lie 1991). Nor does he provide an adequate conceptualization of exploitation specific to any 'forms of integration'. In these ways, then, Polanyi fails to provide a coherent theory of social or institutional change.

The Institutional Division Between Economic and Political Spheres

Polanyi's relatively uncritical acceptance of the orthodox de-socialized conception of the market, combined with his failure to go beyond a moral critique exposes his inability to comprehend how under capitalism 'social' (or political) and 'economic' processes are institutionally separate, but functionally integrated and co-constitutive. Their institutional separation conceals an essential unity, based upon the specifically capitalist social relations of the commodity of labour power – its ability to sell at its full price in the market while simultaneously generating surplus value in production.

In contrast to Polanyi and liberal economics, Marx, by employing his labour theory of value, observed the circulation of labour power in the market place, its expenditure in the workplace and how these two spheres were systemically co-dependent.

> The consumption of labour-power is completed, as in the case of every other commodity, outside . . . the sphere of circulation. Accompanied by Mr. Moneybags [the capitalist] and by the possessor of labour-power [the worker], we therefore take leave for a time of this noisy sphere, where everything takes place on the surface and in view of all men, and follow them both into the *hidden abode of production*, on whose threshold there stares us in the face 'No admittance except on business'. (Marx 1990, 279–80 emphasis added)

Polanyi, unfortunately, obeys the capitalist order to stay outside the hidden abode and is thus left to observe the sphere of circulation. For Marx, the capitalist market place generates the appearance of a realm of freedom of exchange – of 'fictitious' and 'real' commodities where formal contracts govern relations between freely choosing individuals – the 'very Eden of the innate rights of man . . . Freedom, Equality, Property and Bentham' (Marx 1990, 280). Here, labour power is bought and sold on the market for its full value (its socially determined costs of production), as are all other commodities. The institutional separation of the spheres of circulation and production – the former where the worker appears to be, and is nominally, an equal of the

153

capitalist, and the latter where the worker is firmly subordinated to the capitalists' objectives of competitive capital accumulation and where surplus value is generated and extracted – necessitates, for any profound analysis of capitalism, the ability to distinguish between essential social relations and their institutional forms.

But, by conceptually separating the two spheres, and assuming that the economy has its own distinct laws, it is then possible for Polanyi to present 'society' as potentially in opposition to the economy under capitalism. But it is precisely this momentary split between the exploitation of labour (in production) and the realization of profit (in circulation) that generates an appearance under capitalism of an institutional separation between spheres, and constitutes what is historically peculiar about the form of exploitation under capitalism (Wood 1995). And here we confront another significant weakness in Polanyi's understanding of market society: the existence of labour power as a commodity does not 'just' require the separation of the direct producers from the means of production, but it also requires the political, economic and social subordination of labour to capital. As we shall see below, this also requires that the sellers of (commodified) labour power be overwhelmingly poor.

Polanyi's difficulties in explaining the emergence and functioning of market economy and society is, in part, a product of his reluctance to investigate how different forms of exploitation operate across societies. This stems from his rejection, alongside the labour theory of value, of Marx's conception of the mode of production. As already noted, Marx identified different modes of production by specifying '[t]he specific economic form, in which unpaid surplus-labour is pumped out of direct producers'. Polanyi criticized this as 'the historically untenable stages theory of slavery, serfdom and wage labour that is traditional with Marxism – a grouping which flowed from the conviction that the character of the economy was set by the status of labour'. Polanyi argued that Marxist theory of social development', based on the labour theory of value, is problematic because: 'the integration of the soil into the economy should be regarded as hardly less vital' (Polanyi 1957, 256). Polanyi further criticized Marx for following Ricardo 'in defining classes in economic terms' which 'led to a crude class theory of social development' (2001, 158). For Polanyi:

> Actually, class interests offer only a limited explanation of long-run movements in society. The fate of classes is more frequently determined by the needs of society than the fate of society is determined by the needs of classes. (Polanyi 2001, 159)

154

But this is to conflate a conception of class-interests derived from Weber with Marx's conception of class relations, the latter of which was designed to explain the material requirements for the formation, existence and transformation of different class societies. Hence, Polanyi's is an approach which conflates apparently similar distributive mechanisms while obscuring fundamentally different social relations of production and exploitation. For example, he groups together diverse societies according to their organizational/institutional principles of redistribution. '[R]edistribution occurs for many reasons, *on all civilizational levels*, from the primitive hunting tribe, to the vast storage systems of ancient Egypt, Sumeria, Babylonia or Peru . . .' (Polanyi et al. 1957, 254; cited in Godelier 1986). Put differently, Polanyi does not connect his analysis of different organizing principles of resource allocation with that of how wealth is produced, and surpluses concentrated in the hands of certain classes as opposed to, and at the expense of, others. For these reasons then, class, or the nature of production is for Polanyi of secondary importance compared to distributive mechanisms, in understanding how societies reproduce themselves. Godelier therefore charges Polanyi with being unable to search 'beneath the diversity of resemblances or differences, for an underlying order, the invisible logic of the objective properties of social relations and their laws of transformation' (Godelier 1986, 200). And Douglas North criticizes Polanyi for providing 'an account of reciprocity and redistributive systems which [are] inherently changeless' (1977, 715).

These weaknesses arguably derive from Polanyi's application of Weber's ideal-type methodology, which, as Allen observes, generates 'entirely formal categories around which large segments of history are grouped' and thus contributes to the substitution of 'typologies for real explanations of how societies change' (Allen 2004, 79, 80). In a similar vein Voss (1987, 130, cited in Dale 2010, 120) argues that Polanyi's analysis of redistribution 'ignores the fact that the same centralizing phenomenon – the concentration and dispersion of goods – can have very different results and intentions'.

Polanyi's blindness to the role of the exploitation across class societies in general, and under capitalism in particular, disables him from understanding how it is not exclusion from the market (from access to employment), as a consequence of commodification of labour, but inclusion in the market as a holder of labour-power that can yield surplus value, that determines the (re)production of widespread poverty among modern proletarians across market societies.

155

Exploitation and Poverty

'Where do the poor come from'? asks Polanyi (2001, 94). One of *TGT*'s central objectives is to explain the widespread immiseration associated with the rise of market society, in Britain and in its colonies. As part of his critique of 'vulgar Marxism', Polanyi distinguishes sharply between commodification and exploitation, arguing that 'it is precisely this emphasis put on exploitation which tends to hide from our view the even greater issue of cultural degeneration' (Polanyi 2001, 166). He applies this distinction in his analysis of immiseration in colonial India:

> Indian masses in the second half of the nineteenth century did not die of hunger because they were exploited by Lancashire: they perished in large numbers because the Indian village community had been demolished. That this was brought about by forces of economic competition ... the permanent underselling of hand-woven chaddar by machine-made piece goods, is doubtless true; but it proves the opposite of economic exploitation, since dumping implies the reverse of surcharge. (Polanyi 2001, 167)

Putzel (2002, 3) re-states the primacy of commodification (and cultural degradation) over exploitation: 'The impulse toward social protection is not only and perhaps not even primarily protection against economic exploitation. It is protection against the destruction of human dignity.' And while Michael Burawoy (2010, 307) concurs, this distinction represents a fundamental weakness in Polanyi, rooted in his superficial comprehension of capitalism.

The dichotomy of commodification and cultural degradation vs exploitation, as alternative explanations for root causes of the plight of the Indian masses in the nineteenth century, is unnecessary if we comprehend this, and other examples of immiseration, as consequences of global competitive capital accumulation, in which British industry was the pre-eminent leader. British textiles achieved international competitive advantage with help from the British state, and then overwhelmed the Indian market through a number of inter-linked processes – all detailed by Marx in *Capital*: a lucrative slave trade between West Africa and the Americas and the production by slaves in the Americas of cotton; an expanding trade in cotton between the southern United States and Britain; the establishment of a large, highly exploited working class in northern England working on technologically advanced machinery; military/political conquest of the Asian subcontinent by British capital and state; the despoliation of Indian industry (for example banning Indian textile exports); land grabbing (and the beginnings of de-peasantization) by Indian and British landlords and a rising exploitation of the Indian peasantry driven by British demands for rent (Marx 1990; Hobsbawm 1969; Patnaik 1990; Saul 1960; Ahmad 1994). Understood from this vantage point, a distinction between commodification and exploitation obscures the specificity of capitalist expansion, which entails simultaneous commodification and exploitation driven by economic and non-economic forces.

And yet Polanyi's focus is primarily on commodification. For example, in explaining the prevalence of poverty in Britain, Polanyi argues that mass unemployment is a consequence of the subordination of the fictitious commodities of labour to the laws of supply and demand, through 'excess fluctuations of [unregulated] trade'. The supply of and demand for goods and labour is subject to the laws of the market, which in turn subjects large sections of the population to misery as they are unable to find employment (Polanyi 2001, 95). There is no doubt that labour's market dependence makes it vulnerable to forces beyond its control, but is this the only cause of mass poverty within market society?

In *Capital* Marx demonstrates how the establishment of capitalist labour markets (the centuries-long process of 'primitive accumulation') emerged through a combination of 'de-peasantization' and the ruthless oppression of those 'vagabonds' who could not find work. 'Free' workers 'fortunate' enough to find employment were subject to a barrage of parliamentary legislation designed to *force down* wages:

> The rising bourgeoisie needs the power of the state, and uses it to 'regulate' wages, i.e. to force them into the limits suitable for making a profit, to lengthen the working day, and to keep the worker himself at his normal level of dependence. This is an essential aspect of so-called primitive accumulation. (Marx 1990, 899–90)

In chapter 28 of *Capital*, aptly entitled '*Bloody legislation against the expropriated since the end of the Fifteenth Century: The Forcing Down of Wages by Acts of Parliament*' Marx details how '[a] tariff of wages was fixed by law for town and country, for piece-work and day-work ... It was forbidden, on pain of imprisonment, to pay higher wages than those fixed by the statute' (Marx 1990, 900–1). Adam Smith had also recognized how 'We have no acts of parliament against combining to lower the price of labour; but many against combining to raise it' (1976, 1, 74–5). Trade unions were effectively

157

banned until 1825 (Marx 1990, 901). Only in 1813 were 'the laws for the regulation of wages . . . repealed' as '[t]hey became an absurd anomaly as soon as the capitalist began to regulate his factory by his own private legislation . . .' (Marx 1990, 901, 902).

British and other European elites were not only concerned with establishing a market society based upon the reproduction of fictitious commodities to service the expanding industrial revolution. They aimed, systematically, to keep the mass of the population poor and politically weak, in order to maximize their economic exploitation. In the leading industrial sectors, where supply of and demand for labour might have led to relatively scarce, more highly skilled workers bargaining for higher wages, 'production processes were devised to transform workers into simple instruments of production, so-called 'hands' (Sohn-Rethel 1978, cited in Halperin 2004). As Halperin (2004, 295) notes '[t]o maintain control of labour, dominant classes sought to keep labour poor and in excess of demand' and '[d]ominant classes kept peasants and rural workers poor and weak by blocking land reform.'

Commodification of labour and its exploitation were, and are, two sides of the same process. Economic exploitation and the extraction of surplus value from labour by capital was simultaneously an 'economic' process (in the realms of the private, capitalist workplace) and a 'political' process, supported and instituted by pro-capitalist states as they sought to raise the competitiveness of their economies in relation to other capitalist economies. The commodification of labour power enabled its sale and purchase on the labour market, but the extraction of surplus value required a complex and ever changing apparatus of state laws and strict management of the capitalist labour process.

Conclusions

For Polanyi, socialism was on the agenda in the post-war world. But what kind of socialism? As Dale (2010, 205–6) notes, Polanyi's conception of socialism was broad-ranging, embracing Stalinist Russia, the social democracy of the UK's Labour government, community, guild and Christian socialism. These represent, using Hal Draper's (1966) analogy, a variety, and a contradictory amalgam of socialism's 'from above' and 'from below'. The way Polanyi presents the decommodification of labour in *TGT* reveals further his ambiguous conception of the capital–labour relation:

To take labour out of the market means a transformation as radical as was the establishment of a competitive labour market . . . Not only conditions in the factory, hours of work, and modalities of contract, but the basic wage itself, are determined outside the market . . .' (1957, 251)

Is Polanyi suggesting here an end to the wage–labour relationship, as Marx's vision of socialism entailed, or is he simply advocating its regulation by non-market actors (such as governments)? If the latter, then the extent of his conception of decommodification is very limited. Following the second world war, East, West and South, a whole range of mechanisms – including minimum wages set by governments, the institutionalization of collective bargaining between trade unions and employers overseen by government ministries, state commitments to full employment, rules regulating the employment contract and conditions of employment – generated, what by Polanyi's definition, was the decommodification of labour. Lacher (2007) notes, however, that the post-war world's institutionalization of capital–labour relations entailed only a 'slight transformation'. And that transformation was, arguably, even slighter across the emerging Third World. To be sure, a slight transformation is better than no transformation, but it should not be equated with a great transformation, such as the transition to socialism. Nor should it obscure ways in which movements and struggles that were attempting to generate such a great transition were disabled (forcefully repressed) from doing so by modernizing capitalist states that used the slight transformations of capital–labour relations to enhance their legitimacy and to spread and deepen capitalist social relations.

Perhaps one of the reasons that Polanyi's conception of socialism was so broad-ranging, and therefore vague, was that he had no overarching theory of capitalism, or of a potential transition beyond capitalism. This contrasts with Marx's identification of labouring classes as agents of socialist transformation, rooted in their struggles against, and potentially beyond, capitalist exploitation. This critique, however, should not detract from the genuine strengths of Polanyi's work.

Polanyi provides us with an immensely powerful critique of liberal economics. His critique, because it is based on a moral aversion to commodification and the subjection of real humans to abstract market forces, mirrors many rejections of aspects of capitalism that are observable across the contemporary crisis-stricken world, in particular religion-based movements. His assertion that socialism is a preferable and possible alternative to capitalism opens up debates

159

over the form, content and politics of transformation to an alternative, future society.

However, there are limits to Polanyi's critique of capitalism. His lack of comprehension of the centrality of exploitation at the heart of capitalism, combined with his under-socialized and quite technical understanding of the market economy, prevents him from getting to the roots of the dynamics of capitalist expansion and reproduction. His understanding of capitalism leads to an ambiguous and even contradictory conception of socialism.

A Marxist conception of capitalism – understood as a system based upon the exploitation of labour by capital in production and facilitated through the (re)production of the commodity of labour power for sale on the market – provides a more satisfactory account of what causes and reproduces the commodification of labour under capitalism. It also helps explain how the poverty of working classes under capitalism is a pre-condition and corollary of their exploitation.

The line that fundamentally divides Polanyi from Marx is his conception of society as an organic whole in contrast to the latter's class analysis. This divide manifests itself in Marx's historical materialism, conception of modes of production, analysis of class-based exploitation and vision of socialism 'from below', in contrast to Polanyi's institutionalism, his ideal-type categorization of different historical systems of exchange, vision of society as an organic whole and his vague conception of re-embedded markets and socialism based upon a societal counter-movement.

Polanyi's moral aversion to the commodification of labour (land, and money) is a necessary starting point for an effective critique of capitalism. But if a focus on commodification is detached from the analysis of exploitation, it will disable movements that seek to transcend capitalism. If, however, Polanyi's critique of liberal economics is combined with Marx's deconstruction of the mechanisms of capitalist exploitation, then critics and opponents of capitalism will find themselves better equipped as they seek to establish a society based on the upholding and expansion of human dignity.

DEVELOPMENT WITHIN OR AGAINST CAPITALISM? A CRITIQUE OF AMARTYA SEN'S *DEVELOPMENT AS FREEDOM*

Expansion of freedom is viewed, in this approach, both as the primary end and as the principal means of development. (Sen 1999)

Amartya Sen is arguably 'one of the greatest public intellectuals of our time' (Corbridge 2002, 183), and his contribution to development thinking and practice is immense. Sen's vision of development is radically different to those conceptions based upon rapid economic growth, catch-up and industrial transformation (as argued in various ways by List, Gerschenkron and Schumpeter). Like Polanyi and Marx, Sen understands development as a process of human flourishing. Quite significantly, Sen's vision is not confined to intellectual arguments. He was one of the figures responsible for the formulation of the Human Development Index (HDI), which sought to reconceptualize development as a process of expansion of human abilities. The HDI comprehends the development process as one based upon increases to the life expectancy, education and income of the populations of developing (and developed) countries (Harriss 2005, 37).

This chapter discusses Sen's (1999) widely acclaimed *Development as Freedom* (henceforth *DAF*). In this powerful book, Sen sweeps away much of the rationale and justification of catch-up, growth-based development as it has been pursued since the industrial revolution, highlighting how such strategies reduce humanity to a means while elevating economic growth to an end, and consequently, limiting human freedoms. Sen argues, as this chapter's epigraph suggests, that expanding human freedoms should be both goals *and means* of development. Sen's vision is immensely appealing. No doubt many theorists and practitioners of development, and many members of social movements struggling for an amelioration of their political and economic conditions will find much to agree with in Sen's vision. However, while they are attractive, this chapter argues that Sen's critique and alternative vision are compromised by his generally favourable portrayal of capitalist markets. Despite his critique of growth-based development he does argue that capitalist markets are both necessary and virtuous in that they facilitate economic growth (with which to provide expanding populations with the material goods they require to avoid depredation), and that they constitute realms of freedom where individuals can make choices leading to the improvement of their lives. Sharing some ground with Polanyi, Sen recognizes that 'the operation of the market economy can certainly be significantly defective under many circumstances' (Sen 2006, p.137). He concludes, however, that they can be regulated and controlled for the common good, and that '. . . market forces, can be seen as operating *through* a system of legal relations' (Sen 1982, 166, original emphasis).

This chapter argues that Sen's conception of development as the expansion of *individual* freedoms is internally contradictory because it is based on a liberal conception of capitalist markets. It supports this argument by showing how Sen's own work on famines (Sen 1982) undermines his later conception of the potentially benign nature of capitalist markets, adopted in *DAF*. It also argues that the contradictory nature of Sen's approach is exacerbated by his use of Adam Smith and Marx to support his case.

Despite these substantial weaknesses in his conception of the relationship between individuals and the capitalist market, this chapter argues that Sen's vision is still realizable, but only if wedded to Marx's conception of the political economy of labour, and post-capitalist development, as noted in chapter 3. Hence, I recognize with Fine (2004, 97) Sen's brilliance, but agree that 'the key issue now is how his contributions will be taken forward.'

Against Growth-Based Development

As noted in chapter 1, a common conception of development is economic 'catch-up' – where poor countries experience rapid economic growth and technological uptake, thus enabling them to take their place alongside already developed countries. For example, the 2001 New Partnership for Africa's Development (NEPAD), describes how Africa is 'backward', 'underdeveloped' and 'marginalized' from the world economy, and asserts that its primary goal, in order to 'bridge the gap' and 'catch up' with the advanced countries, is the achievement of a continent-wide 7 percent Gross Domestic Product (GDP) growth rate per annum until at least 2016 (NEPAD 2002, Matthews 2004). Sen opposes this logic and argues that development can and should be understood 'as a process of expanding the real freedoms that people enjoy' (1999, 3). He argues neither for freedom in the abstract sense (for example, *Liberté, égalité, fraternité*) nor for the very limited freedom to own property, and to do with it what one pleases, that rests at the heart of liberal political and economic thinking (Nozick 1974). Rather, he argues for *real equal* freedoms for all. Development, therefore, should facilitate the expansion and equalization of the real freedoms of individuals. Sen acknowledges that economic growth may be an important aspect of development, but is adamant that 'If freedom is what development advances, then there is a major argument for concentrating on that overarching objective, rather than on some particular means . . .' (Sen 1999, 3). Economic growth may contribute to the expansion of the freedoms of the poor – but growth alone has at best uneven and at worst detrimental impacts upon the majority of countries' populations.

Historical and contemporary cases support Sen's argument. Navarro (2000, 662), for example, details how during Brazil's economic 'miracle' (1968 to 1981) 'for the top five percent of the Brazilian population the percentage of national consumption increased from 20 percent . . . to 48 percent by the end; [while] for the bottom 50 percent . . . consumption declined from 20 to 12 percent.' The infant mortality rate increased from 70 infant deaths per 1,000 in 1968 to 92 per 1,000 in 1981. Growth in the Brazilian case was based on further concentrating wealth in the hands of the rich and orienting economic activity towards the production of luxury and relatively expensive consumer goods (Kohli 2004).

Contemporary India and China are lauded for their high growth rates by neoliberals and statists alike (Wade and Wolf 2002). However, these countries are experiencing the 'paradox' of rising average incomes, but *falling* living standards for large numbers of urban and rural workers – a process intrinsically linked to rural peasant differentiation and labour regime intensification. Utsa Patnaik provides data showing that while according to official Indian statistics rural income poverty in India declined from 37.3 to 27.4 per cent of the population between 1993–4 and 1999–2000:

Over exactly the same period, a number of interrelated indicators of rural well-being have worsened . . . food grain absorption per head has declined sharply to reach levels prevalent 50 years ago. Rising farm debts have led to loss of assets reflected in a rise in landlessness, and to the historically unprecedented situation of many thousands of farmer suicides . . . Annual food grains availability per head of total population has fallen steeply from 177kg in the early 1990s to only 153kg by 2003–4. (Patnaik 2007, 31–2)

Patnaik explains these trends as emanating from processes associated with capitalist expansion: monetization, peasant differentiation and land dispossession. She notes the increasing rate of monetization of the rural economy and that, as a consequence, wages which had previously been paid in kind have increasingly been paid in cash, which is then used to purchase increasingly expensive foodstuffs. As part of the monetization (and privatization) process, common property and gleaning rights have disappeared. Mehta and Venkataraman (2000) highlight how crop-straw, fuel-wood and fodder, which were previously gleaned by the rural poor or gathered by access to common property, are increasingly purchased at retail rates. Patnaik (2007, 31–2) observes how simultaneous monetization and 'rising farm debts have led to loss of assets reflected in a rise in landlessness . . .' Hence, despite the poor's rising nominal money incomes (if official statistics are to be believed), their purchasing power is falling.

In China, Reddy (2007, 63) observed that during the 1990s nutritional intake worsened for low-income groups, caused by rising food prices 'induced by the liberalization of the grain marketing system, and the abolition of the food coupon system by most provinces in 1993'. Meng et al. (2004, 1) also detail how ' . . . despite the rapid increase in income, the average nutrient consumption of low income urban households declined in the 1990s.' A (banned) Chinese study documents the decline of peasants' per capita farming incomes by 6 per cent since 1997, and concludes that 'given the rising costs of health and education, their real purchasing power has probably fallen still further' (cited in Lian 2005). These average figures, however, disguise processes of peasant differentiation. The *South China Post* estimated that 'the vast majority of the 800 million peasants have incomes of less than US$1 a day' (cited in Hart-Landsberg and Burkett 2005).

In the Indian case, but also as a general hypothesis for industrializing countries, Deaton and Drèze (2009, 43) suggest that such declines in food consumption might be 'due to declining levels of physical activity and possibly also due to various improvements in the health environment'. But this is an implausible explanation considering labour regime intensification during industrialization. Thus, in their study of food consumption trends in Britain between 1770 and 1850, Clark et al. (1995) note how during Britain's industrial revolution rural workers generally displayed better health indicators (for example physical height) than urban industrial workers, and that 'Urbanization and industrialization cut food expenditure and the intake of calories and protein' (Clark et al. 1995, 234). And Frederick Engels observed in 1845 in his *Condition of the Working Class in England*, how:

> The food of the labourer, indigestible enough in itself, is utterly unfit for young children, and he has neither means nor time to get his children more suitable food ... Temporary want of sufficient food, to which almost every working-man is exposed at least once in the course of his life, only contributes to intensify the effects of his usually sufficient but bad diet ... The neglect to which the great mass of working-men's children are condemned leaves ineradicable traces and brings the enfeeblement of the whole race of workers with it. (Engels 2009, 86)

These cases reflect the reality of growth-based capitalist development for the masses. What does Sen propose as an alternative?

Markets, Opportunities and Development as Freedom

Sen argues that development entails the double expansion of freedoms:

> Development consists of the *removal* of various types of unfreedoms that leave people with little choice and little opportunity of exercising their reasoned agency ... However, for a fuller understanding of the connection between development and freedom we have to go beyond this basic recognition ... The intrinsic importance of human freedom, in general, as the pre-eminent objective of development is strongly supplemented by the instrumental effectiveness of freedoms of particular kinds to promote freedoms of other kinds. (Sen 1999)

Sen's conception of positive freedoms rests on expanding individuals' capabilities (abilities) and thus functionings (choices), rather than simply their incomes. Genuine human development therefore requires removing unfreedoms, including practices such as bonded labour (see below). Here Sen stands squarely within the tradition of liberal politics and economics which emphasize the importance of negative freedoms ('freedom from'). Such negative freedoms leave individual producers and consumers *Free to Choose* (Friedman and Friedman 1980). However, Sen also embraces what Berlin (1969) labels positive liberty ('freedom to'), that is, individuals' ability to function well in life, understood in terms of ends that people 'have reason to value', and he supports state actions to expand positive liberties for the masses. Sen lists at least eight 'instrumental freedoms' that he considers essential to any development process: the ability of individuals to live life free of 'starvation, under-nourishment, escapable morbidity and premature mortality, as well as the freedoms that are associated with being literate and numerate, enjoying political participation and uncensored speech and so on' (Sen 1999, 36). Bagchi (2000, 4418), notes that placing these positive freedoms as primary represents a move beyond what Marx would have called 'bourgeois' rights to broad human rights.

In DAF, following Adam Smith, Sen acknowledges that capitalist markets are a source of economic growth, but his principal argument is that they are a source of individual freedom. Smith regarded the market as a mechanism that would free human potential from the stagnation of feudalism. Sen also cites Marx's characterization of the victory of the North in the American Civil War as the great event of nineteenth-century history because it established 'the importance of the freedom of labour contract as opposed to slavery and the enforced exclusion from the labour market' (Sen 1999, 7). Further, 'freedom of exchange and transaction is itself part and parcel of the basic liberties that people have reason to value' (1999, 6). Sen's conception of the relationship between markets, states, and individual

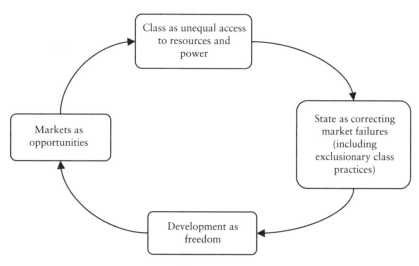

Figure 7.1   Markets as Spheres of Freedom

freedom is shown in figure 7.1 (starting with the top box), which can be understood as a self-reinforcing, closed system. Sen castigates critics of markets as follows:

> To be *generically* against markets would be almost as odd as being generically against conversations between people ... The freedom to exchange words, or goods, or gifts does not need defensive justification in terms of their favourable but distant effects; they are part of the way human beings in society live and interact with each other (unless stopped by regulation or fiat). (Sen 1999, emphasis in original)

However, the (intended?) effect of this formulation is to sideline any discussion of how the freedom to exchange and engage in transactions under capitalism is one not naturally given, but derived from control over things (property). This is a narrow concept of freedom, one which Sen in his attack on growth-based development appears to oppose. *DAF* argues for the expansion of *all* peoples' freedoms to act, to engage in a rich public life and thus to continually expand their freedoms. However, here Sen is elevating the freedom to exchange to a 'basic liberty'. But, as will be discussed later, such freedom represents a partial liberty, based upon institutionalized unfreedoms (for example, the inability of individuals to use *other people's property* in ways that may benefit them). That is, under capitalism, the freedoms of some are maintained and realized through non-freedoms of others (Cohen 1981).

The sources of the division of these freedoms and unfreedoms are, contrary to Sen, a necessary condition and outcome of the capitalist accumulation dynamic. Capitalism is characterized, above all, by competitive accumulation between owners of capital, usually based upon the employment (exploitation) of free wage-labour. Both capitalists and labourers are dependent upon the market for their reproduction (profits and wages). Hence, Robert Brenner notes how 'it is the producers' [employers] commoditizing of their output and their consequent *dependence* upon the market which results in their *subjection* to the creative pressures of competition' (1986, 45 emphases added). Thus, what is portrayed by Sen as *opportunity* is shown by Brenner, to be market dependence, and hence *imperative* (see also Wood 1999). The drive to accumulate capital is a response to an externally determined imperative imposed by market mechanisms of competition and cost-price rationalization. Such competitive pressures manifest themselves through continual attempts to reduce input costs (including labour costs/wages), often realized through limiting workers' freedoms both within and outside the workplace.

Sen's portrayal of capitalism is one where the market system is an arena for choice and a realm of freedom. Central to development, therefore, is the removal of barriers to market access. Hence: 'the crucial challenges . . . in many developing countries today include the need for the freeing of labour from explicit or implicit bondage that denies access to the open labour market.' And later, 'We must . . . examine . . . the persistence of deprivations among segments of the community that happen to remain *excluded* from the benefits of the market-orientated society' (Sen 1999, 7). This formulation represents a residualist, and therefor highly problematic, conception of political economy, as discussed in chapter 1.

Sen's residualist arguments about the liberating potential of labour market access is echoed throughout mainstream development discourse, institutions such as the UN, and various regional country-level Human Development Reports, and inform development strategies for expanding the capabilities of the poor. However, in her discussion of the Arab Human Development Report's conception of women's access to the labour market, Lila Abu-Lughod (2009, 88) argues that:

> The fantasy about the magical value of work for women is a middle-class one – it presumes that jobs are well paid and fulfilling . . . One must ask if work that is badly paid, back breaking, exploitative, or boring liberates women.

To investigate these issues more deeply, and to see why Sen's vision is myopic, we need to turn, again, to the issue of relations between social classes under capitalism.

Social Classes Under Capitalism: Opportunities or Exploitation?

If the capitalist market is a sphere of opportunity, then individuals' occupations must be understood as an outcome of relatively free choice. But if the market is a sphere of compulsion then interactions through it, such as employment contracts, take on a darker hue. Because Sen is wedded to the first axiom, he needs to distort Marx in order to claim that wage labour under capitalism is a source of human freedom. He does this by using Marx's analysis of forms of bonded labour common to feudalism. For example, he quotes Ramachandran's study of agricultural labourers in India to enforce his argument:

> Marx distinguishes . . . the *formal freedom* of the workers under capitalism and the *real unfreedom* of workers in pre-capitalist systems: 'the

freedom of workers to change employers makes him free in a way not found in earlier modes of production'. . . . The extension of the freedom of workers in a society to sell their labour power is an enhancement of their positive freedom, which is, in turn, an important measure of how well that society is doing. (Ramachandran 1990, 1–2, cited in Sen 1999, 29–30, emphasis in original)

To be sure, wage labour under capitalism represents an important improvement in the position of the 'direct producers' compared to say, feudalism or chattel slavery. Wage workers under capitalism are, mostly, free to sell their labour power to whichever capitalist they chose. As G. A. Cohen characteristically puts it 'You cannot be forced to do what you are not able to do, and you are not able to do what you are not free to do' (1981, 14). But that is not the end of the story. Wage labour under capitalism is founded upon a fundamental unfreedom. Generally, workers are not free *not* to sell their labour power, rather, they are forced to do so by the 'dull compulsion of economic relations' (Marx 1990, 809). This is why it is initially curious that Ramachandran's emphasis on the formal freedoms of workers under capitalism is neglected by Sen. However, perhaps it is not so surprising when we consider that such a discussion would ultimately undermine Sen's central claim about the market – that it is a source of expanding human freedom. Thus Cohen comments that 'to think of capitalism as a realm of freedom is to overlook half its nature' (Cohen 1981, 14). Capitalism generates certain freedoms. But it also generates certain unfreedoms.

Before proceeding further it is important to remember that really existing capitalism is often compatible with, based upon and generative of unfree labour. Brass's study of bonded labour in India argues that 'worker attachment is a form of unfreedom, the object of which is to discipline . . . control, and cheapen labour-power by preventing or curtailing both its commodification and the growth of a specifically proletarian consciousness' (Brass 1990, 37). In a similar vein Jan Breman's analysis of evolving rural and urban India finds that 'unfree labour may well and actually does go together with the drive towards capitalist accumulation dominating the economy of both rural and urban India' (Breman 1993, 168). And Jairus Banaji (2003) argues that 'Historically, capital accumulation has been characterized by considerable flexibility in the structuring of production and in the forms of labour used in producing surplus value', and cites examples as varied as sharecropping in colonial Bengal and the forced labour of Polish seasonal workers in Nazi Germany. Moreover Blackburn (1997) shows how the industrial revolution, based upon expanding free wage labour in Britain, stimulated the rapid growth of American slavery. Once we look more closely at the really existing social (class) relations of capitalism past and present we often find forms of unfree labour that would surprise us if we simply adopted Sen's benign approach to capitalist markets.

The nature of freedoms and unfreedoms under capitalism is intimately connected to the question of social class. Sen's comprehension of social classes under capitalism is grounded in a Weberian methodological individualism which, while it enables him to see the effects of class, as in the Bengal and other famines (see below), prevents him from connecting these effects to underlying systemic processes (Fine 2004). For example, in *DAF* he is critical of the activities of powerful interest groups and their abilities to influence public policy to their advantage and other groups' detriment. Such exercise of power is analysed by Weberian-influenced sociology more broadly (e.g. Tilly 1999) where classes are defined by their degree of access to or exclusion from economic opportunities, and the practice that E.O. Wright (2009, 104) labels 'opportunity hoarding': More powerful social classes attempt (and by definition mostly succeed) to monopolize access to wealth, power and status-generating resources, in the process excluding less powerful social classes from access to these resources, the social outcomes of which are visible in numerous spheres – from educational and employment attainment to escaping the worst effects of famines. While this approach understands that 'the economic advantages gained from being in a privileged class-position are causally connected to the disadvantages of those excluded from such positions' (Wright 2009), it does not illustrate how market mechanisms are both guarantor and outcome of exploitative class structures. Rather, it understands these processes as a natural outcome of the struggle for the realization of vested interests. From this angle, Sen argues that Adam Smith 'saw the need to understand the working of markets . . . *as an antidote* to the arguments standardly used by vested interests . . .' (Sen 1999, 121 emphasis added). In this schema, opportunity hoarding and vested interests are phenomena that constrain potentially liberating market mechanisms. But what if market mechanisms guarantee the reproduction of unequal access to resources – from rice to control over the means of production and labour power?

To understand this possibility it is necessary to recap upon Marx's contrast between the appearance of formal equality between capitalists and labourers in the labour market and the reality of class relations where the capitalists' ownership of the productive forces in turn *compels* workers 'to sell their labour power to the capitalists on terms that lead to their exploitation' (Callinicos 2000, 68). Or, as Erik Olin Wright puts it, exploitation is:

Defined by a particular kind of mechanism through which the *welfare* of the exploiters is causally related to the *deprivation* of the exploited. In exploitation, the material well being of exploiters causally depends upon their ability to appropriate the fruit of the labour of the exploited. (1994, 40).

For Marx capitalist exploitation is historically novel because it is generally achieved through economic means (the market) as opposed to extra-economic means (force) utilized under feudalism, slavery and other class societies (Marx 1975). That it is achieved via 'invisible' economic means both enables the existence of legally formal equal rights under capitalism, and makes it appear that these formal equalities are in fact real equalities (Wood 1999).

So while Sen can highlight the horrors of bonded labour, he is blind to those of wage labour. For example, he discusses the violence associated with US slavery, noting that many slaves escaped to join the armies of the North to fight against the South. But he also cites Fogel and Engerman's (1974) study of the conditions of US slaves and notes that:

The commodity basket of consumption of slaves compared favourably ... with the incomes of free agricultural labourers. And the slaves life expectancy too was, relatively speaking, not especially low – 'nearly identical with the life expectation of countries as advanced as France and Holland' and '*much longer* [than] *life expectations [of] free urban industrial workers in both the United States and Europe*'. (cited in Sen 1999, 28, emphasis added)

This passage reveals much about the brutal conditions of wage labourers under early capitalism in the United States and Europe. But, because of his commitment to and understanding of capitalism, Sen cannot investigate these causes further.

When investigating the transition from 'bonded' to 'free' labour, we are, in many ways, trying to understand processes of the widening and deepening of capitalist social relations. This expansion of market imperatives, in Britain and in all countries following its lead after the industrial revolution, has been one of violence and dispossession, rather than one of markets opening up new arenas of choice and freedom for individual actors (Byres, 2005). As Marx comments on the formation of the modern working class in Britain, they were 'forcibly expropriated from the soil, driven from their homes and turned into vagabonds'. And they were 'whipped, branded, tortured by laws so grotesquely terrible, into the discipline neces- sary for the wage system' (Marx 1990, 899). Here Marx points to the interrelation between the expansion of market imperatives and specific, property-based forms of law implemented and upheld by the modern capitalist state. As will be argued below, these observa- tions are crucial to understanding the root causes of famines and contemporary cases of chronic hunger and extreme non-freedom in the context of rapid economic growth and market expansion (see below).

Jairus Banaji (2003) notes that it is Marx's contestation of the concept of 'free' labour under capitalism that distinguishes him from the classical political economists that preceded him (notably Smith) and the neoclassicals and neoliberals that followed him. Marx does this by distinguishing between spheres of capitalist circulation and production. He characterized the former, which include labour markets, as the 'very Eden of the innate rights of man . . . Freedom, Equality, Property and Bentham' (Marx 1990, 280) where formal, individual contracts appear to govern relations between freely choos- ing individuals (employers and workers). But while Sen stops here, Marx goes further. He notes the transformation of the two parties: 'he who was previously the money-owner now strides out in front as a capitalist; the possessor of labour-power follows as his worker' (1990, 280). And, as Lebowitz notes 'They are entering the place of work . . . where the capitalist now has the opportunity to use that property right [the workers' labour power] which he has pur- chased' (Leibowitz 2002, 21). Marx continues and characterizes the employment contract as a 'legal fiction' which 'sustains the appear- ance of independence' (1990, 719). The relationship between 'freely choosing' workers and capitalists is one not between individuals but between social classes:

> In reality, the labourer belongs to capital before he has sold himself to capital. His economic bondage is both brought about and concealed by the periodic sale of himself, by his change of masters, and by the oscilla- tion in the market price of labour-power. (Marx 1990, 723)

Marx describes 'free' wage labour as wage-slavery in order to draw attention to the overriding element of unfreedom that characterizes class relations under capitalism, highlighting how individual workers' 'enslavement to capital is only concealed by the variety of individual capitalists to whom he sells himself' (Marx 1990). Manifestations of the unfreedoms of the capital–labour relationship are myriad, and include the degradation of worker under the capitalist division of labour. Ironically, given Sen's reliance on Smith, it is the latter not the former (despite his infinitely greater knowledge about historical capitalist development) who identified the consequences.

For Smith, the division of labour is 'the necessary, though very slow and gradual consequence of a certain propensity in human nature which has in view no such extensive utility: the propensity to truck, barter and exchange one thing for another' (1976, 25). While the capitalist division of labour gives rise to a significant rise in output, trade, and wealth generation, it also has the effect of degrading the workforce: 'the man whose whole life is spent performing a few simple operations . . . has no occasion to exert his understanding . . . He generally becomes as stupid and ignorant as it is possible for a human creature to become' (Smith 1976, 782)

If the foregoing argument is accepted – that capitalist markets are based intrinsically on combinations of freedoms and non-freedoms determined and mediated by class relations and competitive capital accumulation – then we are better placed to approach Sen's analysis of the relationship between markets and famines. And in doing so we can go beyond Sen in understanding the root causes of famines, chronic hunger and other processes of deepening capability deprivation.

Famines, Markets and Starvation

Sen grew up in British-controlled India and experienced first-hand the Great Bengal Famine where at least three million people perished. His *Poverty and Famines* (1982), where he offers an original interpretation of the causes of famines, is a celebrated text in development studies. It dismantles the food availability decline (FAD) thesis by showing how in cases from Bengal to the Sahel, food was available during famine periods and often in higher quantities than in non-famine periods. In both cases food was hoarded in response to 'market failures' (in particular lack of reliable information), leading to widespread starvation. In place of the FAD thesis Sen proposes the entitlement approach (EA). While this approach does not lead Sen to conclude that markets are sources of structural non-freedoms, I suggest that when placed in a broader historical framework, this is indeed the logical conclusion of his approach – that market dependence is based upon non-voluntary processes of dispossession, that it generates gross vulnerabilities among the poor, and that states play a central role in both generating and guaranteeing it (Peacock 2010). Sen's (1982, 45–46) entitlement approach enables him to illustrate how a family's or an individual's entitlement (access) to food, is determined principally by: (a) the endowment of the family or person, and (b) exchange relations. Endowments refer to individuals' or families' access to or ownership of land and/or their ability to work and sell their labour power in exchange for a wage (in Weberian terms, their control over resources). Exchange relations determine the relative prices of the individual's labour in relation to commodities – in these cases food (rice). Landed peasants can suffer 'direct entitlement failure' under conditions of flooding or drought, which disables them from growing enough food to sustain themselves. Wage workers can suffer 'trade entitlement failure' as a consequence of changes in relative prices between wages and food which disable them from purchasing sufficient food.

Sen (1982) illustrates how the Bengal famine was caused not by crop failure but by rapid price inflation (fuelled by British military and civil construction investments). Price inflation pushed up food prices relative to agricultural wages, leaving agricultural labourers unable to afford food (trade entitlement failure) (Sen 1982, 64–5). Because there was no general crop failure, peasants with access to land were relatively unaffected by price inflation. Non-military or civil-construction wage workers were, by contrast, particularly vulnerable. Consequently, these sections of the wage labour force bore the brunt of the more than three million deaths. The Bengal famine was not exceptional. Bhatia (1985) calculates that during British rule India experienced 25 major famines in which between thirty and forty million Indians perished. Sen also documents how similar dynamics of entitlement failure were at work in the 1974 Bangladesh famine. While food availability had increased and sufficed to feed the population in the first half of the year, flooding in June 1974 contributed to a combination of rising prices for rice, increased unemployment of rural labourers (no longer required to work the flooded land) and food hoarding. Agricultural wages fell, food prices rose and tens of thousands died (Sen 1982, 134; Alamgir 1980).

Inability to afford food stemmed not always from trade entitlement failure, but also from state actions, themselves often designed to expand and/or deepen commodity markets. Sen (1982, 122) observes how in the 1973 Sahel famine, sedentary agriculturalists were not only affected by drought, and thus rising food prices, but also by state taxation. Davis (2001) and Peacock (2010, 67) discuss how in the Egyptian famine of 1878 British authorities continued to collect taxes. Tax collection was not simply a revenue-generating mechanism, but one designed to initiate and then accelerate commercial agriculture (through cash-crop production) and market dependence (through proletarianization of the peasantry). Watts (1983, 276) cites the British governor of Zungeru (Nigeria) who, during the 1905 famine, suggested that 'the experience of hunger will stimulate the people to cultivate larger areas.' Taxation represented a tool for the social transformation of societies and the generation and expansion of market mechanisms favourable to the imperial and industrial centres. These processes constitute the historical background to Sen's analysis of famines:

> It is thus, from the ranks of the peasantry, that wage-labourers are recruited; they have little or no direct food entitlement, are therefore dependent on markets, and are highly vulnerable to price movements and the effects of famine. (Peacock, 2010, 67)

As argued in an earlier part of this chapter, these processes of dispossession (generating market dependence) via marketization and commercialization, are occurring at high speed in contemporary India and China, and the effects are manifested in mass unemployment, falling calorie intake, worsening health and degradation for tens if not hundreds of millions of these countries' poor.

Two important conclusions follow from this discussion. First, if the processes through which peasants become (fully or partially) proletarianized and market dependent, was not a voluntary one, but one generated and re-enforced through increasing competitive pressures and state actions, then clearly the establishment of (labour) markets is one based primarily upon market force(s), rather than participants' free will. Secondly, if market dependence makes wage labourers and poor peasants vulnerable to famine and chronic hunger then the argument that markets promote freedom is undermined.

This is not the only problem with Sen's analysis of famines. His methodological individualist conception of society leaves little room for considerations of collective action. But, as Pritam Singh notes:

> In the 1943 Bengal famine when about 3 million died, the better organized working class in Calcutta forced the then British government in India to arrange for food for them and was thus significantly less affected than the scattered, illiterate and unorganized rural population. (Singh, personal communcation)

Singh continues:

> When the British government decided to demolish the famine refugee camps which eventually worsened the conditions of the victims, the ruthless attention was on the camps housing the rural population and not the more conscious and more organized urban population. (personal communication, December 2011)

Collective action, based on common class experiences and interests, represents then, a key variable in the differential impacts upon 'the poor' of the famine and (regressive) state policy. Class relations are important in other ways too.

Sen proposes that democracy is the key guarantor of the poor's entitlements. But there are many forms of democracy, and the dominant contemporary form is often understood a 'low intensity' variant (Robinson 1996), which guarantees capitalist social property relations and leaves the poor vulnerable to depredation. Fine (2004) asks provocatively whether Sen's solution of more and enhanced democracy could practically, and should normatively, be applied to other commodities such as housing, health, education and employment. Such a move would require a radical social(ist) democracy based on increased labouring class power (see chapter 8). It would be accompanied by widening decommodification – a process whereby owners of capital exercise *decreasing* power over other actors in the market by virtue of their ability to command fewer (commodified) resources (McNally 2002).

While Sen's vision in *DAF* can only be realized through large-scale social change, he rejects such a course of action. Rather, he argues for the extension of market relations through, for example, the 'inclusion' of previously 'excluded' sections of society from the market aided benignly by the capitalist state. Not only does this approach *preclude* greater democracy and contribute to the re-subjection of labouring classes to the capital–labour relation, but, quite paradoxically, it pushes Sen back into a growth-based development paradigm.

Poverty as Capability Deprivation

Sen understands poverty as capability deprivation and fighting poverty as enhancing the poor's abilities 'to do things'. Because Sen dismisses the standard money-metric approaches to absolute poverty (the World Bank's notional US$1 a day), and because he understands development as the expansion of real, equal freedoms to all, he rejects

176

simply focusing on relieving absolute poverty, but aims also to eliminate relative poverty (often defined as those living on less than half the
average wage of any given society (Townsend 1993). Poverty should,
therefore be 'sensibly identified in terms of capability deprivation . . .
[by concentrating] . . . on deprivations that are *intrinsically* important
(unlike low income, which is only *instrumentally* significant)' (Sen
1999, 87). This enhances the 'understanding of the nature and causes
of poverty and deprivation by shifting primary attention away from
means (income) . . . to *ends* that people have reason to pursue, and
correspondingly, to the *freedoms* to be able to satisfy these ends' (Sen
1999, 90, emphases in original). This is a radical position indeed.

Despite these objectives, Sen also utilizes absolute and relative
approaches to poverty alleviation. He argues that the primary focus
of development work must be about the provision and expansion of
the poor's capabilities, which include adequate nutrition, access to
healthcare, acquisition of literacy and education and a low chance
of premature death. And beyond these 'fundamentals' or 'abso-
lutes' he also argues, in a relational vein, that the self-respect and
dignity provided by gainful employment within society are central
to development. And again he draws on Adam Smith. Smith had
argued, contrary to most neoliberals who claim him as their heir, for
a concept of what today would be conceived of as relative poverty,
maintaining that:

> By necessities I understand not only the commodities which are indis-
> pensably necessary for the support of life [neoliberals' absolute poverty
> line], but whatever the custom of the country renders it indecent for
> creditable people, even the lower order, to be without . . . Custom has
> rendered shoes a necessary of life in England. The poorest creditable
> person of either sex would be ashamed to appear in public without
> them. (Smith 1976, 869–70)

The contradiction of employing a relative understanding of poverty
and simultaneously portraying markets as potentially overcoming
such poverty is becoming clearer. On the one hand enabling the poor
to enjoy the basic abilities mentioned above (literacy, health etc.) constitutes something of a base line which benign states can realistically
be expected to aspire towards. Indeed, the institutions are in favour
of enabling the poor achieve these capabilities (via, for example, the
Millennium Development Goals). However, Sen wants more than
these basic, *absolute* capabilities. Dignity and the ability to appear in
public without shame are quintessentially *relational* properties. And
to achieve the latter implies ensuring that no individual lives beneath

the relative poverty line. But this requires a radical, redistributive, political economy.

But, at no point in *DAF* does Sen advocate placing limits on the accumulation of wealth by the rich, nor does he propose radical redistribution of wealth. While this may please his admirers in the neoliberal institutions, it undermines his own approach. This is because as the general wealth of a society increases, so does the median income rise, and, so too does the relative poverty line rise, under which live the poor: the richer a society becomes, the higher the relative poverty line (Townsend 1993).

Capitalism's class-based accumulation dynamic requires and reproduces unequal freedoms across society. Sen's vision of equality of capabilities and the ability to freely and equally make real life choices under capitalism is thus unrealizable. The logic of competitive capital accumulation is that as the rich in society accumulate ever more material goods, the poor will be forced to trail behind in the constant accumulation of goods, or risk 'shame'. The growth and accumulation imperative is back with a vengeance.

Without conceiving of some kind of limits on the wealth of the rich within countries (for example, maximum wage limits and very progressive welfare policies), Sen's vision goes up in smoke. Due to his political timidity Sen is unable to connect his vision to a politics capable of achieving it. However, if we turn to Marx we see a way to re-establish this connection.

Marx, Capabilities and Struggle

When we read Marx in relation to Sen we encounter many similarities. While their closeness enables Sen to quote Marx approvingly in order to bolster his own argument, he can only do so selectively, as a fuller engagement would run up against Marx's foundational critique of capitalism. If we allow ourselves to engage with Marx and Sen with a mind open to possible alternatives beyond capitalism, then we gain more from Marx *and* restore coherence to Sen's position. We also arrive at a very different understanding of the relationships between markets, states and individuals as illustrated in figure 7.2.

The foundation stone of Marxism is the development of human potential – the possibility of humans developing to great heights, unconstrained by oppressions associated with capitalism, in particular class-based exploitation. Hence, wealth in a future society will not be calculated in terms of competitive accumulation, but will be

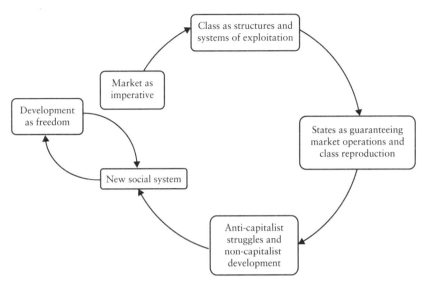

Figure 7.2 Anti-Capitalist Struggles as Process of Development

understood as 'the universality of individual needs, capacities, pleasures [and] productive forces . . .' Note here, that 'productive forces' is last in the list. A future, non-capitalist society is, contrary to Smith, one where

> nobody has one exclusive sphere of activity but each can become accomplished in any branch he wishes, society regulates the general production and then makes it possible for me to do one thing today and another tomorrow, to hunt in the morning, fish in the afternoon, rear cattle in the evening, criticize after dinner, . . . without ever becoming hunter, fisherman, shepherd or critic. (Marx and Engels 1976, 53)

Marx, therefore, views the possibilities and limits to extending humans' abilities and choices as determined by capitalist class relations and the balance of forces between those classes. Contrary to Sen and Smith, he does not regard the extension of these abilities as 'public goods' to be provided by a benign state, but portrays them as outcomes of successful workers' struggles. Unlike Sen, Marx connects explicitly the extension of worker's freedoms under capitalism to their struggles for better conditions. In fact at one time Sen came close to this conclusion himself. At the beginning of *On Economic Inequality*, he acknowledged that 'a perceived sense of inequality is a common ingredient in rebellion in societies . . .' (1973, 1). But to integrate this perspective into *DAF* would require an ideological shift beyond the political (but certainly not intellectual) willpower of Sen.

Conclusions

Development as Freedom represents a bold alternative development narrative. However, by wedding his vision to a conception of capitalist markets as spheres of freedom, Sen undermines his own attempts at seeking out alternative routes to human fulfilment. His framework (methodological individualism, a Weberian conception of class and a limited Smithian understanding of the market) disables him from getting at the root causes of mass deprivation. His critique of growth-based development is made untenable by his commitment to capitalism and private property and his subsequent inability to propose radical, distributive, developmental policies and practices.

An alternative approach rooted in Marxist political economy is potentially able to take up, make coherent and transform Sen's criticisms of capitalist development, into a broad, potentially transformative critique. While Sen weds his vision to the expansion of capitalist markets, Marxist political economy bases itself on the self-activity of the masses and the conviction that it is through such activity that capitalism can be transcended – into a system where development really is a process of a continual expansion of freedom for all.

— 8 —

TOWARDS A LABOUR-CENTRED
DEVELOPMENT

This book has conducted a critical engagement with thinkers who have formulated alternatives to (neo)liberal development theory and practice. Their work undermines monoeconomic and, for the most part, residualist conceptions of development. As liberal concepts of development become increasingly hard to sustain in the context of the current world economic crisis, non-liberal rising powers and mass struggles, their work will continue to represent important referent points for alternative developmental visions.

Friedrich List provides *the* foundational theory for Statist Political Economy, which was extended and contributed to by Alexander Gerschenkron. The former observed how, without state guidance (entailing direct investments, subsidy provision, tariffs, articulation of domestic economic sectors and external economic relations), less-developed countries were destined to remain in the global periphery, dominated economically and politically by industrially advanced countries. Gerschenkron's theoretical addition to these foundational principles was to show how the later the onset of attempted catch-up development, and the larger the development gap between economically advanced and backward countries, then the greater the coordinating role of the state in the process of catch-up. A corollary of this observation was that each subsequent successful case of catch-up development was based upon an institutional innovation (entailing a new set of relations between the state, financial institutions and industrial capital). In this way, Gerschenkron made a fundamental theoretical contribution to Statist Political Economy. However, his stress on (unpredictable) institutional innovations exposes the limitations of SPE's inductive (historically based) methodology. Lessons from yesterday may be necessary for the catch-up attempts of today

181

and tomorrow, but they are not sufficient, and what is sufficient is unspecifiable, precisely because it depends on something new (the institutional innovation).

Both List and Gerschenkron, however, shared the common assumption that workers needed to be manipulated and disciplined by the state, and subject to a labour regime designed to generate rapid productivity increases for capital. They attempted to soften or obscure the political implications of these assumptions by mystifying the catch-up process behind the veil of 'national development'. Marx critiqued List's political economy for, among other things, trying to obscure how raising labour productivity (or, in List's terminology, generating productive power based on mental capital) represented a strategy of raising the rate of exploitation of labour. In fact, SPE cannot conceive of a development strategy that does not rest upon labour exploitation. While it exposes the vacuity of (neo) liberal development theory and practice, it nevertheless has little to offer the world's poor in terms of a genuine human development strategy.

Joseph Schumpeter's great contribution to political economy is his concept of creative destruction. In its original formulation, the concept explains how capitalism is a system of continuous disruption, crisis and transformation. It also illuminates how capitalist competition generates a situation where a few entrepreneurs seize the lion's share of profits derived from industrial innovations, leaving the majority of normal businessmen with little more than 'wages to managers'. The concept suggests how it is perfectly normal to expect capitalism to evolve in the direction of monopoly and the domination of the economy by a minority of giant firms. We noted, however, that Schumpeter purposefully excluded the capital–labour relation from his concept, seeking to naturalize it through a functionalist conception of economic hierarchy, and that he operated within a framework of methodological nationalism, conceptualizing the economy in national, rather than international terms. Marx provides us with the tools to understand creative destruction as operating through sociospatial (class and international) dynamics. This then provides the basis for an analysis of how a few giant firms not only dominate national markets (as suggested by Schumpeter) but also straddle and dominate the global economy, monopolizing Schumpeterian 'rents' or Marx's super/surplus profits. Their domination rests upon their 'governance' (control) of global commodity chains. Such control enables TNCs to integrate and manipulate geographically dispersed but functionally integrated labour systems, with the objectives of using global wage

182

hierarchies to raise the rate of labour exploitation across the entire chain. A Marx-inspired reading of creative destruction illuminates, however, how these global commodity chains are also vulnerable to workers' disruptions of production. While Schumpeter provides no developmental alternative to labouring classes, he undermines, fundamentally, residualist conceptions of capitalist expansion and development.

Karl Polanyi and Amartya Sen provide us with very different understandings of development than the above-mentioned thinkers. Unlike List, Gerschenkron and Schumpeter, they understand development as human development, based upon societies organized around principles of mutual respect (Polanyi) and as a process where individuals are able to expand their freedoms (reducing negative freedoms and expanding positive freedoms) (Sen). Polanyi shows, with great force, how an untrammelled capitalist system undermines any hope of establishing a society based on mutual respect. Sen, in a similar fashion, shows how when development is conceptualized as economic growth or catch-up development, it requires the oppression of the greater part of society through the impositions of unfreedoms by states and firms. Within critical/left liberal and non-Marxist socialist traditions, Polanyi and Sen represent two of the most articulate and radical theorists of development. As we discussed, however, neither is able to incorporate, nor successfully rebut, Marx's analysis of exploitation. While Polanyi understands capitalist disruption as emerging from the subjection of society to market imperatives of profit-maximization and unregulated supply and demand, Sen sometimes slides dangerously close to a residualist conception of development, as when he portrays capitalist markets as potentially benign spheres of free interaction, and argues for development policy to 'integrate' the 'excluded' into these markets.

A consequence, however, of the above thinkers' rejection of Marx's theory of exploitation, is that they adhere in one way or another to elite conceptions of development. Table 8.1 summarizes each of the key thinker's core concerns and their (mostly elitist and exploitative) implications for labouring classes.

This book's argument has been that all of the above thinkers contribute significantly to our comprehension of the limitations and unrealities of (neo)liberal development. However, their alternative visions mostly fail to conceptualize (a) the form and content of unfreedom and exploitation under capitalism, (b) how this unfreedom and exploitation is bound up with unequal development, within and between nation states, and (c) which social classes benefit from

Table 8.1   Key Thinkers in the Political Economy of Development and their Relation to Labour

Key Thinker	Key Development Actor	Relation to Labour	Impacts on Labour
List and Gerschenkron	The State	Subordinate labour to capital accumulation.	Heightened rate of exploitation and initial (and potentially long-lasting) immiseration.
Schumpeter	Bourgeois Entrepreneur	Subordinate labour to entrepreneurial innovation.	Entrepreneurial rents 'trickle down' to labour in the form of higher wages/ better conditions.
Polanyi	Society and the State	Labour as constituent of society, and in potential cooperation with capital and the state.	Better working conditions and less exposure to market forces through instituted capital–labour relations.
Sen	State and Civil Society	State's role in removing labour's unfreedoms (e.g. bonded labour) and instituting 'free' access to markets.	Potentially greater freedom to choose employer.
Marx and Trotsky	Labouring Classes	Labouring class struggles as core determinants of human development.	Struggles for better conditions within, against and beyond capitalism.

and seek to reproduce, and which classes can resist (and potentially transcend) capitalist unfreedom and exploitation.

Only Karl Marx and Leon Trotsky address the above questions, and in doing so provide us with ways to begin thinking about an alternative vision and process of human development, and an alternative academic discipline of development studies. An alternative concept of labour-centred development would place labouring classes centre-stage of the development process and allocate them political primacy. It imagines what kinds of future they can create, and attempts to contribute to these futures by identifying limitations of capitalist development, and sources of workers' power under, and potentially beyond, capitalism.

Mainstream conceptions of capitalist development, either side of the state–market divide, relegate the work of labouring classes to the status of commodity inputs ('human capital') to the accumulation process. They mostly ignore the impacts of their preferred policies upon workers, and when they do focus on them, and (rarely) acknowledge their human costs, these costs are portrayed as 'necessary' but 'transitional' – between the 'tough choices' of today, and the developmental benefits tomorrow. The inescapable paradox of development theory and policy – the advocacy of exploiting, oppressing and constraining the human development of labouring classes, for their benefit – is thus continually reproduced.

An alternative, labour-centred conception of development and development studies does not ignore state and market actors and their attempts at augmenting their power. Rather, it entails at least three steps. It would, first, understand policies and strategies of states and capital as results of and responses to the dialectic of capital–labour relations. Secondly, it would view such actions from the perspective of labouring classes, illustrating, for example, their impacts on workers' human development. Thirdly, it would take sides with labouring classes, theoretically and politically, by, for example, attempting to illustrate potential weaknesses of states and capital, that could be used by workers to enhance their human developmental potential.

Class Relations as Determinants of Human Development

This and following sections discuss how class relations and struggles can be conceptualized as core determinants of human development (and non-development) at three analytically distinct but potentially interconnected registers. This entails conceptualizing and investigating (1) how states and capital determine (or limit) the developmental potential of labouring classes, (2) how labouring classes can extract developmental gains from states and capital and (3) how labouring classes can collectively challenge and potentially supersede capitalist social relations. This discussion is based on a strategic-relational conception of the state (and capital), as discussed in chapter 1, which understands the relations between labour, state and capital as contested and relatively fluid, and therefore containing the potential for labouring classes to generate real developmental gains within and beyond capitalist social relations. The extent of the malleability of capitalist social relations is represented in figure 8.1. It suggests that the extent of labour-centred development depends on the changing balance of class power, as represented by the vertical arrows, and the political economic 'space' that each social class controls. Such struggles will clearly generate social and political conflict and will require a flexible political strategy and tactics by labouring class organizations.

Before proceeding any further, it might be objected that arguing for labouring class organizations to ameliorate their conditions through class struggles against capital presupposes an already-accumulated sum of wealth (held by capital and the state) which can be partly or fully expropriated by labour. If this is correct, then labouring class organizations in poor countries must bide their time until such wealth has been generated, before struggling to get hold of it. Such a line of argument easily falls back into the stagism that Trotsky so effectively critiqued. It also ignores Marx's analysis of the possibilities that the Russian agricultural commune might avoid subsumption to capitalist social relations, and provide the first step towards a post-capitalist transformation.

Such arguments ignore (and sometimes purposefully occlude) the fact that the establishment of capitalist social relations was and is itself a process and outcome of (successful) class struggles from above, which have always been contested by labouring classes from below. In addition, and as highlighted by the strategic-relational conception of the state, these struggles are subsequently institutionalized within state agencies. Just as proponents of capitalist development are clear about their support for the creation of structures which facilitate capital accumulation, so a labour-centred conception of development supports labouring classes' attempts to extract as many concessions as possible from capital and the state within capitalism, and their attempts to challenge and supersede capitalism. The argument that labouring classes should wait for, or actively assist in, large-scale capital accumulation before pressing their claims upon the state and capital is one designed (often purposefully) to demobilize labour and to transform it into a commodity-input within the accumulation process.

The following discussion provides concrete examples of the process of moving from left to right in figure 8.1 – from a situation where labour is a commodity input within the accumulation process, to

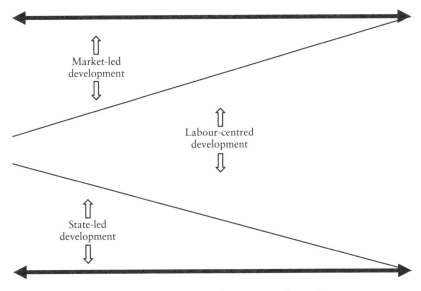

Figure 8.1   Conceptualizing Labour-Centred Development

where labouring classes purposefully generate and direct resources on an increasingly democratic basis. It starts, however, by discussing the capitalist labour process, an area of investigation all but ignored by List, Gerschenkron, Schumpeter, Polanyi and Sen, but central to the work of Marx and Trotsky.

The Capitalist Labour Process

Capital's principal way of determining and limiting labour's human development is through the capitalist labour process and the (re)production of class relations. The labour process represents a sphere of activity where production (of use and exchange values, and of surplus value) and reproduction (of capitalist class relations) occurs. As Marx puts it:

> Our capitalist has two objectives: in the first place, he want to produce a use-value which has exchange-value, i.e. an article destined to be sold, a commodity; and secondly he want to produce a commodity greater in value than the sum of the values of the commodities used to produce it [surplus value]. (Marx 1990, 293)

The implications for the two actors in this process, capital and labour, are first, that 'the worker works under the control of the capitalist to

187

whom [their] labour belongs', and second, that 'the product is the property of the capitalist and not that of the worker.' This is because 'From the instant [s]he steps into [work], the use-value of [her] labour-power, and therefore also its use . . . belongs to the capitalist' (Marx 1990, 291, 292).

Within the capitalist labour process, commodities are produced, surplus value generated and extracted and, most fundamentally, class relations are reproduced:

> On the one hand, the production process incessantly converts material wealth into capital, into the capitalist's means of enjoyment and his means of valorization. On the other hand, the worker always leaves the process in the same state as he entered it – a personal source of wealth [for the capitalist], but deprived of any means of making that wealth a reality for himself . . . *in short, the capitalist produces the worker as a wage-labourer.* This incessant reproduction, this perpetuation of the worker, is the absolutely necessary condition for capitalist production. (Marx 1990, 716, emphasis added)

Because firms relate to each other through constant competition, the labour process is characterized by an endless productivity drive designed to maximize the speed and intensity of the performance of tasks and the 'precision, predictability and quality of transformations being worked . . .' (Brighton Labour Process Group, 1977: 13). Once the employment contract has been signed and workers enter the workplace, managers attempt to ensure that they work as effectively as possible. However, as Smith (2006) observes, labour power is 'indeterminate' in that there is often a disjuncture between the expectations of managers and workers over what exactly needs to be done, how and how fast. Capital must therefore continually re-organize 'a system of power relations the function of which is to define and enforce the discipline of the labour process' (Brighton Labour Process Group, 1977, 13).

Ownership, control and organization of the production process, the means of production, workers' labour and the final commodity by capital are all indispensable in the process of producing surplus value, and are guaranteed by capitalist property relations backed up by capitalist states. Moreover, control over the labour market (the sphere of circulation), by, for example, ensuring that there are sufficient supplies of disciplined and available workers for hire, and at sufficiently low rates of pay as not to reduce capital's profits, is also part and parcel of capital and the state's attempts to structure and ensure the reproduction of the accumulation process. These social relations, which co-constitute the imperatives of competitive accumulation explain why capital will seek to reduce to a minimum, if not eliminate altogether, activities by labour that might limit capital accumulation. They also explain why capital attempts to commodify (to make sellable) everything beyond the workplace, as a means of subjecting all of society and nature to its objectives of profit maximization. Capital accumulation 'is the conquest of the world of social wealth. It is the extension of the area of exploited human material and, at the same time, the extension of the direct and indirect sway of the capitalist' (Marx 1990, 738–9).

As we have seen in chapters 2 and 4, capital in late-developing countries receives significant assistance in these objectives from states through the repression of labour organizations and movements. However, as discussed in chapter 3, Marx also highlights how while capitalists attempt to impose a strict work regime upon labour, the political economy of labour expresses a fundamentally opposed logic to that of capital. For workers 'Free time, disposable time, is wealth itself, partly for the enjoyment of the product, partly for . . . free activity . . .' (Marx, cited in McNally 2002, 185). The co-existence of two political economies, with diametrically opposed objectives, means that the capitalist labour process embodies contradictory, conflicting norms about the nature of human social relations that are sources of myriad forms of class struggle. Moreover, it is within and beyond the workplace that labouring classes possess the capacity to disrupt and potentially subvert capital's objectives.

Within the accumulation process Erik Olin Wright (2002) identifies and distinguishes two sources of power that can be utilized by labouring classes to ameliorate their working and living conditions. Structural power accrues to workers on the basis of their position in the production process and their ability to disrupt it. Associational power is a product of workers' collective organization comprising 'the various forms of power that result from the formation of collective organization of workers' (Wright 2002, 962). While workers' structural power is not automatically transformed into associational power, it can form the basis for generating and augmenting it, as we shall see below.

The Surplus Population

The power of capital to determine the form and content of workers' human development extends beyond the workplace however, as it creates not only a working class, but a large mass of unemployed

189

workers. Hence, '[t]he working population ... produces both the accumulation of capital and the means by which it is itself made relatively superfluous' (Marx 1990, 783). This is the 'relative surplus population' (also referred to as the reserve army of labour) of the unemployed. It is essential to capital since '[m]odern industry's whole form of motion ... depends on the constant transformation of a part of the working population into unemployed or semi-employed "hands"', because 'there must be the possibility of suddenly throwing great masses of men [and women] into the decisive areas without doing any damage to the scale of production in other spheres' (Marx 1990, 786, 785).

The relative surplus population plays both an economic role for capital, through supplying it with an ever-ready pool of labour for employment, and a political role, by 'disciplining' employed workers:

> The industrial reserve army, during the periods of stagnation and average prosperity, weighs down the active labour-army; during the periods of over-production and paroxysm, it holds its pretensions in check. Relative surplus population is therefore the pivot upon which the law of demand and supply of labour works. It confines the field of action of this law within the limits absolutely convenient to the activity of exploitation and to the domination of capital. (Marx 1990, 792)

This unemployed section of the labouring class enables capital to raise the rate of exploitation of employed workers:

> The overwork of the employed part of the working class swells the ranks of the reserve, while conversely the greater pressure that the latter by its competition exerts on the former, forces these to submit to overwork and to subjugation under the dictates of capital. The condemnation of one part of the working class to enforced idleness by the overwork of the other part, and the converse, becomes a means of enriching the individual capitalist. (Marx 1990, 789).

Marx (1990, 794–802) divides the relative surplus population into three sub-categories: the 'floating' section of workers which move from one job to another within modern industrial sectors; the latent surplus population, which is drawn out of agriculture to the industrial centres; and the 'stagnant' population, which finds 'extremely irregular employment' (Marx 1990, 796).

The management of the labour process, the wider labour regime and the generation of a relative surplus population represents capital's ability to determine and limit labour's developmental potential. Conversely, however, labour's structural and associational power within production, and forms of collective action outside the

190

workplace represents its vital source and capacity to begin realizing its own political economy and developmental agenda.

Limiting Labour's Development

Contemporary China provides many stark examples of how the capital–labour relation limits workers' human development. China has achieved major successes in its attempts to break into competitive world markets based on rapid economic growth over the last two decades. This economic 'upgrading' is based upon the exploitation of a fast-expanding labouring class (Hardy and Budd 2012). For example, Foster and McChesney (2012) describe how:

> The KYE factory in China produces manufactured goods for Microsoft and other U.S. factories . . . Workers reported spending ninety-seven hours a week at the factory before the recession . . . Workers race to meet the requirement of producing 2,000 Microsoft mice per shift. The factories are extremely crowded; one workshop, 105 feet by 105 feet, has almost 1,000 toiling workers. They are paid 65 cents an hour, with 52 cents an hour take-home pay, after the cost of abysmal factory food is deducted. Fourteen workers share each dorm room, sleeping on narrow bunk beds. They 'shower' by fetching hot water in a small plastic bucket for a sponge bath.

Microsoft's main rival, Apple, has been found to be relying on child labour in its supply chain (Garside 2013). As noted in the previous section, however, it is not only within the workplace that capital limits workers' human development. It does so too by structuring labour markets in ways designed to fragment potential labour unity and collective action.

India represents another economic 'rising power'. Within its booming economy the construction industry has grown, in terms of its contribution to the labour market, faster than any other sector, employing around 26 million informal workers in the mid-2000s and contributing close to 6 per cent of Indian employment (Pattenden 2012, 166, 7). Many workers in the industry originate from and often return to the agricultural sector. This 'circular migration' reflects broader processes of economic growth, urbanization and expanding non-agricultural employment common across the global south (Lerche 1999, in Pattenden 2012). Pattenden's description of the labour regime in Bangalore's construction sector, encompassing recruitment and on-site work, reveals ways in which capital generates

191

multi-stranded relations within the workforce in order to weaken it and lessen the dangers of collective action:

> Recruitment procedures are . . . central to the fragmentation and control of construction labour, and are part of broader subcontracting chains that offload risks (such as quality control or labour reliability) and minimize costs through a flexible labour force. On most projects a core of indirectly recruited and managed regular unskilled and semi-skilled labour will be supplemented by subcontracting gangs that complete specific tasks . . . on a piece-rate basis. (Pattenden 2012)

Pattenden also observes how:

> Construction capital . . . reduces costs and increases flexibility by hiring labour via intermediaries (maistries). As well as recruiting labour, maistries, who are usually drawn from its ranks, also tend to manage labour on a day-to-day basis . . . They act as a safety-valve for grievances, thereby providing a 'buffer against the entry of trade unionism'. (citing Shivakumar et al. 1991, 35; Pattenden 2012, 168)

A third strategy that capital uses to increase the rate of exploitation, is to employ gender and racial/ethnic differences as part of a hyper-babbagization strategy to further divide labouring classes, as described in chapter 5 (Schumpeter).

Commentators like Jeffrey Sachs, working within the residualist conception of human development discussed in chapter 1, argue that employment under the above-mentioned conditions represents an 'opportunity' for previously unemployed or underemployed workers to escape the poverty trap. But as discussed in chapter 5, it is more plausible to understand the proliferation of such employment practices as the formation of a global labouring class ripe for exploitation by capital (see also Cammack 2002). While a labour-centred approach highlights and explains these practices as rooted in capitalist exploitation, it also points to how workers can, even under very harsh circumstances, engage in collective action.

Labour's Power Under Capital

The ability of labour to disrupt capital accumulation and place demands upon employers and states reflects its structural and associational power. When this power is used effectively, it can begin to change the balance of class power, resulting in developmental gains to labour.

In his analysis of the evolution of capital–labour relations under South Korea's developmental state, and in stark contrast to the SPE tradition discussed in chapters 2 and 4, Dae-Oup Chang (2002) details how workers' struggles against the state and employers rose during the 1980s, reaching a crescendo around 1987. Between 1983 and 1986 real wages increased in manufacturing by about 8.95 per cent per annum. From 1987, at the peak of workers' mobilizations, wage increases in manufacturing accelerated: 10.4 per cent in 1987, 16.4 per cent in 1988, 20 per cent in 1989 and 16.8 per cent in 1990. Furthermore 'working hours decreased from 51.9 per week in 1987 to 47.5 in 1993, without decrease either in the workforce or in [the] real wage' (Chang, D. O. 2002, 18).

Chang also notes, however, that the upward curve of workers' struggles was met by a state/employer counter-offensive designed to weaken trade unions and, once again, raise the rate of exploitation (as under the prior dictatorship).

Working hours, which had continually shortened since 1986 . . . increased from 207 hours per month in 1997 to 226 hours per month by late 1999 . . . Real wage increases . . . slowed down, even showing a 9% real wage decrease in 1998. Increasing competition among workers has also increased the intensity of labour. (Chang, D. O. 2002, 36)

These observations highlight the interrelation between the balance of power between labouring classes, the state and capital, and the extent of the former's human developmental gains.

They are also potentially comparable to the evolution of capital–labour relations elsewhere in Asia. As already noted, contemporary China is characterized by an intense and highly exploitative labour regime where workers' living standards are continually squeezed to ensure rising profits for capital. Consumption as a percentage of Chinese GDP has fallen from 44 per cent to under 39 per cent between 2002 and 2010 (Foster and McChesney 2012). Its one-party system leaves little room for dissenting political organization or expression. Despite this deadening political and economic regime Chinese workers have engaged in mass struggles and have been able to defend and, in many cases, to ameliorate their conditions. The number of mass protests across China have risen over the last two decades – from 10,000 incidents involving 730,000 protestors in 1993 to 60,000 incidents involving more than three million protestors in 2003 (Silver and Zhang (2009, 176). In 2009 there were more than 90,000 mass incidents across China (Chinese Labour Bulletin, 2012). One consequence of these struggles has been that, as *The Economist* reports, '[a] spate of strikes has thrown a spanner into the workshop of the world', leading to manufacturing wages increasing by 17 per cent between 2009 and 2010 (Reinert 2011). Beyond wage increases, Silver and Zhang (2009, 176), argue that these protests have made the Chinese government increasingly fearful of political instability and socio-political breakdown. In response:

> Between 2003 and 2005, the central government and the Chinese Communist Party began to move away from a single-minded emphasis on attracting foreign capital and fostering economic growth at all costs to promoting the idea of a 'new development model' aimed at reducing inequalities among classes and regions as part of the pursuit of a 'harmonious society' . . . Likewise . . . the [state run] All China Federation of Trade Unions, amended its constitution to 'make the protection of workers' rights a priority in 2003'. (Chan and Kwan 2003, in Silver and Zhang 2009)

The nature of these mass incidents across China has also changed. While the majority of actions are defensive (seeking to retain established rights), offensive actions (seeking to establish new rights, conditions and pay rises) have increased, from between 9 per cent and 17 per cent of mass incidents prior to 2010, to around 30 per cent of mass incidents in 2010. These strikes are 'completely unrelated to the activities of the official trade union (the All China Federation of Trade Unions) (Chinese Labour Bulletin 2012,13, 17). However, the Chinese labour movement 'is still fragmented and transitory in nature. Any workers' organization that develops during a protest is usually disbanded after the specific grievances or demands that gave rise to it have been addressed' (Chinese Labour Bulletin 2012, 18). The challenge for the Chinese labour movement is to generate an organizational structure that enables it to formulate and pursue more consistently its aims and objectives, as against those of the Chinese state and national and foreign capital. Whether it is able to do so remains an open question.

An Example of Workers' Power and Human Development in North East Brazil

The Brazilian North East, once synonymous with drought, widespread human misery and paternalist relations between landlords and dependent peasantries, is now home to a fast-expanding zone

194

of export horticulture located within the São Francisco valley.[1] Thousands of hectares of irrigated land enable the production of high-quality grapes and mangoes for northern markets. The valley is but one of many zones of export horticulture production that have emerged across the global south over the last three decades, and that operate within tightly coordinated retailer-dominated supply chains. There are numerous cases, for example in South Africa and Chile, where profitable export horticulture is characterized by domineering farms and precarious conditions for labour – temporary contracts, low pay and limited union recognition or presence. In these cases profits to capital have not translated into improvements for workers.

In the São Francisco valley, however, the local rural workers' union, the *Sindicato dos Trabalhadores Rurais* (STR) has been able to mobilize the workforce in the export grape sector, and has generated significant developmental gains for the sector's workforce. As part of their competitive strategies and within the context of the global 'retail revolution' northern retailers have, since the 1990s, been ramping up requirements across their proliferating supplier base. Suppliers to northern supermarkets need to produce grapes according to an expanding range of buyer-determined requirements, such as fruit size, shape and colour. Meeting such standards requires farms to oversee an increasingly complex labour process. In order to carry out these operations, exporting farms rely on an increasingly skilled and hard-working labour force, of which a large percentage is female.

Initially, working conditions in the valley's export grape sector were very poor, characterized by low and often *ad hoc* pay, lack of employment security and even the use of child labour. As a lawyer from the STR described it:

Before we had the collective agreement, working on grape farms could be very dangerous. Workers were transported to the farms on top of lorries, they had to apply insecticides without using protective clothing, they might hurt themselves at work and not be able to continue working, and then the boss would sack them. Lunch breaks were not specified, with workers sometimes being forced to work throughout the day without a break, and safe drinking water was not provided. (cited in Selwyn 2007, 545)

---

[1] Supporting evidence, quotes and interpretations of this section can be found in Selwyn (2007, 2009 and 2012).

However, in the mid-1990s, the STR began an on-going campaign which has led to improvements in workers' pay and conditions. At the heart of STR's strategy of pressuring employers to ameliorate workers' conditions has been the threat, or use, of strike action. In order to meet retailer demands, exporting farms must implement a strict and precise production calendar, and any delays reduce fruit quality. This represents a strong reliance by farms on dedicated and skilled labour input. It also represents, for workers, a source of structural power, that is, the ability to disrupt production through suspensions of work. Short strikes by workers on exporting farms has deleterious consequences for fruit quality and its sale price. This structural power, which has been augmented by rising retailer demands, has been realized through workers' associational power – their ability to organize through the STR. Early gains made by the STR included commitments by farms to employ only registered workers, leading to pension and other social security contributions such as the rights for women workers to take paid maternity leave, specified working hours, payment above the minimum wage, higher pay for overtime, the provision of protective clothing to workers and the right for the STR to represent, organize and visit workers on farms during the working day. Subsequent gains have included the provision of crèche care, safe transport to and from work and the rights of workers to pursue an education outside work, implying the need for workers to be able to leave the farms on time.

Workers represented by the trade union enjoy substantially better conditions than prior to the STR's mobilization, and better conditions than unrepresented workers elsewhere in the fruiticulture sector. While these victories do not mark the end-point of the STR's campaign for ameliorating the pay and conditions of its members, they do demonstrate the developmental gains that can be won for workers by their own, collective, action.

Beyond the Formal Sector

The above examples have focused on formal-sector workplaces. However, as noted in this book's introduction, under contemporary capitalism, the growth of the global labouring class has taken many forms, including a fast-expanding informal sector, often located within or around the 'planet of slums' and experiencing particularly harsh conditions. These sections of the global labouring class reflect the inability of contemporary capitalism to generate a living wage across much of the world, and they correspond to Marx's description

196

of sections of the relative surplus population discussed above. But they have also shown their abilities to shape their own environments, through organizing against employers, and in the process ameliorating their own human development. As Gallin (2001, 538) notes 'what is true of workers in general is true of informal sector workers: they will organize whenever they have a chance to do so, and they are best organized by their own.' Organization takes myriad forms, within and beyond the workplace.

Instructive examples of informal-sector worker organization can be found in Brazil. The Landless Labourers Movement (*Movimento dos Trabalhadores Rurais Sem Terra*/MST) is perhaps the best-known case. Since its foundation in 1984 and the mid-2000s the MST's membership has grown to over one million. It is composed of former small farmers and rural wage labourers and their families who are unable to get access to land. The organization contests the highly unequal land structure in Brazil, where by 2008 around 3 per cent of the population owned over 60 per cent of all arable land (Zobel 2009). The MST has pursued a long-term strategy of occupying and cultivating unused land and claiming land-rights from the state. By the mid-2000s it had gained land-titles for more than 350,000 families. The MST has faced repression from the Brazilian state, and hostility from much of the Brazilian media. Nevertheless, it has demonstrated the ability of members of the surplus population to organize collectively, and to generate human developmental gains.

The MST, like all mass movements, contains contradictory tendencies. On the one hand its members include former small-scale farmers who want to re-establish themselves as such. While they challenge Brazil's agrarian property relations, they potentially also aspire to employing wage labour as part of their livelihoods/business model. On the other hand, the movement contains many former wage labourers who view gaining access to the land as their best hope of securing a livelihood, but who do not necessarily see themselves as future employers (see Wolford 2010). That the MST contains such contradictory elements is not surprising. The challenge for its more radical members is to envision and pursue a political economic strategy that does not go down the road of class differentiation (as is implied by the small-farmer project of potentially establishing wage–labour relations), and rather, continues to challenge Brazilian agrarian property relations and constructs (rural and urban) political alliances, whilst establishing for themselves viable rural livelihoods. The MST has, in turn, influenced other unemployed workers' movements in Brazil.

Between 1997 and 2005 homeless workers' organizations in São Paulo mobilized 10,000 people to occupy and live in empty buildings (Levy 2011, 74). The best known of these organizations is the *Movimento dos Trabalhadores Sem Teto* (Homeless Workers' Movement, MTST). As its name suggests, the movement originates from the MST and works closely with it. Just as the MST organizes its members to occupy land, the MTST organizes unemployed and informal-sector workers in urban areas to occupy and live in vacant buildings, hence establishing the basic essentials of a livelihood. De Souza (2007, 323) notes how squatting (of buildings and of land) represents a challenge to the 'capitalist order of private ownership' (see also Weinberg 2007). In the early 2000s the MTST also began establishing 'rurban' (rural-urban) settlements on the peripheries of cities on which its participants could combine agricultural activities (rearing animals and planting crops) with the search for urban-based work (De Souza 2007, 323).

Elsewhere in Brazil there are cases where relatively isolated workers have been incorporated into organized workers' movements. Approximately 5 per cent of the Brazilian population are employed as domestic workers, of whom 95 per cent are women and 60 per cent black. Many suffer from irregular and below minimum wage payments and lack social security provision (Gonçalves 2010, 64, 65). Gonçalves notes how:

> Paid domestic work does not constitute a choice for these women. Many of them start working when they are children, and when they become adults they have no chance of social mobility. Many of these women have grandmothers and mothers who work as domestic workers. (Gonçalves 2010, 68)

Despite their physical isolation and the myriad emotional ties between them and 'their' employing families that act as barriers to self-organization, domestic workers in Brazil have been able to mobilize over the last three decades. From the early 1980s with the formation of the National Front of Domestic Workers, to the formation of the National Federation of Domestic Workers (FENETRAD) in 1997, these organizations have been able to press the federal state to enhance their conditions. For example, during the establishment of the post-dictatorship constitution in 1988, and in the context of heightened mobilizations by trade unions and the (then politically radical) workers' party (PT), an 'alliance with the feminist and the women's movement resulted in many victories for the domestic workers being inscribed in the constitution' (Gonçalves 2010, 67).

These included a right to the minimum wage and maternity leave. Through further campaigning FENETRAD has been able to extend these rights to include the right to unemployment compensation, twenty days' paid holiday per annum and job guarantees for pregnant women (Gonçalves 2010). That these rights have been inscribed in the constitution and in law does not mean that all domestic workers experience them. Nevertheless, these legal provisions provide a basis for continuing mobilization and attempts by domestic workers' organizations to spread these gains.

Labour Against and Beyond Capital

So far we have discussed labour's ability to extract concessions from states and capital, thus generating developmental gains through partial alterations in the balance of class power, but while remaining subordinate to capital. This only represents a starting point in conceptualizing how labour can generate its own developmental trajectory, within, against and potentially beyond capital. Transcending capital, however, necessarily implies myriad contradictions in the human development process, as potentially new forms of organization and action are compromised and undermined through interaction with the old regime. As Marx argued:

> It must be kept in mind that the new forces of production and relations of production do not develop out of nothing, nor drop from the sky, nor from the womb of the self-positing Idea; but from within an antithesis to the existing development of production and the inherited, traditional relations of property. (Marx 1990, 278)

Following Marx, Michael Lebowitz (2010) uses the concepts of 'inroads' and 'encroachments' into capital's power over labour. Such inroads might entail, for example, labouring classes taking over capital's decision-making functions, such as resource allocation and investment. While such actions potentially represent the first move beyond capital, they remain within, and reproduce themselves through interaction with the broader capitalist political economy. This reproduction is contested and can lead in various directions – to further inroads and encroachments over, or to retreat in the face of capital.

Potential examples of movements that have attempted to make the kind of inroads that Lebowitz mentions are to be found in recent struggles in Venezuela, Bolivia, Egypt and Argentina respectively. In

199

Venezuela in 2010, the National Workers' Union campaigned for the central government to enact reforms providing full legal status to worker-run factories, reduce the legal working day from 8 to 6 hours and to allow paid time for participation in workers' councils and for political education (Duckworth 2010). In the early days of the Egyptian revolution, President Mubarak was overthrown, and workers' organizations began demanding radically new forms of industrial organization. One account reported how:

> Egypt's Iron and Steel workers . . . issued a statement of demands including the confiscation of private companies to be run by a new management by workers and technicians. They also called for a workers' monitoring committee in all workplaces monitoring production, prices, distribution and wages and a general assembly of all sectors and political trends of the people to develop a new constitution and elect real popular committees. (*Socialist Worker* 2011)[2]

Potentially more concrete examples of attempted inroads into capitalist property relations can be observed in recent struggles in Bolivia, in an echo of the Russian communes' struggles to pursue their own developmental path independent of encroachments by state and capital. As one of the poorest Latin American countries, albeit with an abundant resource base, successive Bolivian governments from the mid-1980s onwards embarked upon programmes of privatization, assisted by transnational development agencies, including the IFIs, bi-lateral aid agencies and a raft of NGOs, in an attempt to implement a new development 'model' from above (Perreault 2006, 152). However, resistance to the privatization of natural resources flourished during the 1990s culminating in the successful water and gas 'wars', in 2000 and 2003 respectively, where increasingly combative social movements forced the Bolivian government to rescind its plans to privatize these natural resources, and also began constituting a broader challenge to Bolivian neo-liberal capitalism. As Jeff Webber notes:

> [L]eft indigenous forces from 2000 to 2005 represented a *combined liberation struggle* which clarified the overlapping of racial oppression and class exploitation and was rooted in the experience of the traditional Bolivian working class, the urban informal proletariat and the poor and/or landless indigenous peasantry. (Webber 2008, 61)

---

[2] See Achcar (2013) for the most incisive account to date of the Arab uprisings.

The water and gas wars represented part of a broader 'revolutionary moment' in Bolivia's recent history which entailed the overthrowing of presidents and the election of a potentially radical new political party – the Movement Towards Socialism (MAS). They revealed, also, an alternative conception of human development. Webber documents how the *cocaleros* (coca-leaf growers), who had borne the brunt of the US-led, but locally implemented 'war on drugs' formulated a list of demands on the Bolivian state:

> They demanded the reassertion of popular collective control over privatized natural resources then in the hands of transnational capital, the recognition of indigenous land and territory, the free trade and industrialization of the coca leaf, democracy and social justice, human rights for the indigenous population, popular sovereignty for the Bolivian state (meaning both Bolivian independence from imperial impositions and the popular sovereignty of indigenous nations within the Bolivian state as against élite domination by a white-*mestizo* ruling class), the re-nationalization of privatized state enterprises, and a general rejection of the neoliberal economic model. (Webber 2008, 68)

The Bolivian case also reinforces how the expansion of capitalist social relation entail not just exploitation within the workplace, but simultaneously extended commodification beyond the workplace.

So far the above examples have been of demands on the state and capital made by labouring class movements. There are further, more concrete examples of how labouring class power has generated ameliorations in human livelihoods that cannot be conceptualized within elite-led conceptions of development. Argentina experienced a mass political uprising following the economic collapse of 2001. The uprising despatched several governments within weeks, and gave rise to numerous cases of industry controlled directly by workers. In the Neuquén province, for example, the Zanon tile factory was occupied:

> In October 2001, the workers officially declared the factory to be 'under workers' control'. By March 2002, the factory fully returned to production. . . . During the period of workers' control, the number of employees has increased from 300 to 470, and wages have risen by 100 pesos a month, and the level of production has increased. Accidents have fallen by 90%. (Elliot 2006)

The experience at Zanon was mirrored across Argentina where hundreds of workplaces, ranging from metallurgical companies, food- and meat-processing plants, printing companies, hotels and supermarkets to health and educational services, were taken over in response to the threat of closure and termination of employment. The process of occupation generated an alternative work ethic:

> Workers defend their own power over the organization of production and the decision-making process by proudly stressing their freedom from direct/supervisory control, the existence of egalitarian relations and the benefits of democratic participation. (Atzeni and Ghigliani 2007, 659)

In these cases hierarchical power structures have been replaced by workplace assemblies where all workers meet to discuss and decide questions of workplace management, and management councils, which are elected by the assemblies, to takes charge of daily administration, commercial responsibilities and legal representation (Atzeni and Ghigliani 2007, 660).

These examples of worker-cooperatives under self-management are not free from contradiction precisely because, as Michael Lebowitz highlights, they are cases of 'contested reproduction' and represent 'inroads' into capitalist socialist relations, rather than their transcendence. That is, workers' control exists within a broader context of societal reproduction determined by the imperatives of competitive capital accumulation. For example, while the labour process has become less intense, working hours have often lengthened, as cooperatives seek to meet client demands for products based on quality, timing of delivery and lowest price. While workers have gained an enhanced degree of freedom in work – within the sphere of production – they are still subject to the laws of the capitalist market in the sphere of circulation. Atzeni and Ghigliani conclude that:

> The absence of the capitalist, of hierarchy, of intermediate managerial layers and forms of direct control, expel the despotic rationality of capital from the sphere of production and open up a new space for workers' intervention. This tends to be directed to the establishment of a more democratic, egalitarian and participatory decision-making process at all levels, emphasized by the central role assigned to the general assembly and epitomized by the redistribution of income generated in equal parts. (Atzeni and Ghigliani 2007)

On the other hand, however:

> Once the collective of workers is confronted with the market, those spaces of autonomy and control, gained by workers after the expulsion of capital from the sphere of production, tend to be reduced. (Atzeni and Ghigliani 2007, 667–8)

202

Opponents of workers' control would argue that these examples demonstrate the limitations of such ventures and the superiority of strict, capitalist discipline within the workplace. But an alternative conclusion can be drawn. Workers' control of industry – from a single workplace, to a geographical region – will never translate into a non-capitalist form of human development as long as the capitalist market predominates in the sphere of circulation. Baldacchino (1990, 473) argues for strategies designed to prevent the degeneration of such cooperatives into worker-run capitalist enterprises through the creation of 'counter-institutional support' for workers' cooperatives. Such measures might include the establishment of mutual services, pooling of finance, research and development. And, in a similar vein, Egan (1990) argues that the relationship between workers' cooperatives and capitalist markets is mediated and determined by the broader societal balance of class power.

These examples raise two further questions, upon which this book draws to a close. How far can the political economy of labour be extended against capital before it supersedes it, and what forms of human development would arise from such transformations?

Human Development Beyond Capitalism

In chapter 3 (Marx) and in previous sections of this chapter we have discussed how the balance of class power exists within and beyond the capitalist workplace, and entails broader social relations encompassing resource generation, allocation, distribution and consumption. The extent of workers' control within and beyond the workplace corresponds in one way or another to the extent and nature of democracy within the broader political economic formation. Just as the relation between capital and labour takes various forms within the workplace, determined by the balance of class power, so there are various forms of democracy, entailing various distributions of political economic power.

At this point it may be objected that to identify the balance of class power as the core determinant of human development is to ignore the economic base upon which any form of development – capital-centred, state-led or labour-centred – must occur. Indeed, a core stated objective of statist and market-orientated development policy is to establish a 'productive' national economy that generates and allocates resources in ways that contribute, at some (ill-defined) point in the future, to human development. That is, the 'economy' provides the foundations for 'society'. It is in the establishment of this competitive and productive economic base that statists and market-centred economists justify their arguments about the need for labour exploitation and repression.

Such arguments are based upon assumptions of 'national' economic development. Human development under capitalism, however, is constituted through many determinations, ranging from local to national to global. To think of labour-centred development in purely national terms is to potentially retreat into a narrow stage-ist conception of development, that was so effectively criticized by Trotsky. Rather labour-centred development should be considered a global project, where labouring classes attempt to alter the balance of class power in their favour in the national sphere, while attempting to facilitate a more general global shift in the balance of class power. It is implausible to hope that a major shift of power towards labour in any single nation state would not attract the attention of international institutions, hegemonic powers and transnational capital, with the objectives of reversing the shift and re-establishing an economic regime more favourable to capital accumulation. International labour-centred development would require, and is predicated upon, international labour solidarity and cooperation between more and less economically advanced countries and regions. If such cooperation is successful, then it is possible to visualize how a shift in class power could be transformed into a radically new development regime.

The democratic control by labour over and redistribution of wealth, assets and investment decisions could generate the reduction and perhaps even eventual elimination of activities that do not con-tribute to the needs of labouring classes. Such activities might include advertising, duplication of production as a result of competition, mili-tary spending and luxury goods production (Kidron 2002). Instead of resources being wasted they could be diverted into socially useful activities such as enabling workers on the land to secure ecologically sound and sustainable productivity-enhancing technology, the appli-cation of labour-saving technology to the production of essential goods (food and clothes), investments in social housing, healthcare and education.

Greater democratic control over resources could lead to the re-allocation of benefits derived from productivity increases to labour, through shorter working hours, rather than to capital through higher profits. Not only could such a development strategy acceler-ate employment generation, it could also allow time for workers to formulate ever more advanced systems of work (thus raising productivity further), community-based democracy and, perhaps most importantly, increased leisure time, through which to further expand human development (Albert 2004; McNally 2002). Under such a development regime the concept of economic efficiency would be radically redefined. Instead of referring to capital accumulation, its criteria would be based on meeting human and environmental needs (Callinicos 2003, 110–11). It could potentially lead to a situation where lower growth rates yield proportionately higher increases in human well-being than under contemporary capitalism, and in so doing begin to address seriously the question of environmental degradation. While capitalism's productive dynamism is an outcome of blind competitive accumulation between capitals, the productive dynamism that would sustain a post-capitalist society could come from a radically different source: it could emerge from the generation of a feedback process between heightened democratic participation and the identification of the requirements for real human development. While the enhancement of productivity under capitalism is based on the democratic exclusion of labouring classes from the production process, post-capitalist dynamism would be based upon workers' ever greater democratic control over investment, production, distribution and consumption.

At this point it might be argued that the above vision might be applicable to societies or countries with a rich resource base, but not to poor countries that still need to establish such a resource base. However, it is worth re-emphasizing that resource constraints faced by poor countries are themselves often 'political' rather than 'natural'. As noted in Chapter 1 of this book, Sub-Saharan African countries, which are often uppermost in people's minds when discussing the need for economic development, are net creditors through capital flight, to the rest of the world. A fundamental shift in the balance of class power towards labouring classes, entailing some forms of democratic control over the banking systems in African countries, could entail reclaiming these lost funds and putting them to the service of real human development. Such objectives would require, and be predicated upon, international cooperation – both to avoid imperialist interventions to destabilize non- and anti-capitalist forms of development, and also as a means for fledgling democratic economies to reproduce themselves on an expanded scale, through reclaiming resources lost through capital flight. Changes in the balance of class power entail new forms of human development and new democratic systems.

Towards Economic Democracy

Atilio Boron (2005) identifies a range of democratic forms which potentially contribute to generating a labour-centred conception of development. The first three forms are compatible with and are possible under capitalism, while the fourth represents a fundamental encroachment upon the power of capital, so much so that it might be considered a transitional form, somewhere between capitalism and a future non-capitalist society. These forms are:

(1) Electoral Democracy – where elections are held on a regular basis but only act to fill the posts of executive and legislative functions of the state who then serve 'market forces'. This is a system described by Noam Chomsky (1991) as 'Low Intensity Democracy'.
(2) Political Democracy – where some degree of effective political representation, a genuine division of powers and improvements in the mechanisms of popular participation in decision making occur. For example, writers such as Heller (2001) view the participatory budgeting that emerged in Porto Alegre in the 1990s, based in the prior struggles of the 1970s and 1980s for political and economic democratization, as representing a significant democratic advance beyond simple electoral democracy.
(3) Social Democracy – where elements of the first two forms are combined with a 'social citizenship'. The latter embodies the 'granting of a wide spectrum of [decommodified] entitlements' in terms of living standards and universal access to educational, housing and health services' (Boron 2005, 52). Decommodification means that a person can survive 'without depending on the market's capricious movements' (ibid.). A more advanced system of social democracy might include the guarantee of full employment, and the provision of a basic income (Weeks 2011). As Gøsta Esping-Andersen (1990) argues, this form of democracy 'strengthens the worker and debilitates the absolute authority of the employers' (cited in Boron 2005, 52).
(4) Economic Democracy – where private firms, or 'the economy' are subject to public, democratic control. Producer-consumer cooperatives might begin playing a role in the generation, allocation and employment of resources (Sklair 2011; Albert 2004), and crucially, would enable the kinds of 'counter-institutional support' noted above, to worker-managed industries necessary

to prevent the latter sliding back into the logic of capitalist cost-benefit rationalization.

If it is theoretically inconclusive whether economic democracy entails the transcendence of capitalism it is because it has not yet been experienced.

However, the history of capitalist development and labouring class struggles, and the theoretical insights gleaned from Marx and Trotsky, suggest that such a form of political economic organization will only come about through a fundamental shift in the balance of class power. In all probability this will take the form of one or several revolution(s), since capitalist firms and states have proven time and again their ability to subvert attempts at reforming them from below by labouring classes, or those that aim to act on their behalf. During such a transformation there will be, in all probability, further societal debates about the possibilities of extending democracy into previously hierarchical (state or private) spheres.

The above schema is not intended to imply a sequence of 'stages' where less-developed countries move from lower to higher stages of democracy. As the recent revolutions of the 'Arab Spring' demonstrate, struggles against dictatorship contain within them myriad forces and potentialities, ranging from counter-revolutions to the implementation of shallow Western-backed electoral democracies, to attempts at constructing more developed economic democracies. As with all struggles, the particular democratic and political economic forms that emerge will depend on the power, strategies and capacities of the contending forces to demonstrate to wider society that their programme represents the most realizable strategy and path to real human development. They will also depend on the international configuration of class forces.

Capitalist development (entailing capital accumulation, industrial diversification and augmentation of state power), which is either the objective of or underlies most conceptions of human development, 'distort[s] the worker into a fragment' of a person (Marx 1990, 799). In contrast to this miserable existence, Marx argued for the need to create an alternative political economic system organized to achieve maximum collective and individual fulfilment, based on the 'the absolute working out of [her] creative potentialities', where 'the development of all human powers [is].. the end itself' (Marx 1993, 488). This system would establish a society where 'the free development of each is the condition for the free development of all' (Marx and Engels 1967 [1848], 105). Such a social system remains

207

a possibility. However, to create it requires an immense effort. That effort, based upon the resistance to capitalist exploitation, entails and requires an alternative process of labour-centred human development. The transformative possibilities of such development are potentially immense. In the act of producing their lives, Marx noted, 'the producers change, too, in that they bring out new qualities in themselves, develop themselves in production, transform themselves, develop new powers and new ideas, new modes of intercourse, new needs and new language' (Marx 1993, 494).

The core argument of this book has been that the extent and nature of human development is determined, fundamentally, by class relations under (and potentially beyond) capitalism in general, and the balance of class power in particular. The struggle against exploitation takes myriad forms and has many outcomes. The challenge of a labour-centred development is to conceptually connect these struggles and their potential outcomes to a vision of human development free from exploitation.

REFERENCES AND FURTHER READING

Abu-Lughod, L. 2009. 'Dialects of Women's Empowerment: The International Circuitry of the Arab Human Development Report 2005'. *International Journal of Middle East Studies*, 41 (1): 83–103.

Achcar, G. 2013. *The People Want: A Radical Exploration of the Arab Uprising*. London: Saqi Books.

Ahmad, A. 1994. *In Theory: Classes, Nations, Literatures*. London: Verso.

Alamgir, M. 1980. *Famine in South Asia: Political Economy of Mass Starvation*. Cambridge, MA: Oelgeschlager, Gunn and Hain.

Albert, M. 2004. *Parecon: Life After Capitalism*. London: Verso.

Allen, K. 2004. *Max Weber: A Critical Introduction*. London: Pluto.

Amsden, A. 1989. *Asia's Next Giant: South Korea and Late Industrialization*. New York: Oxford University Press.

— 1990. 'Third World Industrialisation: Global Fordism or a New Model?' *New Left Review* 1 (182): 5–31.

— 2007. *Escape from Empire: The Developing World's Journey Through Heaven and Hell*. Cambridge, MA: MIT Press.

Anderson, B. 2004. 'In the World-Shadow of Bismarck and Nobel'. *New Left Review*, 28 (July–August): 85–129.

Anderson, K. 2010. *Marx at the Margins: On Nationalism, Ethnicity and Non-Western Societies*. Chicago: University of Chicago Press.

Anderson, P. 1974. *Lineages of the Absolutist State*. London: New LeftBooks.

Applebaum, R. 2008. 'Giant Transnational Contractors in East Asia'. *Competition and Change*, 12 (1): 69–87.

Araghi, F. 2000. 'The Great Global Enclosure of our Times: Peasants and the Agrarian Question at the End of the Twentieth Century'. In *Hungry for Profit: The Agribusiness Threat to Farmers*, ed. J. B. Foster and F. Buttel, 145–60. New York: Monthly Review.

— 2003. 'Food Regimes and the Production of Value: Some Methodological Issues'. *Journal of Peasant Studies*, 30 (2): 41–70.

Arrighi, G. 2007. *Adam Smith in Beijing: Lineages of the Twenty-First Century*. London: Verso.

Arrighi, G. and G. Drangel, 1986. 'Stratification of the World-Economy: An Explanation of the Semiperipheral Zone'. *Review*, 10 (1): 9–74.

Arrighi, G. and J. Moore, 2001. 'Capitalist Development in World Historical Perspective'. In *Phases of Capitalist Development: Booms, Crises, and Globalization*, ed. R. Albritton et al., 56–75. New York: Palgrave.

Arrighi, G., B. Silver and B. Brewer, 2003. 'Industrial Convergence, Globalization, and the Persistence of the North–South Divide'. *Studies in Comparative International Development*, 38 (1): 3–31.

Ashman, S. 2006. 'From World Market to World Economy'. In *100 Years of Permanent Revolution: Results and Prospects*, ed. B. Dunn. and H. Radice, 88–104. London: Pluto.

— 2009. 'Capitalism, Uneven and Combined Development and the Transhistoric'. *Cambridge Review of International Affairs*, 22 (1): 29–46.

Atzeni, M. and P. Ghigliani, 2007. 'Labour Process and Decision-making in Factories Under Workers' Self-Management: Empirical Evidence from Argentina'. *Work, Employment & Society*, December, 21 (4): 653–71.

Babbage, C. 1835. *On the Economy of Machinery and Manufactures. Fourth Edition*. London: Charles Knight.

Babones, S. 2002. 'Population and Sample Selection Effects in Measuring International Income Inequality'. *Journal of World-Systems Research*, VIII (I): 8–28.

Bagchi, A. 2000. 'Freedom and Development as End of Alienation?' *Economic and Political Weekly*, 9 December, 50 (35): 4408–20.

Bair, J. 2005. 'Global Capitalism and Commodity Chains: Looking Back, Going Forward'. *Competition and Change*, 9 (2): 153–80.

Bairoch, P. 1993. *Economics and World History: Myths and Paradoxes*. Brighton: Wheatsheaf.

Bairoch, P. and R. Kozul-Wright, 1996. *Globalization Myths: Some Historical Reflections on Integration, Industrialization and Growth in the World Economy*. UNCTAD Discussion Papers, 113. http://biblioteca.hegoa.ehu. es/system/ebooks/7376/original/Globalization_Myths._Some_Historical_Refle ctions_on_Integration.pdf [accessed 25 September 2011].

Baldacchino, G. 1990. 'A War of Position: Ideas on Strategy for Worker Cooperative Development'. *Economic and Industrial Democracy*, 11 (4): 463–82.

Banaji, J. 2003. 'The Fictions of Free Labour: Contract, Coercion and So-Called Unfree Labour'. *Historical Materialism*, 11 (3): 69–95.

Baran, P. and P. Sweezy, 1966. *Monopoly Capital*. New York: Monthly Review.

Barboza, D. 2010. 'Foxconn Increases Size of Raise in Chinese Factories'. *New York Times*, 6 June. http://www.nytimes.com/2010/06/07/business/ global/07foxconn.html [accessed 1 March 2012].

Barker, C. 1998. 'Industrialism, Capitalism, Value, Force and States: Some Theoretical Remarks'. Anglo-Bulgarian Comparative History Seminar, Wolverhampton University.

— 2006. 'Capital and Revolutionary Practice'. *Historical Materialism*, 14 (2): 55–82.

— ed. 1987. *Revolutionary Rehearsals*. London: Bookmarks.

Bensaïd, D. 2002. *Marx for Our Times: The Adventures and Misadventures of a Critique*. London: Verso.

Berger, S. 2008. 'Circular Cumulative Causation (CCC) à la Myrdal and Kapp: Political Institutionalism for Minimizing Social Costs'. *Journal of Economic Issues*, 42 (2): 357–65.

Bergquist, C. 1986. *Labour in Latin America: Comparative Essays on Chile, Argentina, Venezuela and Colombia*. Stanford: Stanford University Press.

Berlin, I. 1960. 'Introduction'. In *Roots of a Revolution: A History of the Popular and Socialist Movements in Nineteenth Century Russia*, ed. F. Venturi, trans. F. Haskell, 1–4. London: Weidenfeld & Nicolson.

— 1969. *Four Essays on Liberty*. Oxford: Oxford University Press.

Bernard, M. and J. Ravenhill, 1995. 'Beyond Product Cycles and Flying Geese Regionalization, Hierarchy, and the Industrialization of East Asia'. *World Politics*, 47 (January): 171–209.

Bernstein, H. 1992. 'Poverty and the Poor'. In *Rural Livelihoods: Crises and Responses*, ed. H. Bernstein, B. Crow and H. Johnson, 13–26. Oxford: Oxford University Press.

— 2005. 'Development Studies and the Marxists'. In *A Radical History of Development Studies*, ed. U. Kothari, 11–137. London: Zed.

— 2009. 'Agrarian Questions from Transitions to Globalization'. In *Peasants and Globalization: Political Economy, Rural Transformation and Agrarian Question*, ed. H. Akram-Lodhi and C. Kay, 239–61. London: Routledge.

— 2010. *Class Dynamics and Agrarian Change*. Halifax: Kumarian Press.

Bhatia, B. M. 1985. *Famines in India: A Study in Some Aspects of the Economic History of India with Special Reference to Food Problems*. Delhi: Konark.

Bienefeld, M. 1991. 'Karl Polanyi and the Contradictions of the 1980s'. In *The Legacy of Karl Polanyi*, ed. M. Mendell and D. Salee, 3–28. Basingstoke: Palgrave.

Binns, P. and M. Gonzalez, 1980. 'Cuba, Castro and Socialism'. *International Socialism Journal*, 2 (8): 1–36.

Blackburn, R. 1997. *The Making of New World Slavery from the Baroque to the Modern, 1492–1800*. London: Verso.

Blaug, M. 1973. 'Was There a Marginalist Revolution?' *The Marginal Revolution in Economics*. In ed. C. Black, A. Coats and D. Goodwin. Durham, NC: Duke University Press.

— 1985. *Economic Theory in Retrospect. Fourth Edition*. Cambridge: Cambridge University Press.

Block, F. 2001. 'Introduction'. In K. Polanyi, *The Great Transformation*, xviii–xxxviii. Boston, MA: Beacon Press.

Bolsinger, E. 2004. 'The Foundation of Mercantile Realism: Friedrich List and the Theory of International Political Economy'. Paper presented at the 54th Political Studies Association Annual Conference, University of Lincoln.

Booth, D. 1985. 'Marxism and Development in Sociology: Interpreting the Impasse'. *World Development*, 13: 761–87.

Bornschier, V. 1992. 'The European Community's Uprising: Grasping Towards Hegemony or Therapy Against National Decline in the World Political Economy?' Paper presented at the First European Conference of Sociology, Vienna.

Boron, A. 2005. 'The Truth About Capitalist Democracy'. *Socialist Register*. 28–58.

Bottomore, T. 1992. *Between Marginalism and Marxism: The Economic Sociology of J. A. Schumpeter*. London: Harvester Wheatsheaf.

Boyce, J. and L. Ndikumana 2011. 'African Debt: Funny Money and Stolen

211

Lives'. *African Arguments*. http://africanarguments.org/2011/09/28/african-debt-funny-money-and-stolen-lives-by-james-k-boyce-and-leonce-ndikumana/ [accessed 12 November 2012].

Brady, N. and D. Martin, 2007. 'Workers of the Less Developed World Unite? A Multilevel Analysis of Unionization in Less Developed Countries'. *American Sociological Review*, 72 (4): 562–84.

Brass, T. 1990. 'Class Struggle and the Deproletarianisation of Agricultural Labour in Haryana'. *Journal of Peasant Studies*, 18 (1): 36–67.

Braverman, H. 1998. *Labour and Monopoly Capital: The Degradation of Work in the Twentieth Century*. New York: Monthly Review Press.

Breman, J. 1993. *Beyond Patronage and Exploitation: Changing Agrarian Relations in South Gujarat*. Oxford: Oxford University Press.

Brenner, R. 1977. 'The Origins of Capitalist Development: A Critique of Neo-Smithian Marxism'. *New Left Review*, 104: 25–92.

— 1986. 'The Social Basis of Economic Development'. In *Analytical Marxism*, ed. J. Roemer, 23–53.Cambridge: Cambridge University Press.

Breslin, S. 2011. 'The 'China Model' and the Global Crisis: From Friedrich List to a Chinese Mode of Governance?'. *International Affairs*, 87 (6): 1323–43.

Brett, E. 2009. *Reconstructing Development Theory*. Basingstoke: Palgrave.

Brighton Labour Process Group 1977. 'The Capitalist Labour Process'. *Capital & Class*, (1): 3–22.

Brezinski, Z. 2007. *Second Chance: Three Presidents and the Crisis of the American Superpower*. New York: Basic Books.

Buckley, P. and P. Ghauri, 2004. 'Globalisation, Economic Geography and the Strategy of Multinational Enterprises'. *Journal of International Business Studies*, 35: 81–98.

Bukharin, N. 1925. *Historical Materialism*. New York: International Publishers.

— 1973. 'Imperialism and World Economy'. *New York Monthly Review*.

Burkett, P. and M. Hart-Landsberg, 2003. 'A Critique of "Catch-Up": Theories of Development'. *Journal of Contemporary Asia*, 33 (3): 147–71.

Burawoy, M. 1985. *The Politics of Production: Factory Regimes Under Capitalism and Socialism*. London: Verso.

— 2003. 'For a Sociological Marxism: The Complementary Convergence of Antonio Gramsci and Karl Polanyi'. *Politics and Society*, 31 (2): 193–261.

— 2010. 'From Polanyi to Pollyanna: The False Optimism of Global Labour Studies'. *Global Labour Journal*, 1 (2): 301–13.

Byres, T. J. 1991. 'The Agrarian Question and Differing Forms of Capitalist Transition: An Essay with Reference to Asia'. In *Rural Transformations in Asia*, ed. J. Breman and S. Mundle. Oxford: Oxford University Press.

— 2005. 'Neoliberalism and Primitive Accumulation in Less Developed Countries'. In *Neoliberalism: A Critical Reader*, ed. A. Saad-Filho, 83–90. London: Pluto.

Callinicos, A. 1993. 'Bourgeois Revolutions and Historical Materialism'. In *Marxism and the Great French Revolution*, ed. P. McGarr and A. Callinicos, 113–71. London: Bookmarks.

— 1995. *Race and Class*. London: Bookmarks.

— 2000. *Equality*. Cambridge: Polity.

— 2003. *Anti-Capitalist Manifesto*. Cambridge: Polity.

Callinicos, A. and C. Harman, 1989. *The Changing Working Class*. London: Bookmarks.

Cammack, P. 2002. 'Attacking the Poor'. *New Left Review*, 13 (January–February): 125–34.

Capps, G. 2010. 'Tribal Landed Property: The Political Economy of the BaFokeng Chieftaincy, South Africa, 1837–1994'. PhD Dissertation, Development Studies Institute, London School of Economics.

Cardoso, F. H. and E. Faletto, 1979. *Dependency and Development in Latin America*. Berkeley: University of California Press.

Catephores, G. 1994. 'The Imperious Austrian: Schumpeter as Bourgeois Marxist'. *New Left Review*, 205 (l): 3–30.

Ceruti, C. 2007. 'Divisions and Dependencies Among Working and Workless'. *South African Labour Bulletin*, 31 (2): 22–4.

Chan, A. 2007. 'Organizing Wal-Mart in China: Two Steps Forward, One Step Back for China's Unions'. *New Labour Forum*, 16 (2): 87–96.

Chan, S. and D. Kwan, 2003. 'Union's New Approach Puts Workers' Rights First'. *South China Morning Post*, 12 September.

Chandrasekhar, C. P. 2005. 'Alexander Gerschenkron and Late Industrialization'. In *The Pioneers of Development Economics*, ed. K. S. Jomo, 181–92. London: Zed Books.

Chang, D.-O. 2002. 'Korean Labour Relations in Transition: Authoritarian Flexibility'. *Labour, Capital and Society*. 35 (1). 10–40.

Chang, H. J. 2002. *Kicking Away the Ladder? Development Strategy in Historical Perspective*. London: Anthem.

— 2005. *The East Asian Development Experience: The Miracle, the Crisis, and the Future*. London: Third World Network and Zed Press.

— 2007. 'Protecting the Poor'. *Prospect*, 136. http://www.prospect-magazine.co.uk/article_details.php?id=9653 [accessed 5 May 2008].

— 2012 'Africa Needs an Active Industrial Policy to Sustain its Growth'. *Guardian: Comment is Free*, 15 July. http://www.guardian.co.uk/commentisfree/2012/jul/15/africa-industrial-policy-washington-orthodoxy [accessed 13 May 2013].

Chang, H. J. and I. Grabel, 2004. *Reclaiming Development: An Alternative Economic Policy Manual*. London: Zed Press.

Chase-Dunn, C. 1989. *Global Formation: Structures of the World Economy*. London: Basil Blackwell.

Chibber, V. 2005. 'Reviving the Developmental State: The Myth of the "National Bourgeoisie"'. *Socialist Register*, 41: 144–65.

Chinese Labour Bulletin, 2012. *A Decade of Change: The Workers' Movement in China 2000–2012*. Hong Kong.

Chomsky, N. 1991. *Deterring Democracy*. London: Verso.

Clark, G., M. Huberman and P. Lindert, 1995. 'A British Food Puzzle, 1770–1850'. *Economic History Review*, 48 (2): 215–37.

Cliff, T. 1963. 'Deflected Permanent Revolution'. *International Socialism*, 12 (Spring): 1–18.

— 1974. *State Capitalism in Russia*. London: Pluto.

— 1979. 'The Balance of Class Forces in Recent Years'. *International Socialism Journal*, 2 (6). http://www.marxists.org/archive/cliff/works/1979/xx/balance1.htm [accessed 5 June 2011].

213

— 1990. *Trotsky. Vol 2: The Sword of the Revolution 1917–1923*. London: Bookmarks.

— 1995. 'In the Balance'. *Socialist Review*, February, 15–19. http://pubs.socia listreviewindex.org.uk/sr183/cliff.htm [accessed 13 February, 2012].

— 1999. *Trotskyism After Trotsky: The Origins of the International Socialists*. London: Bookmarks.

Cohen, G. A. 1981. 'Freedom, Justice and Capitalism'. *New Left Review*, 1/126 (March–April): 3–16.

Collier, P. 2007. *The Bottom Billion. Why the Poorest Countries Are Failing and What Can Be Done About It*. Oxford: Oxford University Press.

Collins, C., C. Hartman and H. Sklar, 1999. *Divided Decade: Economic Disparity at the Century's Turn*. http://www.economiajusta.org/files/pdf/DivDec.pdf [accessed 20 July 2012].

Corbridge, S. 2002. 'Development as Freedom: The Spaces of Amartya Sen'. *Progress in Development Studies*, 2 (3): 183–217.

— 2007. 'The (Im)Possibility of Development Studies'. *Economy and Society*, 36 (2): 179–211.

Cowen, M. and R. Shenton, 1995. 'The Invention of Development'. In *Power of Development*, ed. J. Crush, 27–43. London: Routledge.

— 1996. *Doctrines of Development*. London: Routledge.

Cruddas, J. 2012. 'Jon Cruddas on Building the New Jerusalem'. *The New Statesman*, 30 September. http://www.newstatesman.com/politics/politics/2012/09/jon-cruddas-building-new-jerusalem?page=1 [accessed 1 November 2012].

Dale, G. 2004. *Between State Capitalism and Globalisation: The Collapse of the East German Economy*. Bern: Peter Lang.

— 2008. 'Karl Polanyi's The Great Transformation: Perverse Effects, Protectionism and Gemeinschaft'. *Economy and Society*, 37 (4): 495–524.

— 2010. *Karl Polanyi: The Limits of the Market*. Cambridge: Polity.

— 2012. 'The Growth Paradigm: A Critique'. *International Socialism Journal*, 134. http://www.isj.org.uk/index.php4?id=798&issue=134 [accessed 1 May 2012].

Davidson, N. 2005. 'How Revolutionary Were the Bourgeois Revolutions?' *Historical Materialism*, 13 (3): 3–38.

— 2006. 'From Uneven to Combined Development'. In *100 Years of Permanent Revolution: Results and Prospects*, ed. B. Dunn and H. Radice, 10–26. London: Pluto.

— 2010. 'From Deflected Permanent Revolution to the Law of Uneven and Combined Development'. *International Socialism*, 128 (Autumn). www.isj.org.uk/?id=686 [accessed 6 April 2011].

Davies, J., S. Sandström, A. Shorrocks and E. Wolff, 2008. *The World Distribution of Household Wealth*. UNU-WIDER Discussion Paper 03.

Davis, M. 2001. *Late Victorian Holocaust: El Niño Famines and the Making of the Third World*. London: Verso.

— 2006. *Planet of Slums*. London: Verso.

Dawidoff, N. 2002. *The Fly Swatter: How my Grandfather Made his Way in the World*. New York: Pantheon Books.

Day, R. and D. Gaido, eds. 2011. *Witness to Permanent Revolution*. Leiden: Brill.

Deaton, A. and J. Drèze, 2009. 'Food and Nutrition in India: Facts and Interpretations'. *Economic and Political Weekly*, 44 (7): 42–65.

Dedrick, J., K. Kraemer and G. Linden, 2008. 'Who Profits from Innovation in Global Value Chains? A Study of the iPod and Notebook PCs'. Presented at Sloan Industry Studies Annual Conference. Boston, MA. http://web.mit.edu/is08/pdf/Dedrick_Kraemer_Linden.pdf [accessed 15 January 2012].

De Long, B. 1988. 'Productivity, Growth, Convergence, and Welfare: Comment'. *The American Economic Review*, 78 (5): 1138–54.

Denning, M. 2004. *Culture in the Age of Three Worlds*. London: Verso.

Department for International Development, 2005. *Trade Matters in the Fight Against Global Poverty*. http://www.dfid.gov.uk/global-issues/how-we-fight-poverty/trade [accessed 24 June 2009].

De Souza, M. 2007. 'Social Movements as "Critical Urban Planning" Agents'. In *City: Analysis of Urban Trends, Culture, Policy, Action*. 10 (3): 327–42.

Dezzani, R. 2002. 'Measuring Transition and Mobility in the Hierarchical World-Economy'. *Journal of Regional Science*, 42 (3): 595–625.

Draper, H. 1966. 'The Two Souls of Socialism'. *New Politics*, 5 (1): 57–84.

Duckworth, J. 2010. 'Venezuela: Thousands Demand Passing of Radical Labour Law'. *Green Left Weekly*, 14 November. http://www.greenleft.org.au/node/46103 [accessed 13 May 2013].

Dunaway, W. and D. Cleland, 1995. 'Review of Commodity Chains and Global Capitalism'. *Journal of World Systems Research*, 1. Online only http://jwsr.ucr.edu/archive/vol1/v1_r5.php [accessed 1 November 2011].

Dunkerley, J. 1988. *Power in the Isthmus: A Political History of Modern Central America*. London: Verso.

Dunn, B. 2005. *Global Restructuring and the Power of Labour*. Basingstoke: Palgrave Macmillan.

— 2009. 'Myths of Globalisation and the New Economy'. *International Socialism*, 121 (Winter, 75–97. http://www.isj.org.uk/index.php4?id=509&issue=121 [accessed 2 February 2011].

Dunn, B. and H. Radice, 2006. *100 Years of Permanent Revolution: Results and Prospects*. London: Pluto.

Edwards, P. and P. Elger, eds. 1999. *The Global Economy, National States and the Regulation of Labour*. London and New York: Mansell.

Edwards, P., J. Belanger and L Haiven, 1994. 'The Workplace and Labour Regulation in Comparative Perspective'. In *Workplace Industrial Relations and the Global Challenge*, ed. J. Belanger et al., Ithaca, NY: ILR Press.

Egan, D. 1990. 'Toward a Marxist Theory of Labour-Managed Firms: Breaking the Degeneration Thesis'. *Review of Radical Political Economics*, 22 (4): 67–86.

— 2011. 'Egyptian workers challenge the boss's control'. *Socialist Worker*, 15 February. http://www.socialistworker.co.uk/art.php?id=23944 [accessed 19 February 2011].

Eisenstadt, S. 2000. 'Multiple Modernities'. *Daedulus*, 129 (1) (Winter): 1–29.

Elliot, J. 1980. 'Marx and Schumpeter on Capitalism's Creative Destruction: A Comparative Restatement'. *Quarterly Journal of Economics*, 95 (1): 45–68.

Elliot, P. 2006. 'Zanon Workers in Argentina Still Waiting for Security'. *Upside Down World*, 26 June. http://upsidedownworld.org/main/argentina-archives-32/336-zanon-workers-in-argentina-still-waiting-for-security [accessed 22 November 2012].

Engels, F. 1847. *Draft of a Communist Confession of Faith*. http://www.marxists.org/archive/marx/works/1847/06/09.htm [accessed 13 November 2012].

— 2009. *The Condition of the English Working Class in 1844*. London: The Echo Library.
Escobar, A. 1995. *Encountering Development*. Princeton: Princeton University Press.
Esping-Andersen, G. 1990. *The Three Worlds of Welfare Capitalism*. Princeton: Princeton University Press.
Evans, P. 1995. *Embedded Autonomy: States and Industrial Transformation*. Princeton: Princeton University Press.
Feeley, D. 2008. 'Everything's on the Line at AAM'. *Against the Current*, 134 (May/June). http://www.solidarity-us.org/current/node/1472 [accessed 15 July 2012].
Financial Times, 2004. *Report*. http://www.ft.com/cms/s/0/7e477 06a-84da-11db-87e0-0000779e2340.html#axzz2CfITuDtB [accessed May 2012].
Fine, B. 1999. 'The Developmental State is Dead: Long Live Social Capital'. *Development and Change*, 30 (1): 1–19.
— 2004. 'Economics and Ethics: Amartya Sen as Starting Point'. *The New School Economic Review*, 1 (1): 151–62.
Fishlow, A. 2003. [Review of Gerschenkron, A. 1962.] '*Economic Backwardness in Historical Perspective*', EH.Net Economic History Services. http://eh.net/bookreviews/library/fishlow [accessed 14 February 2009].
Fogel, R. and S. Engerman, 1974. *Time on the Cross: The Economics of American Negro Slavery*. Boston, MA: Little Brown.
Foster, J. B. 1984. 'The Political Economy of Joseph Schumpeter'. *Studies in Political Economy*, 15 (Fall): 5–42.
— 2010. *The Ecological Rift: Capitalism's War on the Earth*. New York: Monthly Review.
Foster, J. B. and R. McChesney, 2012. 'The Global Stagnation and China'. *Monthly Review*, February (63): 9. http://monthlyreview.org/2012/02/01/the-global-stagnation-and-china [accessed 16 March 2012].
Freeman, R. 2006. 'The Great Doubling: The Challenge of the New Global Labour Market'. Draft, Harvard University. http://emlab.berkeley.edu/users/webfac/eichengreen/e183_sp07/great_doub.pdf [accessed 21 July 2012].
Friedman, M. and R. Friedman, 1980. *Free To Choose*. Harmondsworth: Penguin.
Frierie, P. 1996. *Pedagogy of the Oppressed*. London. Penguin.
Gaillard, J. 1977. *Paris, La Ville 1852–1870*. Lille-Paris: Honoré Champion.
Galambos, L. 2011. 'A Comment on Nathan Rosenberg's Question: "Was Schumpeter a Marxist?"' *Industrial and Corporate Change*, 20 (4): 1223–7.
Gallagher, K. 2005. *Putting Development First: The Importance of Policy Space in the WTO and the IFI's*. London: Zed Books.
— 2008. 'Understanding Developing Country Resistance to the Doha Round'. *Review of International Political Economy*, 15 (1): 62–85.
Gallin, D. 2001. 'Propositions on Trade Unions and Informal Employment in Times of Globalisation'. *Antipode*, 33 (3): 531–49.
Gammon, E. 2008. 'Affect and the Rise of the Self-Regulating Market'. *Millennium*, 37 (2): 251–78.
Garside, J. 2013. 'Child labour uncovered in China's supply chain'. *The Guardian*, 25 January. [http://www.guardian.co.uk/technology/2013/jan/25/apple-child-labour-supply].

216

Gereffi, G. 1994. 'The Organization of Buyer-Driven Global Commodity Chains: How U.S. Retailers Shape Overseas Production Networks'. In *Commodity Chains and Global Capitalism*, ed. G. Gereffi and M. Korzeniewicz, 95–122. Westport CT: Praeger.

— 2001. 'Shifting Governance Structures in Global Commodity Chains, with Special Reference to the Internet. *American Behavioral Scientist*, 44 (10): 1616–37.

Gereffi G. and M. Korzeniewicz, eds. 1994. *Commodity Chains and Global Capitalism*. Westport, CT: Praeger.

Gereffi, G., J. Humphrey and T. Sturgeon, 2005. 'The Governance of Global Value Chains'. *Review of International Political Economy*, 12 (1): 78–104.

Gerschenkron, A. 1943. *Bread and Democracy in Germany*. Berkeley and Los Angeles: University of California Press.

— 1962. *Economic Backwardness in Historical Perspective*. Cambridge, MA: Harvard University Press.

Giddens, A. 2000. *The Third Way and its Critics*. Cambridge: Polity.

Glenn, J. 2007. *Globalization: North–South Perspectives*. Oxford: Routledge.

Gluckstein, D. 2006. *The Paris Commune: A Revolution in Democracy*. London: Bookmarks.

— 2011. 'Workers' Councils in Europe: A Century of Experience'. In *Ours to Master and to Own: Workers' Control from the Commune to the Present*, ed. I. Ness and D. Azzellini, 32–47. Chicago: Haymarket.

Godelier, M. 1986. *The Mental and the Material: Thought, Economy and Society*. London: Verso.

Gonçalves, T. 2010. 'Crossroads of Empowerment: The Organisation of Women Domestic Workers in Brazil'. *IDS Bulletin*, 41 (2): 62–9.

Guscina, A. 2006. *Effects of Globalization on Labor's Share in National Income*. IMF Working Paper 06/294. Washington, DC: International Monetary Fund.

Halperin, R. 1984. 'Polanyi, Marx and the Institutionalist Paradigm in Economic Anthropology'. In *Research in Economic Anthropology*, ed. B. L. Isaac, 6: 245–72.

Halperin, S. 2004. *War and Social Change in Modern Europe: The Great Transformation Revisited*. Cambridge: Cambridge University Press.

Hamilton, A. 1791. *Report of the Secretary of the Treasury on the Subject of Manufactures*. Philadelphia: William Brown.

Hanieh, A. 2011. 'Egypt's Uprising: Not Just a Question of "Transition"'. *The Bullet*, 462. http://mrzine.monthlyreview.org/2011/hanieh140211.html [accessed 20 March 2011].

Hann, C. and K. Hart, eds. 2009. *Market and Society: The Great Transformation Today*. Cambridge: Cambridge University Press.

Hardt, M. and T. Negri, 2000. *Empire*. Cambridge, MA: Harvard University Press.

Hardy, J. and A. Budd, 2012. 'China's Capitalism and the Crisis'. *International Socialism Journal*, 133 (Winter): 65–100.

Harman, C. 1974. *Bureaucracy and Revolution in Eastern Europe*. London: Bookmarks.

— 1984a. 'The Balance of Class Forces'. *Socialist Review*, February (62): online only http://www.marxists.org/archive/harman/1984/01/nga.htm [accessed 15 February 2011].

— 1984b. *Explaining the Crisis: A Marxist Re-Appraisal*. London: Bookmarks.

217

— 1989. 'From Feudalism to Capitalism'. *International Socialism Journal*, 45 (Winter): 35–87.

— 1999. *A People's History of the World*. London: Bookmarks.

— 2004. 'The Rise of Capitalism'. *International Socialism Journal*, 102: 53–86. http://www.isj.org.uk/?id=21 [accessed 5 June 2010].

Harman, H. 2008. 'Theorising Neo Liberalism'. *International Socialism Journal*, 117 (Winter): 25–49.

Harris, N. 1978. *The Mandate of Heaven: Marx and Mao in Modern China*. London: Quartet.

— 1987. *The End of the Third World: Newly Industrialising Countries and the Decline of an Ideology*. Harmondsworth: Penguin.

Harriss, J. 2005. 'Great Promise, Hubris and Recovery: A Participant's History of Development Studies'. In *A Radical History of Development Studies*, ed. U. Kothari, 17–46. London: Zed.

Hart-Landsberg, M. and P. Burkett, 2005. 'China and the Dynamics of Transnational Accumulation'. Paper presented at conference on 'The Korean Economy: Marxist Perspectives', Gyeongsang National University, Jinju, South Korea.

Harvey, D. 2003. *Paris, Capital of Modernity*. New York and London: Routledge.

— 2005. *A Brief History of Neoliberalism*. Oxford: Oxford University Press.

— 2010. *A Companion to Marx's Capital*. London: Verso.

Hayek, F. A. 1949. *Individualism and Economic Order*. London: Routledge & Kegan Paul.

— 2010 [1944]. *The Road to Serfdom*. New York: Routledge.

Haynes, M. 1997. 'Was there a Parliamentary Alternative in Russia in 1917?' *International Socialism Journal*, 76 (Autumn): 3–66.

— 2002. *Russia: Class and Power, 1917–2000*. London: Bookmarks.

— 2011. 'Global Cities, Global Workers in the 21st Century'. *International Socialism Journal*, 132 (Autumn): online only http://www.isj.org.uk/index.php4?id=760&issue=132 [accessed 5 April 2012].

Heller, P. 2001. 'Moving the State: The Politics of Democratic Decentralization in Kerala, South Africa, and Porto Alegre'. *Politics and Society*, 29 (1): 131–63.

Heller, H. 2011. *The Rise of Capitalism*. London: Pluto.

Henderson, J. P., M. Dicken, M. Hess, N. Coe and H. Yeung, 2002. 'Global Production Networks and the Analysis of Economic Development'. *Review of International Political Economy*, 9 (3): 436–64.

Henderson, W. 1983. *Friedrich List: Economist and Visionary, 1789–1846*. London: Frank Cass.

Herod, A. 2001. 'Implications of Just-in-Time Production for Union Strategy: Lessons from the 1998 General Motors–United Auto Workers Dispute'. *Annals of the Association of American Geographers*, 90 (3): 521–47.

Hilferding, R. 1981 [1910]. *Finance Capital: A Study of the Latest Phase of Capitalist Development*. London: Routledge & Kegan Paul.

Hirschman, A. O. 1958. *The Strategy of Economic Development*, New Haven, CT: Yale University Press.

— 1981. *Essays in Trespassing: Economics to Politics and Beyond*. Cambridge and New York: Cambridge University Press.

Hobsbawm, E. J., ed. 1965. *Pre-Capitalist Economic Formations: Essays by Karl Marx*. London: Lawrence and Wishart.

— 1969. *Industry and Empire*. London: Pelican.

— 1989. *The Age of Empire: 1875–1914*. New York: Pantheon Books.

— 1994. *Age of Extremes: The Short Twentieth Century*. London: Penguin.

Hobson, J. 2011. 'What's at Stake in the Neo-Trotskyist Debate? Towards a Non-Eurocentric Historical Sociology of Uneven and Combined Development'. *Millennium Journal of International Studies*, 40 (1): 147–66.

Holmes, C. 2012. 'Problems and Opportunities in Polanyian Analysis Today'. *Economy and Society*, 41 (3): 468–84.

Hore, C. 1991. *The Road to Tiananmen Square*. London: Bookmarks.

Humphrey, J. and H. Schmitz, 2002. 'How Does Insertion in Global Value Chains Affect Upgrading in Industrial Clusters?' *Regional Studies*, 36 (9): 1017–27.

Hunt, D. 1989. *Economic Theories of Development: An Analysis of Competing Paradigms*. Hemel Hempstead: Harvester Wheatsheaf.

Hymer, S. 1972a. 'The Internationalisation of Capital'. *Journal of Economic Issues*, 6 (1): 91–111.

— 1972b. 'The Multinational Corporation and the Law of Uneven Development' In *Economics and World Order*, ed. J. Bhagwati, 113–40. New York: Macmillan.

ILO, 1999. *Decent Work*. Report of the Director-General to the 89th Session of the International Labour Conference, Geneva.

— 2013. *Global Wage Report 2012/2013*. Geneva.

ILO/KILM, 2011. *Working Poverty in the World*. http://kilm.ilo.org/2011/download/Chap1AEN.pdf [accessed 15 April 2013].

Itoh, R., R. Westra and A. Zuege, eds. 2004. *Clean up your Computer: Working Conditions in the Electronics Industry*. London: CAFOD.

James, C. L. R. 1989. *The Black Jacobins*. New York: Vintage Books.

Jessop, B. 1982. *The Capitalist State*. Oxford: Basil Blackwell.

— 2001. 'Institutional Re(turns) and the Strategic-Relational Approach'. *Environment and Planning A*, 33 (7): 1213–35.

— 2008. *State Power: A Strategic-Relational Approach*. Cambridge: Polity.

Jomo, K. S., ed. 2005. *The Pioneers of Development Economics: Great Economists on Development*. London: Zed.

Jomo, K. S. and B. Fine, eds. 2006. *The New Development Economics: After the Washington Consensus*. London: Zed.

Jomo, K. S. and E. Reinert, eds. 2005. *The Origins of Development Economics: How Schools of Economic Thought have Addressed Development*. London: Zed.

Jonas, A. 1996. 'Local Labour Control Regimes: Uneven Development and the Social Regulation of Production'. *Regional Studies*, 30 (4): 323–38.

Kabeer, N. 1994. *Reversed Realities: Gender Hierarchies in Development Thought*. London: Verso.

Kaldor, N. 1972. 'The Irrelevance of Equilibrium Economics'. *Economic Journal*, 82 (328): 1237–55.

Kaplinsky, R. 2005. *Globalization, Poverty and Inequality: Between a Rock and a Hard Place*. Cambridge: Polity.

Kaplinsky, R. and M. Morris, 2001. *A Handbook for Value Chain Research*. http://www.ids.ac.uk/ids/global/ [accessed 1 December 2010].

Kapsos, S. 2007. *World and Regional Trends in Labour Force Participation. Methodologies and Key Results.* Geneva: ILO.
Karshenas, M. 1996. 'Dynamic Economies and the Critique of Urban Bias'. *Journal of Peasant Studies*, 24 (1–2): 60–102.
Kay, C. 1989. *Latin American Theories of Development and Underdevelopment.* London: Routledge.
— 2002. 'Why East Asia Overtook Latin America: Agrarian Reform, Industrialisation and Development'. *Third World Quarterly*, 2 3(6): 1073–102.
Keynes, J. M. 1936. *The General Theory of Employment, Interest and Money.* London: Macmillan.
Khan, S. and J. Christiansen, 2011. *Towards a New Developmentalism: Markets as Means Rather than Master.* Abingdon: Taylor and Francis.
Kidron, M. 2002. 'Failing Growth and Rampant Costs: Two Ghosts in the Machine of Modern Capitalism'. *International Socialism Journal*, 96 (Winter): 87–103. http://pubs.socialistreviewindex.org.uk/isj96/kidron.htm
Kidron, M. and E. Gluckstein, 1974. 'Waste: US 1970'. In *Capitalism and Theory*, ed. M. Kidron, 35–60. London: Pluto.
Kiely, R. 1995. *Sociology and Development: The Impasse and Beyond.* London: Routledge.
— 2007. *The New Political Economy of Development: Globalisation, Imperialism, Hegemony.* Basingstoke: Palgrave.
Kitching, G. 1989. *Development and Underdevelopment in Historical Perspective.* London: Routledge.
Klein, N. 2000. *No Logo.* London: Flamingo.
— 2009. 'Why We Should Banish Larry Summers From Public Life'. http://www.naomiklein.org/articles/2009/04/why-we-should-banish-larry-summers-public-life [accessed 8 April 2012].
Knei-Paz, B. 1978. *The Social and Political Thought of Leon Trotsky.* New York: Oxford University Press.
Kohli, A. 2004. *State-directed Development: Political Power and Industrialization in the Global Periphery.* Cambridge: Cambridge University Press.
Korzeniewicz, R. and W. Martin, 1994. 'The Global Distribution of Commodity Chains'. In *Commodity Chains and Global Capitalism*, ed. G. Gereffi and M. Korzeniewicz, 67–91. Westport, CT: Praeger.
Lacher, H. 1999. 'Embedded Liberalism, Disembedded Markets: Reconceptualising the Pax America'. *New Political Economy*, 4 (3): 343–60.
— 2007. 'The Slight Transformation: Contesting the Legacy of Karl Polanyi'. In *Reading Karl Polanyi for the Twenty-First Century: Market Economy as a Political Project*, ed. A. Bugra and K. Agartan, 343–60. Basingstoke: Palgrave Macmillan.
Lal, D. 1984. *The Poverty of Development Economics.* London: Institute of Economic Affairs.
Lazonik, W. 2011. 'Comment on Nathan Rosenberg, "Was Schumpeter a Marxist?"' *Industrial and Corporate Change*, 20 (4): 1229–33.
Lebowitz, M. 1992. *Beyond Capital: Marx's Political Economy of the Working Class.* London: Macmillan.
— 2002. 'Karl Marx: The Needs of Capital vs. the Needs of Human Beings'. In *Understanding Capitalism: Critical Analysis from Karl Marx to Amartya Sen*, ed. D. Dowd, 85–104. London: Pluto.

— 2005. *Building Socialism in the Twenty First century*. New York: Monthly Review Press.

— 2010. *The Socialist Alternative: Real Human Development*. New York: Monthly Review Press.

Lenin, V. 1917. *Imperialism: The Highest Stage of Capitalism*. Moscow: International Publishers.

— 1970. *The State and Revolution*. Peking: Foreign Language Press.

Lerche, J. 1999. 'Politics of the Poor: Agricultural Labourers and Political Transformations in Uttar Pradesh'. *Journal of Peasant Studies*, 26 (2–3): 182–241.

— 2012. 'Labour Regulations and Labour Standards in India: Decent Work?' *Global Labour Journal*, 3 (1): 16–39.

Levi-Faur, D. 1997. 'Friedrich List and the Political Economy of the Nation-State'. *Review of International Political Economy*, 4 (1): 154–78.

Levy, C. 2011. 'Ocupando o Centro da Cidade: Movimento dos Cortiços e Ação Coletiva'. In *Otra Economia*, 5 (8): 73–96.

Lewis, W. A. 1954. 'Economic Development with Unlimited Supplies of Labour'. *Manchester School*, 22 (2): 131–91.

Leys, C. 1996. *The Rise and Fall of Development Theory*. Bloomington: Indiana University Press.

Lian, Y. 2005. 'Dark Side of the Moon'. *New Left Review*, 32 (March–April): 132–140.

Lie, J. 1991. 'Embedding Polanyi's Market Society'. *Sociological Perspectives*, 34 (2): 219–35.

Lipsey, R. E. and F. Sjöholm 2005. 'The Impact of Inward FDI on Host Countries: Why Such Different Answers?' In *Does Foreign Investment Promote Development?*, ed. T. H. Moran, E. M. Graham and M. Blomström, 23–43. Washington, DC: Institute for International Economics and Center for Global Development.

List, F. 1856. *National System of Political Economy*. Philadelphia, PA: J. B. Lippincott. [republished by University of Michigan, University Library (n.d.)]

Lowy, M. 1981. *The Politics of Uneven and Combined Development*. London: Verso.

— 2006. 'The Marxism of Results and Prospects'. In *100 Years of Permanent Revolution: Results and Prospects*, ed. B. Dunn and H. Radice, 27–34. London: Pluto.

McMichael, P. 2000. *Development and Social Change: A Global Perspective, Second Edition*. Thousand Oaks, CA: Pine Forge Press.

McNally, D. 2002. *Another World is Possible: Globalization and Anti-capitalism*. Winnipeg: Arbeiter Ring.

Maddison, A. 1991. *Dynamic Forces in Capitalist Development*. Oxford: Oxford University Press.

Mamdani, M. 1996. *Citizen and Subject: Contemporary Africa and the Legacy of Late Colonialism*. Princeton: Princeton University Press.

Mandel, E. 1975. *Late Capitalism*. London: NLB.

— 1980. *Long Waves of Capitalist Development*. London: Verso.

— 1994. *The Place of Marxism in History*. New Jersey. Humanities Press.

Marx, K. 1842. 'The Industrialists of Hanover and Protective Tariffs'. *Rheinische Zeitung*, 326. http://www.marxists.org/archive/marx/works/1842/11/22.htm [accessed 10 July 2011].

221

REFERENCES AND FURTHER READING

— 1846. *Letter from Marx to Pavel Vasilyevich Annenkov in Paris.* http://www.marxists.org/archive/marx/works/1846/letters/46_12_28.htm [accessed 4 November 2012].

— 1847a. *Wage Labour and Capital.* http://www.marxists.org/archive/marx/works/1847/wage-labour/ch09.htm [accessed 5 November 2012].

— 1847b. 'The Free Trade Congress at Brussels'. *The Northern Star.* http://www.marxists.org/archive/marx/works/1847/09/30.htm [accessed 6 July 2011].

— 1848. *On the Question of Free Trade.* http://www.marxists.org/archive/marx/works/1848/01/09ft.htm [accessed 6 July 2011].

— 1853. 'The Future Results of British Rule in India'. *New York Daily Tribune.* http://www.marxists.org/archive/marx/works/1853/07/22.htm [accessed 10 July 2011].

— 1864. *Inaugural Address of the International Working Men's Association.* http://www.marxists.org/archive/marx/works/1864/10/27.htm [accessed 12 July 2011].

— 1867a. *Rules and Administrative Regulations of the International Workingmen's Association.* http://www.marxists.org/archive/marx/iwma/documents/1867/rules.htm [accessed 8 January 2012].

— 1867b. *Address of the General Council of the International Working Men's Association to the Members and Affiliated Societies.* http://www.marxists.org/archive/ marx/iwma/documents/1867/affiliates.htm [accessed 13 May 2013].

— 1870. 'Letter of Marx to Sigfrid Meyer and August Vogt in New York'. In *Marx and Friedrich Engels Selected Correspondence*, 220–4. Moscow: Progress Publishers.

— 1871. *The Civil War in France: March–May 1871.* http://www.marxists.org/archive/marx/works/1871/civil-war-france/index.htm [accessed 15 July 2011].

— 1881. 'Drafts of a Reply to Vera Zasulich'. In *Late Marx and the Russian Road*, ed. T. Shanin, 97–126. New York: Monthly Review Press.

— 1929. 'Marx–Engels Correspondence 1858'. In *Marx and Engels, Works.* Moscow. http://www.marxists.org/archive/marx/works/1858/letters/58_01_16.htm [accessed 11 July 2011].

— 1974. 'Inaugural Address of the International Workingmen's Association'. In *The First International and After: Political Writings, Volume Three*, ed. K. Marx, 76–79. Harmondsworth: Penguin.

— 1975. 'Draft of an Article on Friedrich List's Book Das Nationale System Der Politischen Oekonomie'. In *Collected Works, Vol. 4, 1844–1845*, ed. K. Marx and F. Engels. Moscow: Progress Publishers. http://www.marxists.org/archive/marx/works/ 1845/03/list.htm [accessed 13 May 2013].

— 1981. *Capital, Vol. 3.* New York: Vintage Books.

— 1990. *Capital: A Critique of Political Economy.* London: Penguin.

— 1993. *Grundrisse.* London: Penguin.

Marx, K. and F. Engels, 1848. *The Manifesto of the Communist Party.* http://www.marxists.org/archive/marx/works/1848/communist-manifesto/ch01.htm #007 [accessed 13 May 2013].

— 1967. *The Manifesto of the Communist Party.* London: Penguin.

— 1975. *Selected Correspondence.* Moscow: Progress Publishers.

— 1976. *The German Ideology.* Moscow: Progress Publishers.

Mason, E. 1951. 'Schumpeter on Monopoly and the Large Firm'. *The Review of Economics and Statistics*, 33: 139–44.

Matin, K. 2006. 'Uneven and Combined Development and "Revolution of Backwardness": The Iranian Constitutional Revolution, 1906–11'. In *100 Years of Permanent Revolution: Results and Prospects*, ed. B. Dunn and H. Radice, 119–32. London: Pluto.

Matthews, S. 2004. 'Investigating NEPAD's Development Assumptions'. *Review of African Political Economy*, 31 (101): 497–511.

Mehta, J. and S. Venkataraman, 2000. 'Poverty Statistics: Bermicide's Feast'. *Economic and Political Weekly*, 35 (1): 2377–82.

Meng, X., X. Gong and Y. Wang, 2004. 'Impact of Income Growth and Economic Reform on Nutrition Intake in Urban China: 1986–2000'. Discussion Paper 1448. IZA Institute for the Study of Labour, Bonn.

Migdal, J. 1988. *Strong Societies and Weak States: State–Society Relations and State Capabilities in the Third World*. Princeton: Princeton University Press.

Milberg, W. 2008. 'Shifting Sources and Uses of Profits: Sustaining US Financialization with Global Value Chains'. *Economy and Society*, 37 (3): 420–51.

Miller, M. G. and P. Newcomb, 2013. 'Billionaires Worth $1.9 Trillion Seek Advantage in 2013'. *Bloomberg*, 2 January. http://www.bloomberg.com/news/2013-01-01/billionaires-worth-1-9-trillion-seek-advantage-in-2013.html [accessed 13 May 2013].

Milonakis, D. and B. Fine, 2009. *From Political Economy to Economics*. London: Routledge.

Miyamura, S. 2012. 'Emerging Consensus on Labour Market Institutions and Implications for Developing Countries: From the Debates in India'. *Forum for Social Economics*, 41 (1): 97–123.

Mommsen, W. 1985. 'Capitalism and Socialism: Weber's Dialogue with Marx'. In *A Weber–Marx Dialogue*, ed. R. Antonio and R. Glassman, 583–589. Kansas: University of Kansas Press.

Moore, B. 1967. *Social Origins of Dictatorship and Democracy: Lord and Peasant in the Making of the Modern World*. Harmondsworth: Penguin.

— 2011 'Moving back to America', 2011. *The Economist*, 12 May. http://www.economist.com/node/ 18682182 [accessed 13 May 2013].

Munck, R. 2006. 'Globalisation and Contestation: A Polanyian Problematic'. *Globalizations*, 3 (2): 175–86.

— 2010. 'Globalisation, Labour and Development: A View from the South'. *Transformation*, 72/73: 205–224.

Murphy, K. 2005. *Revolution and Counterrevolution: Class Struggle in a Moscow Metal Factory*. New York: Berghahn.

Myrdal, G. 1956. *An International Economy*. New York: Harper Brothers.

Navarro, V. 2000. 'Development and Quality of Life: A Critique of Amartya Sen's Development as Freedom'. *International Journal of Health Services*, 30 (4): 661–74.

Ndikumana, L. and J. K. Boyce, 2011. *Africa's Odious Debts: How Foreign Loans and Capital Flight Bled a Continent*. London: Zed Books.

NEF. 2010. 'How Poor is "Poor"? Towards a Rights-Based Poverry Line'. *London. New Economics Foundation*.

NEPAD Implementation Committee, 2002. *Communique Issued in Abuja*, 28 March.

Nolan, P. 2003. 'Industrial Policy in the Early 21st Century: The Challenge of the

Global Business Revolution'. In *Rethinking Development Economics*, ed. H. J. Chang, 299–322. London: Anthem.

Nolan, P. and J. Zhang, 2010. 'Global Competition After the Financial Crisis'. *New Left Review*, 64 (July–August): 97–108.

North, D. 1977. 'Market and Other Allocation Systems in History: The Challenge of Karl Polanyi'. *Journal of European Economic History*, 6: 703–16.

Nozick, R. 1974. *Anarchy, State and Utopia*. Oxford: Oxford University Press.

Nurske, R. 1953. *Problems of Capital Formation in Underdeveloped Countries*. New York: Oxford University Press.

Nussbaum, M. 1978. *Aristotle's De Motu Animalium*. Princeton: Princeton University Press.

O'Hearn, D., 1994. 'Innovation and the World System Hierarchy: British Subjection of the Irish Cotton Industry, 1780–1830'. *American Journal of Sociology*, 100 (3): 587–621.

Ortiz, I and M. Cummins, 2011. *Global Inequality: Beyond the Bottom Billion*. New York: UNICEF.

Oxfam, 2013. *The Cost of Inequality: How Wealth and Income Extremes Hurt us All*. London: Oxfam. http://www.oxfam.org/sites/www.oxfam.org/files/cost-of-inequality-oxfam-mb180113.pdf [accessed 25 January 2013].

Özel, H. 1997. 'Reclaiming Humanity: The Social Theory of Karl Polanyi'. Unpublished PhD dissertation, University of Utah.

Panayotakis, P. 2011. *Remaking Scarcity: From Capitalist Inefficiency to Economic Democracy*. London: Pluto.

Panitch, L. and M. Konings, 2009. 'Myths of Neo Liberal Deregulation'. *New Left Review*, 57 (May–June): 67–83.

Panitch, L. and C. Leys, 2001. 'Preface'. In *The Socialist Register 2001*, ed. L. Panitch and C. Leys, V11–X1. London: Merlin.

Pares, B. 1941. *Russia*. London: Penguin.

Patnaik, P. ed. 1990. *Agrarian Relations and Accumulation*. Delhi: Oxford University Press.

— 2005. 'Karl Marx as a Development Economist'. In K. S. Jomo ed. *The Pioneers of Development Economics*. London: Zed.

— 2007. 'Neoliberalism and Rural Poverty in India'. *Economic and Political Weekly* (28 July–3 August): 3132–50.

Pattenden, J. 2012. 'Migrating Between Rural Raichur and Boomtown Bangalore: Class Relations and the Circulation of Labour in South India'. *Global Labour Journal*, 3 (1): 163–90.

Payne, A. and N. Phillips, 2010. *Development*. Cambridge: Polity.

Peacock, M. 2010. 'Starvation and Social Class: Amartya Sen on Markets and Famines'. *Review of Political Economy*, 22 (1): 57–73.

Perelman, M. 2011. *The Invisible Handcuffs of Capitalism*. New York: Monthly Review Press.

Perreault, T. 2006, 'From the *Guerra Del Agua* to the *Guerra Del Gas*: Resource Governance, Neoliberalism and Popular Protest in Bolivia'. *Antipode*, 38 (1): 150–72.

Pfeiffer, K. 1979. 'State Capitalism and Development'. *MERIP Reports*, 9 (7): 3–11.

Plekhanov, G. 1976. *The Materialist Conception of History*. London: Lawrence and Wishart.

Pogge, T. 2003. 'The First UN Millennium Development Goal'. http://www.

carnegiecouncil.org/publications/articles_papers_reports/1076.html/_res/id=sa
_File1/1076_pogge_millenniumgoal2.pdf [accessed 10 May 2012].
— 2010. *Politics as Usual: What Lies Behind the Pro-Poor Rhetoric?* Cambridge: Polity.
Polanyi, K. 1947. 'Our Obsolete Market Mentality'. *Commentary*, 3: 109–17.
— 1957. 'The Economy as Instituted Process'. In *Trade and Market in the Early Empires: Economies in History and Theory*, ed. K. Polanyi, M. Conrad, M. Arensberg and H. W. Pearson, 243–69. Glencoe, IL: Free Press.
— 2001 [1944]. *The Great Transformation: The Political and Economic Origins of our Time*. Boston, MA: Beacon Press.
Polanyi, K., C. Arensberg and H. W. Pearson, 1957. 'The Place of Economics in Societies'. In *Trade and Market in the Early Empires: Economies in History and Theory*, ed. K. Polanyi, M. Conrad, M. Arensberg and H. W. Pearson, 239–42. Glencoe, IL: Free Press.
Polanyi, M. 1966. *The Tacit Dimension: Garden City*. New York: Doubleday and Company.
Polanyi-Levitt, K. 2005. 'Karl Polanyi as a Development Economist'. In *The Pioneers of Development Economics*, ed. K. S. Jomo, 165–80. London: Zed.
— 2006. 'Tracing Karl Polanyi's Institutional Political Economy to its Central European Source'. In *Karl Polanyi in Vienna: The Contemporary Significance of the Great Transformation*, ed. K. Polanyi-Levitt and K. McRobbie, 378–91. Montreal: Black Rose Books.
Post, K. 1978. *Arise Ye Starvelings: The Jamaican Labour Rebellion of 1938 and its Aftermath*. The Hague: Martinus Nijhoff.
Pradella, L. 2010. *L'attualità del Capitale. Accumulazione e Impoverimento nel Capitalismo Globale*. Padua: Il Poligrafo.
— 2011. 'Imperialism and Capitalist Development in Marx's Capital'. Unpublished manuscript. London.
Putzel, J. 2002. *Politics, the State and the Impulse for Social Protection: The Implications of Karl Polanyi's Ideas for Understanding Development and Crisis*. London: Crisis States Programme Development Research Centre, London School of Economics.
Rahim, E. 2009. 'Marx and Schumpeter: A Comparison of their Theories of Development'. *Review of Political Economy*, 21 (1): 51–83
Rainnie, A.S., S. McGrath-Champ and A. Herod, 2010. 'Making Space for Geography in Labour Process Theory'. In *Working Life: Renewing Labour Process Analysis*, ed. P. Thompson and C. Smith, 297–315. Basingstoke: Palgrave Macmillan.
Ramachandran, V. K. 1990. *Wage Labour and Unfreedom in Agriculture: An Indian Case Study*. Oxford: Clarendon Press.
Ravallion, M. 2004. 'Monitoring Progress Against Global Poverty'. *Poverty in Focus*. UNDP International Poverty Centre. September.
Rawls, J. 1999. *A Theory of Justice*. New York: Belknap Press.
Reddy, S. 2007. 'Death in China: Market Reforms and Health'. *New Left Review*, 45 (May–June): 49–65.
Rees, J. 1998. *The Algebra of Revolution: The Dialectic and the Classical Marxist Tradition*. London: Routledge.
Reinert, E. 1998. 'Raw Materials in the History of Economic Policy – Or why List (the Protectionist) and Cobden (the Free Trader) both agreed on Free Trade in

Corn'. In *The Economics and Politics of International Trade: Freedom and Trade*, Volume 2, ed. G. Cook, 275–300. London: Routledge.

— 2011. 'The Rising Power of the Chinese Worker'. *The Economist*, 29 July. http://www.economist.com/node/16693333 [accessed 13 May 2013].

Rist, G. 2008. *The History of Development: From Western Origins to Global Faith*. London: Zed.

Robinson, W. 1996. *Promoting Polyarchy: Globalisation, U.S. Intervention and Hegemony*. Cambridge: Cambridge University Press.

Rosenberg, J. 1996. 'Isaac Deutscher and the Lost History of International Relations'. *New Left Review*, 1 (215): 3–15.

— 2008. 'Anarchy in the Mirror of "Uneven and Combined Development"': An Open Letter to Kenneth Waltz'. Paper presented at the British–German IR Conference, Arnoldshain, Germany.

Rosenberg, N. 2011. 'Was Schumpeter a Marxist?' *Industrial and Corporate Change*, 20 (4): 1215–22.

Rosenstein-Rodan, P. 1943. 'Problems of Industrialization of Eastern and Southeastern Europe'. *Economic Journal*, 53: 210–11.

Rostow, W. W. 1960. *The Stages of Economic Growth: A Non-communist Manifesto*. Cambridge: Cambridge University Press.

Roxborough, I. 1979. *Theories of Underdevelopment*. Basingstoke: Macmillan.

— 1984. 'Unity and Diversity in Latin American History'. *Journal of Latin American Studies*, 16 (1): 1–26.

Ruggie, J. G. 1982. 'International Regimes, Transactions and Change: Embedded Liberalism in the Post-War Economic Order'. *International Organisation*, 36 (2): 379–415.

Sachs, J. 2005. *The End of Poverty: How We Can Make it Happen in our Lifetime*. London: Penguin.

Sachs, W. ed. 1992. *The Development Dictionary*. London: Zed.

Said, E. 1993. *Culture and Imperialism*. London: Vintage.

— 2003. *Orientalism*. London: Penguin.

Sandbrook, R. 2011. 'Polanyi and Post-Neoliberalism in the Global South: Dilemmas of Re-embedding the Economy'. *New Political Economy*, 16 (4): 415–43.

Saul, S. B. 1960. *Studies in British Overseas Trade 1870–1914*. Liverpool: Liverpool University Press.

Schaffer, S. 1994. 'Babbage's Intelligence: Calculating Engines and the Factory System'. *Critical Inquiry*, 21 (1): 203–27.

Schumpeter, J. A. 1934. *The Theory of Economic Development*. Cambridge. MA. Harvard University Press

— [1943] 1987. *Capitalism, Socialism and Democracy*. London: Allen and Unwin.

— 1946. 'Capitalism'. In *Essays: On Entrepreneurs, Innovations, Business Cycles and the Evolution of Capitalism*, ed. R. Clemence, 180–211. London: Transaction Publishers.

— 1949a. 'The Communist Manifesto in Sociology and Economics'. *Journal of Political Economy*, 47 (3): 199–212.

— 1949b. 'Science and Ideology'. *American Economic Review*, 39 (2): 345–59.

— 1951a. *Imperialism and Social Classes*. Oxford: Basil Blackwell.

— 1951b. *Essays on Economic Topics*, ed. R. V. Clemence: Port Washington, New York: Kennikat Press.

— 1954. *History of Economic Analysis*. London: Allen and Unwin.

— 1961. *The Theory of Economic Development: An Enquiry into Profits, Capital, Credit, Interest and the Business Cycle*. Cambridge MA: Harvard University Press.

— 1964. *Business Cycles: A Theoretical, Historical And Statistical Analysis of The Capitalist Process*. New York: McGraw-Hill.

Schwartz, H. 2000. *States Versus Markets: The Emergence of A Global Economy*. Basingstoke: Palgrave.

— 2010. *States vs Markets*. 3rd edn. Basingstoke. Palgrave.

Segre, C. 2001. 'Fascism'. In *The Oxford Companion to Politics of the World*, 274–6. New York: Oxford University Press.

Sell, S. 2002. *Private Power, Public Law*. Cambridge: Cambridge University Press.

Selwyn, B. 2007. 'Labour Process and Workers' Bargaining Power in Export Grape Production, North East Brazil'. *Journal of Agrarian Change*, 7 (4): 526–53.

— 2008. 'Bringing Social Relations Back in: (Re)conceptualising the "Bullwhip Effect" in Global Commodity Chains'. *International Journal of Management Concepts and Philosophy*, 3 (2): 156–75.

— 2009. 'An Historical Materialist Appraisal of Friedrich List and his Modern-Day Followers'. *New Political Economy*, 14 (2): 157–80.

— 2011a. 'Liberty Limited? A Sympathetic Re-Engagement with Amartya Sen's Development as Freedom'. *Economic and Political Weekly*, September, 46 (37): 68–76.

— 2011b. 'Trotsky, Gerschenkron and the Political Economy of Late Capitalist Development'. *Economy and Society*, 40 (3): 421–50.

— 2012. *Workers, State and Development in Brazil: Powers of Labour, Chains of Value*. Manchester: Manchester University Press.

— 2013. 'Social Upgrading and Labour in Global Production Networks: A Critique and an Alternative Conception'. *Competition and Change*, 17 (1): 75–90.

Sen, A. 1973. *On Economic Inequality*. Oxford: Clarendon Press.

— 1982. *Poverty and Famines: An Essay on Entitlement and Deprivation*. Oxford: Oxford University Press.

— 1999. *Development as Freedom*. Oxford: Oxford University Press.

— 2006. *Identity and Violence: The Illusion of Destiny*. New York: W.W. Norton.

Shafaeddin, M. 2005. 'Friedrich List and the Infant Industry Argument'. In *The Pioneers of Development Economics*, ed. K. S. Jomo, 42–61. London: Zed.

Shaikh, A. 1980. 'The Law of International Exchange'. In *Growth, Profits and Property*, ed. E. J. Nell, 204–36. Cambridge: Cambridge University Press.

Shanin, T. ed. 1983. *Late Marx and the Russian Road: Marx and the 'Peripheries' of Capitalism*. New York: Monthly Review Press.

Shivakumar, M., K. Sheng and K. Weber. 1991. 'Recruitment and Employment Practices in the Construction Industry: A Case Study of Bangalore'. *Economic and Political Weekly*, 26 (8): 27–40.

Silver, B. 2003. *Forces of Labour: Workers' Movements and Globalization Since 1870*. Cambridge: Cambridge University Press.

Silver, B. and G. Arrighi, 2003. 'Polanyi's Double Movement: The Belle Époques of British and U.S. Hegemony Compared'. *Politics and Society*, 3 (2): 325–55.

227

Silver, B. and L. Zhang, 2009. 'China as an Emerging Epicentre of World Labour Unrest'. In, ed. H. F. Hung, *China and the Transformation of Global Capitalism*. Baltimore. Johns Hopkins Press.

Singh, P. 1982. 'Who Dies in Famines and Why? A Review of Amartya Sen's *Poverty and Famines: An Essay on Entitlement and Deprivation*'. In *The Tribune* (18 December): 4.

Sklair, L. 1988. 'Transcending the Impasse: Metatheory, Theory and Empirical Research in the Sociology of Development and Underdevelopment'. *World Development*, 16: 697–709.

— 1993. *Assembling for Development: The Maquila Industry in Mexico and the United States*. London. Routledge.

— 2001. *The Transnational Capitalist Class*. Oxford: Blackwell.

— 2011. 'The Transition from Capitalist Globalization to Socialist Globalization'. *Journal of Democratic Socialism*, 1 (1): 1–14.

Smith, A. 1976. *The Wealth of Nations*. Chicago: University of Chicago Press.

Smith, C. 2006. 'The Double-Indeterminacy of Labour Power: Labour Effort and Labour Mobility'. *Work, Employment and Society*, 2 (20): 389–402.

Smith, T. 2004. 'Technology and History in Capitalism: Marxian and Neo-Schumpeterian Perspectives'. In *The Constitution of Capital: Essays on Volume 1 of Marx's Capital*, ed. R. Bellofiore and N. Taylor, 217–42. Basingstoke: Palgrave.

Sohn-Rethel, A. 1978. *Intellectual and Manual Labour: A Critique of Bourgeois Epistemology*. London: Macmillan.

Solow, R. 1956. 'A Contribution to the Theory of Economic Growth'. *The Quarterly Journal of Economics*, 70: 65–94.

South China Post. 2005, Quoted in M.H. Landsberg and P. Burkett, 'China and the Dynamics of Transnational Accumulation'. Paper presented at conference, 'The Korean Economy: Marxist Perspectives', Gyeongsang National University, Jinju, South Korea.

Standing, G. 2007. 'Labor Recommodification in the Global Transformation'. In *Reading Karl Polanyi for the Twenty-First Century: Market Economy as a Political Project*, ed. A. Buğra and K. Ağartan, 67–93. New York: Palgrave Macmillan.

— 2011. *The Precariat: The New Dangerous Class*. London: Bloomsbury.

Stanfield, J. R. 1980. 'The Institutional Economics of Karl Polanyi'. *Journal of Economic Issues*, 14 (3). 593–614.

Steadman, ?., Jones, G. S. 1970. 'The Specificity of US Imperialism'. *New Left Review*, 1 (60) March–April: 59–86.

Stiglitz, J. 1998. 'More Instruments and Broader Goals: Moving Towards the Post-Washington Consensus'. Paper presented at WIDER Annual Lectures, Helsinki.

— 2001. 'Foreword'. In *The Great Transformation*, K. Polanyi, xvi–xvii. Boston, MA: Beacon.

Strange, R. and J. Newton, 2006. 'Stephen Hymer and the Externalisation of Production'. *International Business Review*, 15: 180–93.

Sturgeon, T. 2001. 'How do we Define Value Chains and Production Networks?' *Bulletin: Institute of Development Studies*, 32 (3): 9–19.

Sutcliffe, B. 2004. 'World Inequality and Globalization'. *Oxford Review of Economic Policy*, 20 (1): 15–37.

Szporluk, R. 1988. *Communism and Nationalism: Karl Marx versus Friedrich List*. Oxford: Oxford University Press.
Talbot, J. 2004. *Grounds for Agreement: The Political Economy of the Coffee Commodity Chain*. Lanham, MD: Rowman and Littlefield.
Tax Justice Network, 2012a. *The Price of Offshore Revisited*. http://www.taxjustice.net/cms/upload/pdf/Price_of_Offshore_Revisited_26072012.pdf [accessed 13 May 2013].
— 2012b. *You Don't Know the Half of It*. http://www.taxjustice.net/cms/upload/pdf/Inequality_120722_You_dont_know_the_half_of_it.pdf [accessed 13 May 2013].
Taylor, M. 2006. *From Pinochet to the 'Third Way': Neoliberalism and Social Transformation in Chile*. London: Pluto.
Ticktin, H. 2006. 'Trotsky, 1905, and the Anticipation of the Concept of Decline'. In *100 Years of Permanent Revolution: Results and Prospects*, ed. B. Dunn and H. Radice, 35–47. London: Pluto.
Tilly, C. 1999. *Durable Inequality*. Berkeley: University of California Press.
Townsend, P. 1993. *The International Analysis of Poverty*. London and New York: Harvester Wheatsheaf.
Toye, J. 1987. *Dilemmas of Development*. Oxford: Blackwell.
Trotsky, L. 1957. *The Third International After Lenin*. New York: Pathfinder.
— 1969 [1906]. *The Permanent Revolution and Results and Prospects*. New York: Merit Publishers.
— 1997. *The History of the Russian Revolution*. London: Pluto.
Valensi, L. 1981. 'Economic Anthropology and History: The Work of Karl Polanyi'. *Research in Economic Anthropology*, 4: 3–11.
Van der Linden, M. 2007. 'The "Law" of Uneven and Combined Development'. *Historical Materialism*, 15: 145–65.
— 2008. *Workers of the World: Essays Towards a Global Labor History*. Leiden and Boston, MA: Brill.
— 2013. 'Gerschenkron's Secret: A Research Note'. *Critique: A Journal of Socialist Theory*, 40 (4): 553–62.
Van der Pijl, K. 2006. *Global Rivalries: From the Cold War to Iraq*. London: Pluto.
— 2007. *Nomads, Empires, States*. London: Pluto.
Veblen, T. 1939. *Imperial Germany and the Industrial Revolution*. New York: Viking Press.
Verdoorn, P. J. 1980. 'Verdoorn's Law in Retrospect: A Comment'. *Economic Journal*, 90 (June): 382–5.
Visvanathan, N., L. Duggan, L. Nisonoff and N. Wiegersma, eds. 1997. *The Women, Gender and Development Reader*. London: Zed Books.
Von Laue, T. H. 1969. *Sergei Witte and the Industrialization of Russia*. New York: Colombia University Press.
Voss, J. 1987. 'The Politics of Pork and Rituals of Rice'. In *Beyond the New Economic Anthropology*, ed. J. Clammer, 121–41. Basingstoke: Macmillan.
Wade, R. 2000. 'Out of the Box: Rethinking the Governance of International Financial Markets'. *Journal of Human Development*, 1 (1): 145–57.
— 2001. 'Winners and Losers: The Global Distribution of Income is Becoming More Unequal: That Should be a Matter of Greater Concern than it is'. *The Economist*, 26 April: 79–81.

— 2003. 'The Invisible Hand of the American Empire'. *Ethics and International Affairs*, 17: 77–88.

— 2004. *Governing the Market. Second Edition*. Princeton: Princeton University Press.

— 2005a. 'Globalization, Poverty and Inequality'. In *Global Political Economy*, ed. J. Ravenhill, 373–409. Oxford: Oxford University Press.

— 2005b. 'What Strategies are Viable for Developing Countries Today? The World Trade Organization and the Shrinking of "Development Space"'. In *Putting Development First: The Importance of Policy Space in the WTO and International Financial Institutions*, ed. K. Gallagher, 80–101. London: Zed.

— 2006. 'Choking the South'. *New Left Review*, 38: 115–27.

Wade, R. and Wolf, M. 2002. 'Are global poverty and inequality getting worse? Yes: Robert Wade, No: Martin Wolf'. *Prospect* (March), 16–21.

Wallerstein, I. 1974. *The Modern World-System 1: Capitalist Agriculture and the Origins of the European World-Economy in the Sixteenth Century*. New York: Academic Press.

— 1980. *The Modern World-System 2: Mercantilism and the Consolidation of the European World-Economy, 1600–1750*. New York: Academic Press.

— 1989. *The Modern World-System 3: The Second Era of Great Expansion of the Capitalist World-Economy, 1730–1840s*. San Diego, CA: Academic Press.

— 1991. *Unthinking Social Science: The Limits of Nineteenth-Century Paradigms*. Cambridge: Polity.

— 2001. *Unthinking Social Science. The Limits of Nineteenth-Century Paradigms. Second Edition*. Philadelphia: Temple University Press.

— 2012. 'The World Class Struggle: The Geography of Protest'. http://www.iwallerstein.com/world-class-struggle-geography-protest [accessed 7 June 2012].

Wan, P. Y. 2011. 'Systems Theory: Irredeemably Holistic and Antithetical to Planning?' *Critical Sociology*, published online before print. http://crs.sagepub.com/content/37/3/351.full.pdf+html [accessed 1 June 2012].

Warren, B. 1980. *Imperialism: Pioneer of Capitalism*. London: Verso.

Watts, M. 1983. *Silent Voices: Food, Famine, and Peasantry in Northern Nigeria*. Berkeley: University of California Press.

Weaver, F. S. 2000. *Latin America in the World Economy: Mercantile Colonialism to Global Capitalism*. Boulder, CO: Westview.

Webber, J. 2008. 'Rebellion to Reform in Bolivia. Part II: Revolutionary Epoch, Combined Liberation and the December 2005 Elections'. *Historical Materialism*, 16 (3): 55–76.

— 2011. *From Rebellion to Reform in Bolivia: Class Struggle, Indigenous Liberation, and the Politics of Evo Morales*. Chicago: Haymarket Books.

Weber, M. 1949. *The Methodology of Social Science*. New York: Free Press.

— 1978. *Economy and Society*. Berkeley: University of California Press.

Weeks, J. 1981. *Capital and Exploitation*. Princeton: Princeton University Press.

— 1997. 'The Law of Value and the Analysis of Underdevelopment'. *Historical Materialism*, 1 (1): 91–112.

Weeks, K. 2011. *The Problem with Work*. London: Duke University Press.

Weinberg, K. 2007. 'Brazil: Homeless Occupation Movements in Rio de Janeiro'. In *Upside Down World*. http://upsidedownworld.org/main/brazil-archives-63/830-brazil-homeless-occupation-movements-in-rio-de-janeiro [accessed 10 December 2012].

Weis, T. 2007. *The Global Food Economy: The Battle for the Future of Farming*. London: Zed.

Weiss, L. 1998. *The Myth of the Powerless State*. Ithaca, NY: Cornell University Press.

— 2005. 'Global Governance, National Strategies: How Industrialized States Make Room to Move Under the WTO'. *Review of International Political Economy*, 12 (5): 723–49.

Wheen, F. 1999. *Karl Marx*. London: Fourth Estate

Williamson, J. 1989. 'What Washington Means by Policy Reform'. In *Latin American Readjustment: How Much has Happened*, ed. J. Williamson, 5–20. Washington, DC Institute for International Economics.

Willis, K. 2005. *Theories and Practices of Development*. Abingdon: Routledge.

Wolf, E. 1980. *Europe and the People Without History*. Berkeley: University of California Press.

— 1982. *Europe and the People Without History*. London: University of California Press.

Wolf, M. 2004. *Why Globalization Works*. New Haven, CT: Yale University Press.

Wolford, W. 2010. *This Land is Ours Now: Social Mobilization and the Meanings of Land in Brazil*. Durham, NC: Duke University Press.

Wood, E. 1991. *The Pristine Culture of Capitalism: An Historical Essay on Old Regimes and Modern States*. London: Verso.

— 1995. *Democracy Against Capitalism: Renewing Historical Materialism*. Cambridge: Cambridge University Press.

— 1999. *The Origins of Capitalism*. New York: Monthly Review Press.

— 2003. *Empire of Capital*. London: Verso.

Woodward, D. 2013. 'Incrementum ad Absurdum: Global Growth, Inequality and Poverty Eradication in a Carbon-Constrained World'. *World Economics Association*. Accessed 1 September 2013 at: http://werdiscussion.worldeco nomicsassociation.org/?post=incrementum-ad-adsurdum-global-growth-inequ ality-and-poverty-eradication-in-a-carbon-constrained-world

World Bank, 1993. *The East Asian Miracle*. Oxford: Oxford University Press.

— 1997. *World Development Report*. Oxford: Oxford University Press.

— 2002a. *Globalization, Growth and Poverty: Building an Inclusive World Economy*. Oxford: Oxford University Press.

— 2002b. 'Intellectual Property: Balancing Incentives with Competitive Access'. In *Global Economic Prospects 2002*, 129–149. Washington, DC: World Bank.

— 2009. *Global Monitoring Report 2009 – A Development Emergency*. http:// siteresources.worldbank.org/DEVCOMMINT/Documentation/22148602/DC 2009-0002%28E%29GMR2009.pdf [accessed 5 November 2012].

Wright, E. O. 1979. *Class Structure and Income Determination*. New York: Academic Press.

— 1994. *Interrogating Inequality*. London: Verso.

— 2002. *The Shadow of Exploitation in Weber's Class Analysis*. http://www.ssc. wisc.edu/~wright/Weber-revised.pdf [accessed 6 March 2008].

— 2006. 'Compass Points'. *New Left Review*, 41: 93–124.

— 2009. 'Understanding Class'. *New Left Review* 60 (November–December): 101–116.

Zeilig, L. 2010. 'Tony Cliff: Deflected Permanent Revolution in Africa'.

International Socialism, 126: 159–186. www.isj.org.uk/?id=641 [accessed 20 March 2011.

Zobel, G. 2009. 'We Are Millions'. *New Internationalist Online*, 428: http://newint.org/issues/2009/12/01/ [accessed 6 February 2013].

INDEX

Note: a page number with 'n' indicates a reference in the notes.

Marx's analysis of 28, 53–4
monopolization 126–7
non-beneficial growth 163–4
Polanyi's understanding of 151–3
Schumpeter's justification of 104–5
social relations of 24, 28
staged process of 62–3
    see also accumulation;
    exploitation; liberal economics;
    markets; state capitalism
Capitalism, Socialism and Democracy
    (Schumpeter) 104, 115
Capps, Gavin 68
Carey, Henry 31
    The Harmony of Interests 32
Catephores, G. 112–13
Catholic Agency for Overseas
    Development (CAFOD) 130
Ceruti, Claire 17
Chandrasekhar, C. P. 85–6
Chang, Dae-Oup 193
Chang, Ha-Joon 30
    Kicking Away the Ladder 39
    social movements 45
    SPE development strategy 40–1
Chernyshevsky, N. G. 72
China
    capital-labour relations 193–4
    catch-up industrialization 53
    imperialism and 63, 74
    labour militancy 132
    limiting human development 191
    List and 39
    paradox of growth 163–4
    place in global economy 107
    wages 130
    WWI and 95
Chomsky, Noam 206
Christiansen, J. 135
class see social class
class struggle
    Australia and 65, 66–8
    diversity of structures 65–6
    English industrial workers 65, 68–9
    French commune 65, 69–71
    institutionalization of 99
    non-industrial Russia 65, 72–4
    Owen rejects class hate 137
    rise of capitalism 58–60
    summary of concepts 25–6

Clay, Henry 31–2
Cliff, Tony 20, 50
Cohen, G. A. 169
collective action
    Babbagization and 132
    challenging capital social relations
        185
    power of labour 192–4
    regulation of representation 22
    rural workers in Brazil 194–6
    state and 34–5
    see also trade unions
commodification
    all elements of industry 149
    decommodification 206
    'fictional' nature of 27, 152
    of labour 186, 187–8
    of nature 15
    poverty and 156–8
commodities
    the bourgeois entrepreneur 112
    firms and market shares 125
    global supply chains 19, 126,
        127–8, 134, 182
    Polanyi objects to 'fiction' of 146
communism 30
    Stalin's counter-revolution 20
    state capitalism 50, 51
    The Communist Manifesto (Marx and
        Engels) 4, 112
    pre-capitalism to capitalism 57
    on subjugation 54, 55
comparative advantage model 8
competition
    anti-monopoly policy 117
    dependence on market 167
    levelling and punishing 97
    *Condition of the Working Class in
        England* (Engels) 165
consumption
    downward pressure 90
    freedom of choice and 6
copyrights and patents 39–40
Corbridge, Stuart 21
creative destruction 132–3, 182–3
    Arrighi et al draw on 107–8
    capitalism in motion 115–18
    Schumpeter's concept of 104–5
    spatial/state differences 121,
        124

235

Egypt
  labour in power 199, 200
  state capitalism 51
Eisenstadt, Shlomo 56
Elger, P. 22
Elson, Diane 130
employers
  social organization of labour 22
  see also capitalists
Engels, Friedrich
  The Communist Manifesto (with
    Marx) 4, 54, 55, 57, 112
  Condition of the Working Class in
    England 165
  List and 45
Engerman, S. 171
entrepreneurial innovation
  capitalism in motion 115–18
  development policies 3
  Gerschenkron and 84
  innovations 26
  Schumpeter's response to Marx 112
  social class and 118–21
  summary of concepts 184
environment 10
  capitalist production and 205
  commodification of nature 15
  degradation of 28
  natural capital 38
  resources 205
equality/inequality
  gap increase in economic crisis
    10–13
  socialist vision 20–1
Esping-Andersen, Göta 206
Europe
  Eurocentric modernity 56–8
  Gerschenkron's model 93–4
  rise of capitalism 58–9
Evans, Peter 30
exclusion see inclusion/exclusion
exploitation
  appearance of equality 170–1
  commodification 156–60
  defining 5
  five moments of 14–15
  global value relations 114–15
  inbuilt in capitalism 18
  incorporating into development
    183

informal workplaces 196–9
Polanyi's approach 141, 151,
    155–8
  presented as necessary 185
  resistance to 208
  state and 182
  surplus population 189–91
  surplus value 114–15
  workplace and conditions 191–2
Export Processing Zones 16–17

famines 162
  entitlement approach 173–6
  food availability decline 173
Fanon, Frantz 24
financial institutions
  assymetric investment 126
  Bank Act (England) 145
  global commodity chains 134
  influence on labour relations 128
  liberal ideology and practice 1
  Polanyi's 'counter-movement' 147
  recent economic crisis 135
Fine, B. 109
Fishlow, A. 78
Fogel, R. 171
Food and Agriculture Organization
    (FAO) 12–13
Foster, J. B. 191
France
  imperialism 59–60
  'moderate backwardness' 86
  Paris Commune 65, 69–71, 75,
    108
  peasant struggle 58
Frank, A. G. 7
Free to Choose (Friedman and
    Friedman) 165
freedom
  capitalism's unfreedoms 169
  eight instrumental freedoms 166
  human development 183
  human over market 136
  limitiations of 6
  of market access 167–8
  Polanyi's market critique and
    148
  removal of unfreedom and 165–8
  Sen and 24
  Sen's 162, 163

239